The Self on the Page

also by

Creative Writing in Health and Social Care
ISBN 1 84310 136 X

of related interest

Therapeutic Dimensions of Autobiography in Creative Writing
Celia Hunt
ISBN 1 85302 747 2

Writing Well: Creative Writing and Mental Health
Deborah Philips, Liz Linington and Debra Penman
ISBN 1 85302 650 6

Can You Read Me?
Creative Writing With Child and Adult Victims of Abuse
Edited by Jacki Pritchard and Eric Sainsbury
ISBN 1 84310 192 0

The Therapeutic Potential of Creative Writing
Writing Myself
Gillie Bolton
ISBN 1 85302 599 2

Writing My Way Through Cancer
Myra Schneider
ISBN 1 84310 113 0

The Self on the Page

Theory and Practice of Creative Writing in Personal Development

edited by
Celia Hunt and Fiona Sampson

Jessica Kingsley Publishers
London and Philadelphia

First published in the United Kingdom in 1998
by Jessica Kingsley Publishers
116 Pentonville Road
London N1 9JB, UK
and
400 Market Street, Suite 400
Philadelphia, PA 19106, USA

www.jkp.com

Copyright © Jessica Kingsley Publishers 1998
Second Impression 2002
Third impression 2005

Library of Congress Cataloging in Publication Data
A CIP catalog record for this book is available from the Library of Congress

British Library Cataloguing in Publication Data
The self on the page: theory and practice
Of creative writing in personal development
1.Creative writing – Therapeutic use
I.Hunt, Celia II.Sampson, Fiona
615.8'516

ISBN-13: 978 1 85302 469 6 hb
ISBN-10: 1 85302 469 4 hb

ISBN-13: 978 1 85302 470 2 pb
ISBN-10: 1 85302 470 8 pb

Contents

ACKNOWLEDGEMENTS   8

Introduction   9
Celia Hunt and Fiona Sampson

PART I: CURRENT PRACTICE OF CREATIVE
         WRITING IN PERSONAL DEVELOPMENT   19

1. Writing with the Voice of the Child: Fictional
    Autobiography and Personal Development   21
    Celia Hunt, University of Sussex

2. The Self as Source: Creative Writing Generated
    from Personal Reflection   35
    Cheryl Moskowitz, writer and psychodynamic counsellor

3. The Web of Words: Collaborative Writing
    and Mental Health   47
    Graham Hartill, Poetry and Healing Project, Wales

4. 'Men Wearing Pyjamas': Using Creative Writing
    with People with Learning Disabilities   63
    Fiona Sampson, writer-in-residence, Age Concern, Swindon

5. Writing or Pills? Therapeutic Writing in Primary
    Health Care   78
    Gillie Bolton, University of Sheffield

6. Final Fictions? Creative Writing and Terminally
    Ill People   93
    Colin Archer, freelance writer

7. A Matter of the Life and Death of the Mind:
    CreativeWriting and Dementia Sufferers   104
    *John Killick, Dementia Services Development Centre,
    University of Stirling*

PART II: THEORETICAL CONTEXTS FOR CREATIVE
            WRITING IN PERSONAL DEVELOPMENT   115

8.   The Creative Word and the Created Life:
     The Cultural Context for Deep Autobiography   117
     Peter Abbs, University of Sussex

9.   Thinking about Language as a Way through
     the World: Some Sources for a Model   129
     Fiona Sampson, writer-in-residence, Age Concern, Swindon

10. Writing, the Self and the Social Process   142
     Mary Stuart, University of Sussex

11. The Empty Word and the Full Word:
     The Emergence of Truth in Writing   153
     Trevor Pateman, University of Sussex

12. Transformative Reading: Reconfigurations
     of the Self between Experience and the Text   164
     Jan Campbell, University of Sussex

13. Autobiography and the Psychotherapeutic
     Process   181
     Celia Hunt, University of Sussex

14. Towards a Writing Therapy?
     Implications of Existing Practice and Theory   198
     *Fiona Sampson, writer-in-residence, Age Concern, Swindon
     and Celia Hunt, University of Sussex*

     LIST OF CONTRIBUTORS   211
     SUBJECT INDEX   215
     AUTHOR INDEX   221

For our parents

Acknowledgements

For permission to reprint copyright material the editors gratefully acknowledge the following:

Extract from 'Aunt Julia' from *Collected Poems* by Norman MacCaig reproduced with the kind permission of the estate of Norman MacCaig and Chatto and Windus, London; extract from *Childhood* by Nathalie Sarraute, translated by Barbara Wright, copyright © 1983 by Éditions Gallimard, English translation copyright © 1983 by Barbara Wright, reprinted with the kind permission of George Braziller, Inc., New York, U.S.A. and Calder Publications, London; extracts from 'Sketch of the Past' in *Moments of Being* by Virginia Woolf, copyright © 1976 by Quentin Bell and Angelica Garnett; reprinted by permission of Harcourt Brace and Company, Florida, U.S.A. and HarperCollins, London.

Introduction

Celia Hunt and Fiona Sampson

The idea that engaging in creative writing can be a means of personal development is not new. If one looks back through the history of literature, one can find many examples of celebrated writers for whom the act of writing fiction or poetry has been more than the creating of a work of art. This, for example, is how Virginia Woolf speaks about her obsession with her mother and the way she came to write this out in *To the Lighthouse*:

> It is perfectly true that she obsessed me, in spite of the fact that she died when I was thirteen, until I was forty-four. Then one day walking round Tavistock Square I made up, as I sometimes make up my books, *To the Lighthouse*, in a great, apparently involuntary rush. One thing burst into another. Blowing bubbles out of a pipe gives the feeling of the rapid crowd of ideas and scenes which blew out of my mind, so that my lips seemed syllabling of their own accord as I walked. What blew the bubbles? Why then? I have no notion. But I wrote the book very quickly; and when it was written, I ceased to be obsessed by my mother. I no longer hear her voice; I do not see her. (Woolf 1989, p.90)

She goes on to suppose that: 'I did for myself what psycho-analysts do for their patients. I expressed some very long felt and deeply felt emotion. And in expressing it I explained it and then laid it to rest' (p.90). There is no indication here that Woolf specifically set out on a therapeutic quest; indeed, she would have been unhappy at the idea that her writing might be thought of as in any sense a conscious therapeutic undertaking. She was concerned first and foremost with the creation of works of art and was quite clear about the need to distinguish between 'writing as an art and as self-expression' (Woolf 1928/1972, p.79). Whatever therapeutic benefit she may have derived from her writing came by default rather than by design.

For some writers, on the other hand, creative writing involves a conscious quest for self. In his journal of 1920–21 Hermann Hesse, that most autobiographical of fiction writers, describes creative writing as

> a long, diverse, and winding path, whose goal it would be to express the personality, the 'I' of the artist so completely, so minutely in all its branchings…that this 'I' would in the end be as it were unreeled and finished, that it would have raged and burned itself out. (Hesse 1970, pp.80–82; quoted by Stelzig 1988, p.38)

The quest for the complete and ultimate expression of the self on the page is, from the perspective of current thinking about the self, unrealistic. But Hesse's work stands as a striking example of how the act of placing oneself and one's experience on the page in fictional form can be a means to a deeper self-engagement and self-understanding.

The area we are calling 'creative writing and personal development' embraces the sort of approaches represented by both Woolf and Hesse. But it is much broader than that. In the UK over approximately the past ten years there has been a steadily growing interest in the practice of autobiography and creative writing as a means of gaining insight into oneself, of coping with difficult emotional or psychological problems, or as a way of dealing with difficult life experiences such as emotional traumas, illnesses, ageing and death. This practice is to be found not only amongst individuals working towards personal growth independently or in groups, but also amongst therapists, analysts and counsellors working with patients or clients. It can also be seen amongst writers working in institutions such as prisons, hospitals and day centres, with a wide spectrum of client groups ranging from those with mental health problems or learning disabilities, to older people, stroke victims, dementia sufferers and terminally ill people.

Much of this practice has been carried out in isolation, with individuals, practitioners and user groups developing their own working methods and techniques. However, during the last few years a field has begun to take shape. Papers have begun to appear in professional journals such as the journal of the National Association of Writers in Education (NAWE),[1] or have been delivered at conferences on topics as diverse as contemporary women in

---

1   For example, Morgan (1996) and McLoughlin (1997).

poetry and medical ethics.[2] Practitioner meetings on specific topics, such as writing and mental health, have been held.[3]

In 1994 the Poetry Society established a Special Interests Group on Issues of Health, Healing and Personal Development. This comprised practitioners, academics, researchers, representatives of user groups and interested individuals. In 1996 this group constituted itself into the Association for the Literary Arts in Personal Development – LAPIDUS – with the aim of providing a focus for continued development in this field. 1996 also saw the start of the first academic programme in the UK to look critically at the emerging field: the Postgraduate Diploma in Creative Writing and Personal Development at the University of Sussex Centre for Continuing Education.

LAPIDUS has a large and enthusiastic membership and it is clear that there is a great deal of interest in the field of creative writing and personal development. This has clearly reached some sort of threshold in the UK, where there is now the critical mass and diversity of practices to generate useful discussion of the form and content of the work being carried out, as well as directions it might take in the future. This book is a first attempt to do that, by offering an introduction to the range of current thinking and practice. As well as addressing issues regarding practice, our contributors also propose ways to orientate the new field theoretically. This is an important aspect of the work to be done if the field is to develop, and as yet very little attention has been devoted to it.

The book is divided into two parts. The first provides an overview of current practice in education, therapy and various areas of health care; the second is devoted to the application of theory to practice and to the exploration of possible theoretical frameworks within which practice might be usefully thought through.

Current practice of creative writing in personal development

As Woolf shows us, personal development can be a by-product of engaging in writing for the purposes of creating art, especially when the raw material

---

2   'Kicking Daffodils Conference and Festival', Oxford Brookes University, April 1994; and 'The Royal Society of Edinburgh Workshop', The Wellcome Unit for the History of Medicine, University of Glasgow, May 1994.

3   For example, 'Writers Working in Mental Health' organised by NAWE, Ilkley, Yorkshire, October 1995, and London, January 1996.

used in the writing is the writer's own experience. This is what Celia has observed while teaching creative writing through the use of autobiography as a starting point for fiction. For many people writing fictional autobiography can have a significant and positive impact on their self-understanding and sense of identity. The writing technique which Celia discusses in 'Writing with the Voice of the Child' – the fictionalising of early memories – can provide insight not only into the writer's past but more significantly into the present structure of the writer's personality. The emphasis which creative writing puts on *showing* the feelings and emotions of characters in fiction rather than simply *telling* their story makes it a valuable method for getting in touch with the inner life. However, there are potential dangers in carrying out this work in a straightforward creative writing context. Creative writing classes may become, on occasion, arenas where deep feelings and emotions are unearthed and expressed, and teachers and group leaders may sometimes find themselves in the position of counsellor or therapist, without the appropriate skills to act as such.

In Cheryl Moskowitz's use of creative writing in her practice as a psychodynamic counsellor, therapeutic sessions provide the holding framework for the emergence of deep feelings and emotions. Cheryl also advocates fictionalising the self as a method of self-exploration. Drawing on Robert Louis Stevenson's celebrated story of psychic opposites, Dr Jekyll and Mr Hyde, she focuses on the presence within the personality of different aspects of the self which may be at odds with each other. 'The Self as Source' is a method of creating fictional characters out of opposites within the personality, which might be thought of as the 'good' and 'bad' or 'well' and 'ill' selves. Once objectified on the page, these opposing 'selves' are brought into contact through story, where they engage with each other and ultimately exchange something of significance. Cheryl shows how valuable this technique is in her example of work with a client struggling with the 'ill' and 'well' parts of herself in the aftermath of leukaemia.

Graham Hartill has used his technique, 'The Web of Words', with a wide variety of groups, including sufferers from mental health problems. He takes his inspiration from James Hillman's idea of 'soul-making': the use of words and images to tap into the deep sources of the self. Using 'keys' as a focus, the technique encourages participants to enter their imaginary worlds and to create their own 'metaphors of self'. These metaphors are then linked together through a group reading, the group leader acting as the centre of the 'web' by interspersing the individual readings with a 'chorus'. The result is more akin to a sacred chant than to a literary reading. It can be a deeply moving experience, although Graham is not working as a Jungian therapist.

Whilst the emphasis in Graham's approach is on writing as a form of healing, for the client group Fiona discusses – adults with learning disabilities – the emphasis is on writing as empowerment. Here, engaging in – mostly dictated – creative writing helps to develop verbal, intellectual and imaginative skills, but it can also be a way of excavating identity and of taking an important step into the prevailing discourses to which this client group does not have ready access. The skills of the facilitator – highly developed literary skills and well-formulated ethical procedures – are crucial here to ensure that both process and product work a balance between prioritising the clients' own ways of writing their experiences and the new opportunities and skills which the facilitator can contribute.

Gillie Bolton's work is in the area of primary health care. She discusses the at first sight surprising suggestion that GPs might 'prescribe' creative writing instead of pills to those people who seek help for psychological distress or physical ailments caused by it. This idea has been the subject of a pilot project in Sheffield involving six GPs. Initial feedback from both GPs and patients has largely been positive, and valuable insights have been gained for future provision. The challenge here will be to devise criteria for identifying patients for whom writing is likely to be most effective, and to move beyond the informal and anecdotal to a more solidly based evaluation of the effects of the writing.

Colin Archer takes on the role of scribe in his difficult work with terminally ill people in hospices. Whilst accepting that only a minority of patients will want to avail themselves of his services, Colin finds that there are many reasons why dying people wish to place themselves if not 'on the page' then 'on the line'. Writing can serve as a distraction from pain or as a means of filling time; it can fulfil the desire to leave something behind for the family; or it can address deeper concerns, such as the need to express in writing what is really being felt about illness and approaching death, or help to find a shape and meaning to life. Whether the resulting pieces of writing are 'final fictions' or 'final facts' is not important in this work; rather it is the catharsis and the communication which both process and product can bring about.

In John Killick's work with dementia sufferers the emphasis is more on process than product. John believes that writers working with this group of people are part of a new approach to dementia care, where emphasis is put on the sufferers as individuals with a need to express themselves creatively and to communicate with others. Recording and shaping these people's extraordinarily creative language into prose or poetic form, John often finds himself in the role of editor to people who no longer have reflective powers to bring to bear on their own work. Inevitably, important questions arise here. For whom is the writing being done? Does it have a therapeutic value and, if so, for whom? Does the writer have the right to edit and shape a patient's words? In his chapter 'A Matter of the Life and Death of the Mind', John attempts to answer these questions and speculates on the sources of the creativity he identifies in the people with whom he works.

Theoretical contexts for creative writing in personal development

As the chapters discussed above indicate, some practitioners in the field of creative writing and personal development have already begun to explore theories which might frame their work. Graham Hartill reflects on the writings of analytical psychologist James Hillman. Celia thinks about the literary autobiographical canon as well as about the classroom as a Winnicottian 'good enough' holding environment for personal development; and Fiona works with existing health care practices and deploys critical reading techniques to respond to writing produced in care settings. Other practitioners, such as Cheryl Moskowitz, are using writing and personal development within an existing practice which is already theoretically and ethically informed.

Plainly theory is going to have an important role to play in the constitution of the field. But how can any single theoretical framework, whether borrowed, appropriated or constructed, account for the diversity of practice which Part One marks out? The answer seems to be that this is not possible. In the contemporary field of creative writing and personal development, practices and their contexts are diverse. So are their aims and their ideas about the nature of writing, personality and development. Some practices even seem to contradict each other. Writers in health care settings see individuals' access to creative writing activities as particularly significant at a time when they are vulnerable and alienated from 'normal' life. Members of Survivors' Poetry, on the other hand, argue that opportunities to write and share poetry can only be available in a meaningful sense outside the unequal relationship between care worker and client.

No unifying theory can accommodate such diversity and contradiction. And indeed no single dominant theoretical strand has emerged from the field. Bearing this in mind, Part Two looks at some of the diverse theoretical work being done in and on the borders of the field of creative writing and personal development. This work, informed by discourses as various as sociology, philosophy and psychotherapy, throws up challenges and suggests avenues for debate. However, several key conceptual loci – siting clusters of often contradictory ideas – inform this part of the book. These conceptual sites include the role of autobiography and other textual practices in defining ideas of the self; the significance of feeling; humanism – interpreted as the significance of work centred on the human individual; the status and accessibility of truth; and the self's potential for transformation.

Several of these ideas occur in Peter Abbs' work. To open the theoretical debate he contextualises contemporary developments in the field of writing the self with an examination of three moments in the history of autobiography. His chapter uses canonical texts by Heraclitus, Saint Augustine and Rousseau to map changing ideas about the nature of the self and goes on to argue that the 'self' with which we now work is, therefore, necessarily a historicist construct. Abbs points out that this does not invalidate the work of personal development but rather increases its richness. It is the very nature of his 'self' that the writer working in this field is engaged in producing.

On the other hand Fiona surveys philosophical and theoretical models in which language use is seen as creating the individual discursive space in which the self – however it is constructed – can carry out its own characteristic way of being. Because the stakes of discursive survival are high, ways of thinking and using language struggle with each other for the power to be heard and respected. The vulnerable individual's struggle for her own life in language to be acknowledged may therefore be facilitated by access to a powerful but nevertheless individualist discourse such as creative writing.

Mary Stuart's examination of 'Writing, the Self and the Social Process' prefaces her presentation of writing as social interaction with a general discussion of the role that social interaction may play in defining the individual self. She links structuralist ideas – about the role played by value-laden language and culture in the social construction of the self – to theories of symbolic interactionism, in which what is essentially the conscious self acquires, through interaction with the world, a self-knowledge which will only be destabilised by the essentially unconscious 'me'. Stuart concentrates on the structural role of narrative in the development of the self, and on language and writing practice as providing particularly strong examples of such narratives. Unlike Pateman, who represents such difficulties as manifestations of inner psychic states, she suggests that writers' anxieties about the quality of their work manifest instead the presence, even in language practices, of such determining social interactions as esteem and shame.

In his chapter, suggestively subtitled 'The Emergence of Truth in Writing', Trevor Pateman proposes the process of writing as neither simply a matter of self-discovery nor exclusively a form of self-invention either of author or narrator. Instead he suggests that writing – process and product – is one way in which selfhood is 'enacted'. Writing is one form of human being and the state of the writing self is enacted in the finished text as well as in its production. However, unlike Fiona, who concentrates on the potential of discursive territory as such, Trevor goes on to argue that, in particular, writerly states of dis-ease such as the repression of difficult feelings are enacted *within* the text in the form of the 'empty word'. The 'empty word' lacks the affect lived experience can give to the 'full word', which is often characterised by the vividly sensory world it contains. This way of thinking through the life of the text further allows Pateman to re-read writer's block as a form of repression.

Like Mary Stuart, Jan Campbell recognises that the reader too interacts with the written text. She shows reading as transformative of the reader's experience not only of the world but of her own self. For Campbell, hermeneutic reader response theories – in which the subject/object self, situated within its own reading experience, must constantly reconfigure this self in the light of that experience – combine with a post-structuralist psychoanalysis, in which the analysis itself is one in a series of collaborative fictions, to suggest the significant role that stories and texts may play in the continued construction of the reader's self. She uses her own experiences of reading Toni Morrison's novel *Beloved* to look in more detail at the possibility of a 'transformational space' between text and reader, between the text's implied reader and a reading self constructed by multiple narratives mediating bodily and linguistic experiences.

Whilst Jan Campbell focuses on the relationship between the implied reader and the reading self, Celia explores the relationship between the writing self and the implied author. Drawing on the psychoanalytic theory of Karen Horney and the work of literary critic Bernard Paris, who interprets and applies Horney's ideas to the understanding of character and conflict in literature, Celia suggests that the implied author of autobiographically based writings, when understood as an expression of aspects of the writer's personality, can provide insight into the present state of the psyche. She frames her suggestion within the context of current thinking in psychoanalysis and the theory of autobiography, both of which stress the textuality of the self and the fictional nature of 'personal truth'.

The complex diversity of theoretical work in Part Two suggests a number of potential future orientations of the field of creative writing and personal development. It is not possible to predict whether any one orientation will come to dominate the field, or whether the work which is going on will continue to develop a number of viewpoints in dialogue with each other. Rather, this diversity suggests that the practice itself is situated at a conceptually rich cross-roads between reflective and experiential work as well as between literature, theory and personal development.

It is also, of course, situated between present and future work. And it is to future developments in the field of creative writing and personal development that our last chapter turns. In making a case for ethical practice rigorously underpinned by research, we identify three main strands within the field's activities. We suggest, first, that writing which privileges the literary product in the conventional way, but in which the writer engages in some form of personal development while writing, is a significant presence in this field, even when the writer is not conscious of other related practices. Such practices include, second, artform-led writing activities engaged in because of perceived personal development benefits – examples are individual diary writing and community arts projects – and, third, current and potential future uses of writing within, or as the basis for, a particular therapy.

It is this last idea which is the most controversial. However, at present a writing therapy *per se* – as opposed to the use of writing within formal therapeutic practices – is potential rather than actual practice. And we do not argue that such a therapy is the only form future practice in the field should take. Rather we suggest that, unless a case for writing therapy based on established methodologies and criteria of benefit *can* be made, it will become increasingly hard to argue for benefits which have been identified only in anecdotal form. In the last ten years the field of creative writing and personal development has rapidly achieved a high profile through the development of artform-led activities with perceived personal development benefits. However, developments in the field, which have hitherto been powered in part by novelty, will in the long term be restricted rather than enhanced unless practitioners and theorists can advance convincing arguments for the safety, professionalism and benefits of their practice. And such arguments will necessarily beg the question of why, if such a case can be made, such benefits have not been formalised into a therapy.

Whilst some of our contributors air arguments for the advantages of informal settings for their practice, we suggest that any future emergent writing therapy should legitimate artform-led practices. It may also provide a context in which literary works produced in conjunction with personal development can be read with particular insight and attention. We also suggest that such a therapy may limit the development of writing practices which make inappropriate therapeutic claims.

All this, however, is in the future. In the meantime this book celebrates the practical and intellectual richness of a field characterised by the commitment to personal development as well as by the literary excellence of a Woolf or Hesse. We would like to thank all the contributors for the energy, integrity and enthusiasm with which they have made the field 'come alive'.

References

Hesse, H. (1970) *Gesammelte Werke.* Vol. 11. Frankfurt: Suhrkamp Verlag.

McLoughlin, D. (1997) 'Teaching writing in a hospice day centre.' *Writing in Education 11,* 7–9.

Morgan, P. (1996) 'Whittingham Hospital writer-in-residence.' *Writing in Education 9,* 25–28.

Stelzig, E.L. (1988) *Hermann Hesse's Fictions of the Self: Autobiography and the Confessional Imagination.* Princeton, NJ: Princeton University Press.

Woolf, V. (1928/1972) *A Room of One's Own.* Harmondsworth: Penguin.

Woolf, V. (1989) 'Sketch of the past.' In *Moments of Being.* London: Grafton Books, pp.72–173.

PART ONE

Current Practice of Creative Writing in Personal Development

Writing with the Voice of the Child
Fictional Autobiography and Personal Development

Celia Hunt

My interest in creative writing and personal development arose out of my teaching of a writing course, 'Autobiography and the Imagination',[1] at the University of Sussex Centre for Continuing Education, which advocated the writing of fictional autobiography as a way into fiction. Whilst this course was devised primarily with the aim of enabling people to find their writing voice,[2] it became increasingly obvious to me that, for many people, writing fictional autobiography had a significant and positive impact on their self-understanding and sense of identity. This led me to engage in research into the personal development component of my creative writing course.[3] It also led me to set up the Postgraduate Diploma in Creative Writing and Personal Development in which I explore, with students, the potential of the writing exercises I used in 'Autobiography and the Imagination' for gaining insight into the inner life. One of the writing exercises I have found most useful in this context is 'Writing with the Voice of the Child', which focuses on finding an appropriate voice for early memories.

---

1 In 1994 this course was incorporated into the Certificate in Creative Writing as the first term of a three-term programme. For an outline of the course, see Hunt (1995).

2 For a discussion of the idea of a 'writing voice', see Hunt (1997) and Pateman in this volume.

3 My DPhil on 'The Use of Fictional Autobiography in Personal Development' is due for completion in 1998.

The exercise 'Writing with the Voice of the Child'

I usually begin this exercise by asking students to think about their early memories and to say something about their nature. A few say that they have long tracts of memory from their early lives in linear form. Some claim to have very little early memory or even none at all. The majority report that they have strong memories of individual events or a series of linked events, or that they have fragments of memories of which the full memory is lost. For the purposes of this exercise the fragmentary or episodic nature of early memory is helpful rather than not. The point of the exercise is not to find the *truth* of the past with a capital 'T'. After all, from research on memory we know that, whilst autobiographical memories contain a high degree of self-reference, they are never true in the sense of being literal representations of events. As Martin Conway says, '…they may be accurate without being literal and may represent the *personal meaning* of an event at the expense of accuracy' (Conway 1990, p.9; emphasis added). This means that autobiographical memories are *interpretations of past events from the point of view of the present.* They will therefore include information about current thoughts, wishes and motivations, as well as the beliefs and understanding of the rememberer (p.11). As Paul John Eakin says in his discussion of autobiographical writing, '…the materials of the past are shaped by memory and imagination to serve the needs of present consciousness' (Eakin 1985, p.5), and it is these needs of present consciousness, expressed through the fictions we create about our pasts, which can provide insight into ourselves in the present.

To get students thinking about their early memories, I ask them to bring to the session a small portfolio of old photographs of themselves, their parents and their early environment. They spend up to half-an-hour discussing these with a partner. Then I ask them to put the photographs aside and to identify a particular memory to write about, preferably a fragment or a single image rather than a complete event. For most people the starting point will be a visual image taken from a photograph. I ask them to concentrate on this visual image and to 'walk into it', as it were, and to ask themselves: 'what do I see?', 'what do I hear?', 'what do I smell?', 'what do I taste?', 'what do things feel like under my fingers when I touch them?'[4] I encourage them to spend some time with their eyes closed, immersing themselves in the

---

4   This is a development of an idea suggested in Fairfax and Moat (1981).

memory, expanding it through imagination and experiencing what the memory feels like, or, to put it another way, to engage with the emotional *feeling tone* of the memory.

After they have spent a while feeling their way into the memory and expanding it through imagination, I suggest that they start writing about it, using what I call the 'strong words and phrases method'. This involves writing down individual words and phrases which come readily to mind when associating to the memory. Nouns, adjectives and adverbs which encapsulate the sights, sounds, smells, tastes and tactile impressions are important, as are verbs of motion, particularly present participles, which help to introduce movement into the memory. When students have accumulated a sufficient amount of material, I suggest that they start to develop a more connected piece of writing, whether prose or poetry.

Finding a form for early memories

As examples of different forms which can be used for early memories, we discuss extracts from Virginia Woolf's 'Sketch of the Past' (1989) and Nathalie Sarraute's *Childhood* (1984). For Virginia Woolf, conveying feelings and emotions in words was a central feature of her writing, writing which, as much as it was a creation of works of art, was an attempt to find a clearer sense of her own identity and therefore a kind of autobiography (see McCracken 1994).[5] When, towards the end of her life, she came to write autobiography proper, it was the sensual quality of memory, conveyed particularly through the visual and aural senses and imbued with the emotional 'feeling tone' of the past, which was her vehicle for committing her earliest memories to the page:

> ...the first memory. This was of red and purple flowers on a black ground – my mother's dress; and she was sitting either in a train or in an omnibus, and I was on her lap. I therefore saw the flowers she was wearing very close; and can still see purple and red and blue, I think, against the black; they must have been anemones, I suppose. Perhaps we were going to St. Ives; more probably, for from the light it must have been evening, we were coming back to London. (Woolf 1989, p.72)

5   See Roe (1990) and (1995) for a discussion of the paradoxes implicit in this argument.

This early memory is significant in that it not only gives a powerful, close-up impression of colour and light, but it also captures a sense of closeness to the mother in the way, perhaps, a child experiences the world before it has the capacity to reason. The factual detail is vague and clearly devised by the adult consciousness, which is trying to make sense of the where and when: a train, perhaps, or an omnibus, going to St Ives or coming back to London. The core of the memory, the sensuous feeling-tone, is set in a context which is already hypothetical, mythical. And indeed this mythical context suits Woolf's purposes: fictionalising the memory allows a link to be made to another important early memory:

> ...it is...convenient artistically to suppose that we were going to St. Ives, for that will lead to my other memory, which also seems to be my first memory, and in fact it is the most important of all my memories. If life has a base that it stands upon, if it is a bowl that one fills and fills and fills – then my bowl without a doubt stands upon this memory. It is of lying half asleep, half awake, in bed in the nursery at St. Ives. It is of hearing the waves breaking, one, two, one, two, and sending a splash of water over the beach; and then breaking, one, two, one, two, behind a yellow blind. It is of hearing the blind draw its little acorn across the floor as the wind blew the blind out. It is of lying and hearing this splash and seeing this light, and feeling, it is almost impossible that I should be here; of feeling the purest ecstasy I can conceive. (Woolf 1989 pp.72–3)

In this second part of her earliest memory it is sound which is more significant than sight – the relentless breaking of the waves and the scraping across the floor of the little acorn on the blind-pull – but both sight and sound are part of a great intensity of feeling, the purest ecstasy of feeling. Lying in the nursery behind the pale yellow blind, the writer imagines that her child-self is lying in a grape and looking through a film of semi-transparent yellow, a metaphor that was central to her throughout her life. Woolf seems to find words inadequate to convey these feelings; she would prefer to paint them, in the way the impressionists and post-impressionists did:

> If I were a painter I should paint these first impressions in pale yellow, silver, and green. There was the pale yellow blind; the green sea; and the silver of the passion flowers. I should make a picture that was globular; semi-transparent. I should make a picture of curved petals; of shells; of things that were semi-transparent; I should make curved shapes, showing the light through, but not giving a clear outline. Everything

would be large and dim; and what was seen would at the same time be heard; sounds would come through this petal or leaf – sounds indistinguishable from sights. Sound and sight seem to make equal parts of these first impressions. When I think of the early morning in bed I also hear the caw of rooks falling from a great height. The sound seems to fall through an elastic, gummy air; which holds it up; which prevents it from being sharp and distinct. The quality of the air above Talland House [the family home in St Ives] seemed to suspend sound, to let it sink down slowly, as if it were caught in a blue gummy veil. The rooks cawing is part of the waves breaking – one, two, one, two – and the splash as the wave drew back and then it gathered again, and I lay there half awake, half asleep, drawing in such ecstasy as I cannot describe. (Woolf 1989 p.74)

Woolf refers to these memories as 'pictures' in the mind, then qualifies this word, because 'sight was always then so much mixed with sound that picture is not the right word' (p.75). Her imagination is governed by a synaesthetic way of thinking: it not only links together sights and sounds but, as Sue Roe says, reactivates rhythms and colours in the manner of the imagist poets (Roe 1990, p.44). These sensations coalesce into intensely remembered, intensely felt moments, 'moments of being', as she calls them, which rise out of the cotton-wool of everyday life. They evoke rapture and are much more real to her than the present moment, although she is aware of their partly fictional nature and the extent to which she is creating them in the present:

At times I can go back to St. Ives more completely than I can this morning. I can reach a state where I seem to be watching things happen as if I were there. That is, I suppose, that my memory supplies what I had forgotten, so that it seems as if it were happening independently, though I am really making it happen. (Woolf 1989, p.75)

She toys with the idea that the past is 'an avenue lying behind; a long ribbon of scenes, emotions'(p.75). She would like to be able to fit a plug into the wall and listen in to the past, not just catching these individual moments, but being able to 'live our lives through from the start'(p.76). This, of course, is impossible, but what she does instead is to step back into the old memories and draw them into the present through fictionalising.

Whilst in 'Sketch of the Past' Woolf re-creates the sense impressions of the child's world in the voice of the adult, in her autobiography, *Childhood*, Nathalie Sarraute attempts to re-inhabit the emotions of her child-self and to speak them with the voice of the child. At the same time, however, she steps outside of the child's voice and gives the reader her adult reflections on the child's words and feelings, so that the child's and the adult's points of view form a dialogue. Here is a typical example:

Outside that luminous, dazzling, vibrant garden, everything seems to be covered in a pall of greyness, it has a rather dismal, or rather, a sort of cramped air...but it is never sad. Not even what I still remember of the nursery school...a bare courtyard surrounded by high, sombre walls, round which we marched in Indian file, dressed in black overalls and wearing clogs.

Here, however, looming up out of that mist, is the sudden violence of terror, of horror...I scream, I struggle...what has happened? What is happening to me?

'Your grandmother is coming to see you'... Mama told me that... My grandmother? Papa's mother? Is that possible? is she really going to come? she never comes, she is so far away...I don't remember her at all, but I feel her presence in the affectionate little letters she sends me from over there, in the softwood boxes with pretty pictures carved in them, whose hollowed-out contours you can trace with your finger, in the painted wooden cups covered by a varnish that is soft to the touch... 'When will she come? when will she be here'... 'Tomorrow afternoon... You can't go out for your walk...'

I wait, I watch out for her, I listen to the footsteps on the stairs, on the landing...there, here she is, the bell has rung, I want to rush out, I'm stopped, wait, don't move...the door to my room opens, a man and a woman dressed in white overalls grab hold of me, I've been put on someone's knees, I'm being held, I struggle, they press a piece of cotton wool over my mouth, over my nose, a mask, from which something atrocious, asphyxiating, emanates, suffocates me, fills my lungs, rises to my head, dying, that's what it is, I'm dying... And then, I am alive again, I'm in my bed, my throat is burning, my tears are flowing, Mama is wiping them away... 'My little kitten, you had to have an operation, you know, they took something out of your throat, it was harming you, it was bad for you...go to sleep now, it's all over...'

– How long did it take you to realise that she never tried – unless very absent-mindedly and clumsily – to put herself in your place?...

– Yes, curiously enough that indifference, that casualness, were part of her charm, in the literal sense of the word, she charmed me... No word, however powerfully uttered, has ever sunk into me with the same percussive force as some of hers.

'If you touch one of those poles, you'll die...'

– Perhaps she didn't say it exactly in those terms...

– Perhaps not...but that was how it reached me. If you touch that, you'll die...

We are going for a walk somewhere in the country, I don't remember where, Mama is walking slowly, on Kolya's arm...I am behind, rooted to the spot in front of the wooden telegraph pole... 'If you touch that, you'll die,' Mama said that...I have an urge to touch it, I want to know, I'm very frightened, I want to see what it will be like, I stretch out my hand, I touch the wood of the telegraph pole with my finger...and, immediately, that's it, it's happened to me, Mama knew it, Mama knows everything, it's certain, I'm dead, I run up to them screaming, I hide my head in Mama's skirts, I shout with all my strength: I'm dead...they don't know it, I'm dead... But what's the matter with you? I'm dead, dead, dead, I touched the pole, there, it's happened, the horrible thing, the most horrible thing possible was in that pole, I touched it and it passed into me, it's in me, I roll on the ground to get it to come out, I sob, I howl, I'm dead...they pick me up in their arms, they shake me, kiss me... No, no, you're quite all right...I touched the pole, Mama told me...she laughs, they both laugh, and this calms me... (Sarraute 1984, pp. 17–20)[6]

As in the Woolf extract, sense impressions are very important here: colours, sounds and feelings loom large – the luminous, dazzling, vibrant garden; the clogs clattering on the bare courtyard; the cramped air which is never sad. Like Woolf's 'moments of being', they rise up out of the 'pall of greyness' which surrounds them. The immediacy of events is intensified by the use of the present tense and the switching into the child's voice. In those moments Sarraute becomes the child, naive, taken in by her mother's soft but insistent untruths. The child's experience requires exaggeration in order to convey the extremity of it: the struggle with the doctors, the shock of asphyxiation, the sensation of dying. In the second incident, where she touches the electricity pylon, she is certain that she is dead. Death is the spectre stalking the colourful memories of childhood. Then, in between the memories, the dialogue between two aspects of the adult: the 'me' and the 'you', debating between themselves the rights and wrongs of the mother's treatment. These

---

6   I am indebted to Abbs and Richardson (1990) for drawing my attention to this extract.

two adult selves seem to represent Sarraute's ambivalence towards her mother: she wants to damn her cruelty, but she can also appreciate her charm. The voices of child and adult are consistent, authentic, wholly self-contained. The switch from one to the other is made by subtle cues in the language used: the short, breathless sentences of the child and the calmer, much more leisurely sentences of the adult.

These two extracts are very different in form, but what they have in common and what is particularly useful for our purposes is that both Woolf and Sarraute seek to re-create early childhood memories by stepping inside them, re-inhabiting them. They use sense impressions and the techniques of fiction to draw the memories into the now and bring them alive. In this way they create fictions of the self which contain feelings and emotions which belong as much to the present as they do to the past, and can be used to throw light on the present configuration of the personality.

Students' responses to 'Writing with the Voice of the Child'

Students taking the Certificate and the Diploma have made interesting use of the exercise 'Writing with the Voice of the Child', using Woolf and Sarraute as models. Tania Waghorn,[7] for example, used the extract from Woolf as a model to re-create the feeling tone of a very important person in her childhood, her great-grandmother. The piece opens with Tania's struggle to place herself inside the fragment of memory which is her starting point:

It is difficult to fix my mind upon a time and a place, or moreover to distinguish between what I have been told to remember and what I really do remember. It is hard to place the entirety of me now as part of a snatched fragment in my mind then; an elusive fragment that slips from my grasp, indeed the grasp itself slips so that my recollection exudes a lack of my own significance; a lack of my own voice, yet I am central to the piece I try and recall. I try and climb into my memory, but it is like a discoloured or yellowed photograph hazy with age. Perhaps the day itself was grey, which is why its imprint is bleary, but my predominant recollection is a sense of a lack of participation; an absence of substantial mental presence and contribution. I was more a spectator; a child without

7   I am grateful to Tania for allowing me to quote from 'Earliest Memory', as well as from her essay which discussed this and other pieces of writing.

a voice; a piece that merely has cause and effect externally. I remember feeling weak and dominated.

Already in the attempt to re-inhabit the memory, Tania has a sense of herself as being absent rather than present. As we shall see in a moment, this sensation is important in terms of what she draws from the memory overall. Having struggled to get into the memory, she begins to sketch out first what she sees and hears, but it is the feelings of the memory which predominate:

The house to my right was mine and an equal, the woman was not. Strength and austerity oozed from her as I recall her marching me in a pram along sheltered, fir-lined roads. Was it really possible to march a three year old? Perhaps it was. It made me small, it made me minus three. It was all achingly silent, yet I was cocooned not necessarily in love, but in duty – in the womb of the adult; the authority; the relation. She was my great-grandmother who I never even spoke to in my life, as she died soon after this. I remember nothing of her but from that day and the connotations her name had later on.

Having fixed the location and the person, she then takes a further step into the memory itself and tries to use the other senses, smell and touch, but strangely they are lacking:

No real colour stands from that day – more a smeared and anaemic smudge of shades. I can feel the stillness now in my recollection and my lack of voice; my minus three; my lack of part. I can attempt to imagine smells. I could climb into the nostrils of the day and excite autumnal crispy tangs and the sharp, clear freshness of grey drizzle on grass and roads and fallen leaves. But the smell in recollection is grey too – cold and indistinguishable. An image of bursting shrubbery dominates the ground of my memory, alongside the backdrop of my home. I should have been in a pram yet my sensation is that I was looking on, seeing the tallness of my great-grandmother poised in rocks. She had more roots than the shrubbery; more foundation than the house. She strangles the memory so that the growth around me has no colour. How strange that I should recall no green, no flush of any boldness. The impact is her height, the aura a silent force which holds the whole gummy image in a suspension of still outlines; a captured focus; a capsuled moment; a snapshot in my mind.

What emerges from the memory is an impression of power and domination, which render the world colourless. The adult Tania understands why her great-grandmother was like that:

> The only voice is age; a certain history; a great-grandmother erect and upstanding. The dimness calls up the history. I think of war, of women's work, of trenches, strength and bitterness born from suffering, women's suffering. I think of silence, defiant continuance amidst oppression and acres of destruction, humility, submission, heads held high, chins held firm, knarled hands stiff with drudgery. The images play around the height of her; the strength of her; the knowledge of her, and they scoop the motionlessness of my memory and tell me why it is still.

But whilst she understands how difficult a woman's position must have been in her great-grandmother's time, she feels strongly that her coldness and colourlessness was a damaging experience in her own childhood. Because this woman did not relate to her, she seems to be saying, she as a child was not able to get a sense of herself; she felt alone, isolated. The piece does not tell us anything about other people in Tania's childhood, such as her parents, so the reader does not know how formative the relationship with the great-grandmother would have been. But if we assume, as we have noted above, that autobiographical memories are shaped to a considerable degree by the needs of present consciousness, then what is important for Tania is not whether the memory is objectively 'true', but rather what it tells her about herself in the present. As she says in her essay, it is the 'very real precariousness in the child's sense of [her] own worth and significance' which she takes away from this piece, and a realisation that part of herself continues to feel that way. From a personal development point of view, this was a significant piece of writing for Tania in that it enabled her to identify the important theme (for her) of self-fragmentation, and to lay the foundation for other pieces she was to write later, in which she sought to bring the fragmented parts of herself together, on the page.

Tania's piece is particularly successful in its effective conveying of feelings which are part of memory. Whilst, in recovering the memory, she certainly inhabits it, she does not speak it with the voice of the child but, like Woolf, draws the feelings of the child into present consciousness through imagination and speaks them with the voice of the adult. Christine Roberts,[8] on the other hand, uses Sarraute's approach to *inhabit* the feelings and sensations of a memory and to speak them with the voice of the child, although the language she uses is a mixture of the child's and the adult's.

My tongue is pressed against my lower lip in the effort of concentration. My fingers, whose lack of motor control I sense but do not understand, struggle to split the slender wilting stem of the daisy I have picked in an effort to create an eyehole through which to thread another daisy stem. It is important to pick them close to the ground to give myself the best chance of splitting the stems cleanly. My daisies come away in my fumbling fingers with an inch long stem, barely enough for the dexterous process needed to convert flower into jewellery.

The pain of the effort rises through my cramped knees, bent back at an angle beneath my smocked cotton dress. I long to release the tension, to give up the struggle, but I can't. It is as if I am nailed to the ground. Ten, eleven, twelve daisies, and the chain is finished. I offer it to my sister.

I stand up. I brush the grass mowings from my grubby knees which now bear the indented mesh of grass stems and the hard clayey ground.

Now I am sitting close by the rose bed. I am dwarfed by these rose bushes – Hybrid Teas as I can now name them. Their woody stems form a cruel forest of thorny branches – the kind that protect sleeping princesses in turreted castles. But the air surrounding this barbed growth is heady with a warm scent which envelopes and reassures me. I embark upon a perilous task. My skinny brown arm cautiously weaves its way in and out of the tough spiky branches in search of prickles. I am making a prickle chain. The older, larger prickles trace white scratches on my arm as my hand seeks out the new growth, the softer prickles. Finding them, the trick is to bend them sideways until they snap off and then to add them to a small collection of prickles in the soft gingham folds of my skirt. Then begins the painful process of creating the prickle chain.

I push each thorn into the exposed base of the last until the chain resembles an article of medieval torture quite unlike the slender delicate creation made out of daisies. It seemed at the time, and again the tension in the muscles and the tautness of the tongue and lips tell me this was so, crucial to tackle this brutal task. Is it simply a desire to emulate my older

8   I am grateful to Christine for allowing me to quote from 'Daisy Chains and Prickle Chains', as well as from her essay which discussed this and other pieces of writing.

sister, so competently creating her prickled artefact at my side? I find it difficult but am driven by this desire to complete the task, however painful, however complex.

'Daisy Chains and Prickle Chains' is an effective piece of writing which captures the intense physicality of concentration and purpose. Christine was intrigued by the fact that it contained such destructive and painful images relating to childhood play, when the photograph which sparked it off, of herself at the age of seven or eight, showed her 'smiling and nonchalantly leaning on a fork in our garden'. Thinking about this, she was 'surprised at just how many memories of play were associated with pain and discomfort'. Rather than trying to draw conclusions from this for her childhood, she found it more useful to relate the contrasting imagery in the piece to her present experience and to see the piece 'as a metaphor for my own writing personality at this stage'. Seen in this way, the strenuous physical sensations conveyed in the piece – the tension in the muscles, the tautness of tongue and lips – seem to represent a struggle, of which Christine became increasingly aware during the first term of the Diploma, between the desire to write spontaneously with the senses and the blocking of this desire by what she refers to as her 'arrogant intellect,'[9] which turns writing into a 'brutal task' that brings pain and discomfort. Thus what the piece provides is a powerful picture of different aspects of the present personality in conflict with each other.

The value of fictionalising from self

In both these examples, exploring early memories leads to insights into the present structure of the psyche and provides both writers with new avenues to pursue in their self-exploration. The value of this exercise seems to lie in the scope it offers for creating powerful images of oneself through a combination of fact and fiction, fantasy and reality.[10] The key factor here is the role of fiction in providing access to feelings and emotions. As I have said elsewhere (Hunt 1997), one of the most important elements of good mimetic fiction is that it should be *emotionally felt*. This means that the reader is enabled not only to get into the minds of the characters portrayed, but also to

9   This is a term used by Natalie Goldberg (1986).

10   For a discussion of the self as a kind of fiction, see my chapter 'Autobiography and the Psychotherapeutic Process' in this volume.

experience the emotions of the characters, as if they were real people. In order to achieve this effect, writers have to be able to immerse themselves in the feelings they are trying to portray, to 'show' rather than to 'tell' (see Booth 1991, chapter 1). When writing autobiographical fiction, the requirement that we should 'show' rather than 'tell' means that we are forced to enter into *our own* feelings and emotions in a way which we may not be able to do simply by writing about the facts of our lives. Thus fictionalising from ourselves and finding a satisfactory form for our fictions helps us to engage more deeply with our inner life, opening up possibilities for greater insight and self-understanding.

Implications for creative writing teaching

There are, needless to say, risks involved in encouraging people to engage more closely with their inner lives: taking a step into their feelings and emotions may be painful, even frightening, as well as exciting and liberating. Within a therapeutic environment, safeguards are normally built into the process. Teachers of creative writing, however, who engage in this kind of work, will need a considerable degree of awareness of the possible problems which may arise. If they have not undergone some kind of counselling or therapy training, they will need to be aware of the importance of creating in the classroom a 'holding environment', to use Winnicott's term,[11] within which participants can feel safe enough to engage more closely with their inner worlds. This can be done by organising peer support within the writing group itself, or through the availability of individual consultations with the tutor, or by having available counselling or psychotherapeutic back-up which can be used when necessary. As the work of educationalist James Britton suggests, any teacher needs to be a sort of 'good enough mother' in the Winnicottian sense (see Wyatt-Brown 1993), to develop working methods and a relationship with students which provide both support and guidance, and which acknowledge the difficult task they face of engaging with their inner worlds. This is even more so when the teacher is encouraging the use of creative writing for personal development.

11   See Pateman (1997) re educational practices which seek to create a 'holding environment'.

References

Abbs, P. and Richardson, J. (1990) *The Forms of Narrative.* Cambridge: Cambridge University Press.

Booth, W. (1991) *The Rhetoric of Fiction.* Harmondsworth: Penguin.

Conway, M.A. (1990) *Autobiographical Memory.* Buckingham: Open University Press.

Eakin, P.J. (1985) *Fictions of the Self: Studies in the Art of Self-Invention.* Princeton, NJ: Princeton University Press.

Fairfax, J. and Moat, J. (1981) *The Way to Write.* London: Elm Tree Books.

Goldberg, N. (1986) *Writing Down the Bones.* Boston and London: Shambhala Publications.

Hunt, C. (1995) 'Autobiography and the imagination.' *Writing in Education 7,* Winter, 25–26.

Hunt, C. (1997) 'Finding a voice – exploring the self: autobiography and imagination in a writing apprenticeship.' *Auto/Biography 1–3,* 169–179.

McCracken, L. (1994) '"The synthesis of my being": autobiography and the reproduction of identity in Virginia Woolf.' In E. McNees (ed) *Virginia Woolf: Critical Assessments Vol. IV.* Mountfield: Helm Information.

Pateman, T. (1997) 'Space for the imagination.' *Journal of Aesthetic Education 31,* 1, 1–8.

Roe, S. (1990) *Writing and Gender: Virginia Woolf's Writing Practice.* Hemel Hempstead: Harvester/Wheatsheaf.

Roe, S. (1995) 'The mind in visual form: sketching *The Waves.' QWERTY 5,* 241–251.

Sarraute, N. (1984) *Childhood.* London: John Calder.

Woolf, V. (1989) 'Sketch of the past.' In *Moments of Being.* London: Grafton Books, pp.69–173.

Wyatt-Brown, A.M. (1993) 'From the clinic to the classroom: D.W. Winnicott, James Britton, and the revolution in writing theory.' In P.D. Rudnytsky (ed) *Transitional Objects and Potential Spaces.* New York: Columbia University Press.

CHAPTER 2

The Self as Source
Creative Writing Generated from Personal Reflection

Cheryl Moskowitz

Writing is not an accidental act. It comes out of a desire to communicate and a need to express one's self in all its complexities. Freud opened his paper 'Creative Writers and Day-Dreaming', with his curiosity to know '…from what sources that strange being, the creative writer, draws his material, and how he manages to make such an impression on us with it and to arouse in us emotions of which, perhaps, we had not even thought ourselves capable' (Freud 1959, p.143).

Creative writing is almost always fuelled by personal experience and so carries profound truths behind the fiction. Inherent in the process is the power to transform, and make positive use of, some of life's most perplexing and painful issues.

Some years ago I was approached by an acquaintance, Ruth,[1] who had just gone into remission after a period of suffering from a severe form of leukaemia during which time she had spent almost a year, on and off, in a hospital isolation ward whilst receiving treatment for her illness. During this time Ruth had struggled constantly with the very real possibility that she might die and now wanted to find a voice to express the many fears and strong emotions this possibility aroused. She was offered counselling by the NHS on her discharge from hospital but many of the feelings were still too close and frightening to find adequate expression in this setting and she had

---

[1]   Special thanks to Ruth for her permission to make references to our work together.

an instinct that what she really wanted to be able to do was to write creatively about her experience.

Ruth approached me as she knew I was a writer and asked if I had any ideas which might enable her to put pen to paper. It became clear in talking to her that the illness had caused a feeling of total disintegration, like that which is experienced after any major crisis, physical or emotional. She felt herself to be split in many ways; fearful and hopeful, living and dying, loving and hating, angry and forgiving. She talked about herself in relation to how she was before the illness and now, how changed she felt in its aftermath. I began to work on an exercise with her which we called the 'ill self' and the 'well self'. She explored each of these sides to herself as if they were different people. Together we brainstormed words, ideas and phrases that fitted each, and later searched for visual images and verbal metaphors to flesh them out. The next stage was to give each of these sides to herself, these split parts that had now become separate people in their own right, an identity and a name. She christened the ill self 'Eileen' and the well self 'Sally'. We endowed the two characters with biographical details: age, profession, physical characteristics and personality, place to live, car to drive, personal likes and dislikes.

The third stage of the exercise was to create a way, through story, for Eileen and Sally to meet one another. The objective of the story was for the two women to exchange something of mutual value. The story could be anywhere and the exchanges could be anything, material or in the form of ideas or quality of self. The introduction of story at this point provided Ruth with a way of distilling and reintegrating these disparate and painfully opposing aspects of herself. Fiction had rendered the truth more bearable and not only that but had offered up new and creative ways of coping with it.

The discovery for myself as a writer of fiction was that the creation of characters from split parts of the self provides a richness of emotion and spirit as well as an essential believability that defies initial imagination or pure invention. These characters, once created and given dimension, do not remain static in their approach or reaction to changing circumstances around them. They are changed by events and, in fact, become people with the same real contradictions and splits from which they were initially created. It was this discovery and the moving experience of working as writing partner and enabler with Ruth that led me to develop a writing practice and theory based around the concept of 'The Self as Source'.

'The Self as Source' is a creative writing technique which relies on inward reflection and an identification of different and conflicting parts of the self as the main source of inspiration for the work. The method proceeds from the basic premise that personal development is achieved through self-exploration, investigation and understanding, and that looking closely at disintegrated parts of ourselves and our experience not only opens up vast new roads of fictional possibilities, but puts us in touch with hidden truths about ourselves and new ways of managing them.

In the following passage from Robert Louis Stevenson's portrait of moral duplicity, *The Strange Case of Dr Jekyll and Mr Hyde*, the author's unfortunate hero, Henry Jekyll, asserts his notion of the duality of human nature as he makes his final statement about the case:

> With every day, and from both sides of my intelligence, the moral and the intellectual, I thus drew steadily nearer to that truth…that man is not truly one, but truly two. I say two, because the state of my own knowledge does not pass beyond that point. Others will follow, others will outstrip me on the same lines; and I hazard the guess that man will ultimately be known for a mere polity of multifarious, incongruous and independent denizens. (Stevenson 1979, p.82)

In the words of his protagonist, Stevenson offers this statement of man's variegated nature as a way of understanding and perhaps justifying why he, the morally just and upstanding Dr Jekyll, felt compelled to breathe life into his depraved counterpart, Mr Hyde. 'If each…,' he explains, 'could but be housed in separate identities, life would be relieved of all that was unbearable…' (p.82). Dr Jekyll confesses that he had, for some time, dwelt on the possibility of separating these two extreme elements in himself, the good and the evil, savouring the idea as 'a beloved daydream'.

Indeed, the idea for the story itself came to Stevenson in the form of a dream, or rather more of a nightmare, during which he imagined the essential components of this gothic tale. It has often been suggested that the dreamer is always subject in his or her dreams, no matter how diverse or radically different from themselves the characters in the dream may appear. It would seem that Stevenson, a man whose short life oscillated between illness and health and whose Calvinist upbringing meant that issues of good and evil were omnipresent, had dreamed up two characters, Jekyll and Hyde, who could perfectly embody his own different and conflicting parts. Whether giving separate identities to these 'polar twins' of his own consciousness in his novel achieved for Stevenson Dr Jekyll's dream of relieving life of all that was unbearable, the artistic brilliance and creativity of the work cannot be overlooked.

Robert Louis Stevenson wrote his book several years before the advent of psychoanalysis. However, many of the ideas put forward by Sigmund Freud and his followers attempt to explain in a different way the duality or multiplicity of human nature. Freud described the human personality as being made up of three basic and very separate structures: the id, the ego and the super-ego. The id is ruled by the *pleasure principle* and is driven by a constant desire for instinctual gratification. The ego is governed by the *reality principle* and serves as a check on the unruly behaviour generated by the id, whilst still seeking valid and effective ways of achieving satisfaction. The super-ego in Freudian terms is the moral and judicial branch of personality, which manifests itself in the idealistic and conscientious behaviour of an individual.

At the same time as Freud was formulating his concepts, his contemporary, Carl Jung, was discovering a *collective unconscious* from which human experience can be communicated and understood through a recognition of common archetypal images and symbolic representations. Jung had also developed a definition of self in which the public face, the *persona*, is stalked by a darker, less presentable *shadow.* He believed in the duality of human nature and thus proposed the idea of *anima* and *animus* as archetypal images which reveal themselves as contra sexual manifestations in the male and female psyche. In other words, Jung believed that every male has a female side and every female, too, the propensity for maleness.

Most thinkers today would agree that the human personality cannot be defined singularly but rather that it is made up of many, sometimes opposing and conflicting, parts. Most would also agree, however, that it is the integration of these parts into some kind of harmony that leads to a healthy mind and creative functioning and that a lack of such integration can lead to psychological confusion, torment and anguish as the separate parts of the self engage in a destructive battle on the mental site of the individual.

There are as many routes to self-integration as there are theories about the origins of the universe, but all start from the basic premise that something must be disparate before it is whole. Inherent also in the process of integration and harmony is the idea of creativity. To put something together, to make something new by identifying and fitting many different parts together, is a creative and productive act. It is from this platform of thought that I propose the use of 'The Self as Source' as one way of generating writing which is both creative and integrative.

Splitting the self: the creation of character

> There was a little girl and she had a little curl
> Right in the middle of her forehead;
> When she was good, she was very very good,
> But when she was bad, she was horrid.

Most of us can see ourselves reflected in the picture portrayed of the child in this nursery rhyme. It is inherent in our natures as human beings that we have the propensity to possess wildly different and opposing qualities within our same person. It is also, however, a feature of social law and etiquette that we learn to suppress certain parts of our being in favour of others.

When Robert Louis Stevenson created the split person of Dr Jekyll and Mr Hyde, he was responding to the opposing forces of good and evil in his own conscience and upbringing. Through the narrative he was able to give both the acceptable and the unacceptable parts of himself legitimate space to function. When Ruth created Eileen and Sally she was guided by her physical and emotional struggle between illness and health. Separating them gave her the opportunity to be objective about her subjective sense of self and to discover that there was value to be had from the experience of being ill, just as there was from being well, and released her from having to idealise one and denigrate the other. The starting point for the creation of two or more characters from the self must be the location of internal difference or conflict. In other words, it is necessary before any imaginative work can begin to identify an area in one's own personality or behaviour which can be split.

Whether working with a group or an individual, it is almost always useful in the first instance to agree a role identity. That is, in a group of people, a common role identity should be found, that is, we are all students...we are all mothers...we are all teachers...we are all someone else's children. For an individual, a role that defines the self in a particular context should be identified and owned, that is, I am a doctor...I am a writer...I am a sister...I am a neighbour...I am a wife. Choosing a role identity is a way of making the subject matter (the self) containable. Within any role, of course, live a myriad of others, but the chosen role provides a good starting point.

It is now necessary to locate an area of conflict or polarity within that role and this can be done by referring to archetypes. Because they form what Jung calls the 'collective unconscious' and are therefore universally representative as mental images, archetypes can be used to define the self in deep and meaningful ways. Archetypal images such as Good and Bad, Love and Hate, Life and Death can be applied as definitions of role identities. For example, someone may feel themselves to be both a good mother and a bad mother, a loving sister and a hateful sister, a lively writer and a lifeless one.

Imaging and the sensual self: description of character

Having established a role and an archetypal polarity to attach to it, the journey of exploration of these two sides of the self can begin. This journey of exploration is carried out by a process called *imaging*. Imaging can be done with pictures and objects as well as with words, and I often use both. Imaging is basically the application of metaphor to embellish description and intensify understanding of character. Photographs, pictures cut from magazines, the fronts of postcards and even actual objects can be sorted through and selected as belonging to one or other of the polarised sides of the self. When creating literary metaphors to describe the two sides of the self, I encourage the use of a third person pronoun, that is, *she is*...as a way of prefixing the found image in words. The following lines, taken from Norman MacCaig's (1990) poem, 'Aunt Julia', provide an excellent example of this kind of character imaging:

> She was buckets
> and water flouncing into them.
> She was winds pouring wetly
> round house-ends.
> She was brown eggs, black skirts
> and a keeper of threepennybits
> in a teapot.

When imaging her ill self and well self in the creation of Eileen and Sally, Ruth used some of the images shown in Table 2.1.

Table 2.1: Finding Personal Metaphors

Eileen (ill self)	Sally (well self)
She is…	She is…
…black clouds and thunder in the closet	…sunshine
…a snake with a forked tongue	…a bouncing ball
…an unexploded bomb awaiting gentle diffusion	…a waterfall of unharnessed energy
…hailstones that can melt into water	…a light-footed gazelle
	…golden, sunny, starry

The process of imaging requires full application of the senses. To the five that we know about – sight, smell, sound, touch and taste – something further can be added which could be referred to as the sixth sense of *emotion*. Referring to each of these senses in turn can guide the process and enrich the resulting images. Ask questions about each of the characters, such as: what do they look like to themselves, to others? What colours would they be painted in? What kinds of smell would evoke their presence? Are they smooth, slippery, prickly, hard, cold, soft or warm? Are they salty, sweet, bitter or sour? What makes them angry? What makes them happy? What makes them sad?

Birth and christening: releasing and naming the characters

With cries of labour I gave birth to this hymn…

(Enheduanna 2300BC)

These 4000-year-old words taken from the writings of a Sumerian moon priestess, the earliest named and recorded writer, draw a comparison between the creation of a piece of writing and childbirth. The two processes, of course, are astoundingly similar. The seed is sown, the idea or child conceived and then held on to and nurtured in the internal space, before it is finally delivered painfully and miraculously into the world as something separate from, but still part of, the self.

Having split the self and begun to do some imaging around the two parts, it is time to name each part and let them live and breathe lives of their own. The giving of names is as important a ritual as the cutting of the umbilical cord of an infant. It means that the character that has been created is no longer a partial aspect of the self or the 'mother' from whom it was born, but has its own identity which can grow away from, and without attachment to, its original source.

Stevenson named his good self 'Dr Jekyll' and his evil self 'Mr Hyde'. The titles and the names chosen may well carry the unconscious wishes or aspirations of the writer. Mr Hyde represented the side of his personality he longed in vain to be normal (a common Mr) but then literally needed to hide (Hyde) away. Dr Jekyll was a doctor, a do-gooder whose hard-earned title could earn respect by a mere mention.

Ruth called her well self 'Sally' and her ill self 'Eileen'. Both names carry associations and connotations as well as meanings recognised by the conscious and unconscious mind of the person choosing them. Similarly, any parents, however cognisant they are of the reasons, will have their own motivation for choosing a particular name for their child. The motives may be driven by aspects of wish-fulfilment, expectation, hope, fear and even aggression.

In the process of naming each part of the self, more specific biographical issues such as age, gender, class and background may also be decided. What kind of clothes do they wear, what is their occupation, who are their friends, where do they live and how do they live? It is useful at this point to attempt a brief summation of each by writing short passages charting 'A Day in the Life of…' both characters.

For Sally, Ruth began: 'I woke up this morning and the sun was streaming through the window. I stretched my body, which felt good…'

In contrast, Eileen began her day thus: 'I am awoken harshly from a fitful sleep by the children squabbling'.

Sally, we learn, does not have children. Rather, she focuses on her own needs and those of Jim, her attentive lover, who looks on dotingly as she spends her day, plentiful with leisure time, toning and preening her enviously fit body.

Eileen, on the other hand, is starved of sleep by the insistent needs of her fretful children. She does not have the time or the will to bother about the way she looks. She is unsupported in her mothering role and longs to be a child again, cared for and looked after herself.

Sketching out a typical day for each character builds on poetic imaging and adds more flesh to the bones of the creation. It is also a crucial step in achieving separation: in allowing for the discovery and recognition of the varying wants, needs and even lifestyles required of the different parts of the self, it is possible to work creatively on individuation, acceptance and co-existence. Renaming split parts of the self and endowing each new identity with qualities, attributes and drives that go beyond initial conception involves a sense of wonderment and horror.

Mary Shelley's *Frankenstein* is a graphic account of the creation of life formed literally from bare bones. In this gothic tale, the being that is created or 'given birth to' by the idealistic Frankenstein not only achieves life, strength and emotion beyond the wildest imaginings of its creator but proves that beside the capacity to love and honour is also the capacity to hate and destroy, and thus the monster acknowledges himself: '...fallen angel becomes a malignant devil' (Shelley 1818, p.221).

Marrying the self: seeking resolution and integration in the creation of story

'No man is an island, entire of itself,' wrote John Donne. These words might just as well apply to characters created out of parts of the self as to the self as a whole. Each part of the self must be able to co-exist, interact with, tolerate, provide for, and be provided by, others. Just as we are physically, socially and emotionally dependent on one another as human beings, so the parts of ourselves are interdependent on one another for healthy survival.

To conceive, feed and nurture, christen and eventually give independence to disparate, and perhaps deeply troubling or uncomfortable, parts of oneself can be a painful, frightening, but also joyful experience. However, unless these newly created saints, monsters, angels and devils can be configured in such a way as to form a unified understanding of the self and its many contradictions, they can serve no purpose except to perpetuate a sense of lack of wholeness and disintegration on the part of the individual.

The final stage of the exercise, then, is to find a way through story or fictional narrative to bring split parts of the self back together into some kind of productive union. In a sense this process is like a marriage, albeit an arranged one, where two separate and different individuals discover, in the course of being together, the ways in which they can either fulfil or frustrate each other's needs. Because bringing together split parts of the self can almost be like trying to reunite a divorced couple, the task is not an easy one and it takes a great deal of creative thought, understanding and powers of manoeuvre to achieve successfully.

Every story told has three parts: a beginning, a middle and an end, as well as three components: a setting, a conflict and a resolution. These three components can be thought of as the questions, where, what and how? In thinking about placing the newly created characters into a story setting, then, these questions can be applied as a way of planning and deciding the narrative. *Where* does it happen, *what* happens and *how* is the situation handled?

A story must have a setting, that is, a place where it begins from or happens within. For the purposes of this exercise, one has to decide on a place, real or imagined, where these two characters, born from split parts of the self, may chance or be forced to meet. The choice of setting will, of course, shape the narrative. Is it on neutral ground or will the meeting take place on one or other of the character's territories? Is the setting a restful or chaotic environment? A desperate one or a hopeful one? Again, applying the senses to the creation of setting, what smells, tastes, sounds, sights and feelings are present or evoked by this setting?

Having established a place for the characters to be, a metaphorical stage for them to play upon, they must make their entrances. They must be brought into contact and, by necessity, conflict. Bringing the two together is much like the carrying out of a scientific experiment. Despite having hypotheses based on the information given, it is impossible to know, until tested, what will actually happen when these two forces or elements meet. Will they repel, attract, combine or combust? What conditions must be present for any or all of these things to happen?

The final stage of any story is resolution, even if the only resolution possible is dissolution. As a way of guiding and shaping this part of the story, it is useful to introduce a dictate, namely that the characters must exchange something of mutual value before parting. In this way the split parts of the self are made to look beyond their differences and to uncover, however momentarily, a point of understanding and identification which will allow this exchange to take place. The exchange may be an exchange of ideas, thoughts or words, or some more material gift such as an object, food or a piece of clothing. The characters will each possess very different qualities and resources and therefore whatever is given by each to the other can be similar only in value and not in type.

This process of meeting and establishing at least partial reconciliation with split and opposing parts of the self through creative writing can be likened to the journey taken by an individual in psychoanalysis or psychotherapy. Joyce McDougall, author and analyst, has written lucidly about what she calls the 'psychic theatre', a person's inner world which is peopled by a host of differing and opposing characters and within which gets played out a rich tapestry of emotions and experiences. In the prologue of her book, *Theatres of the Mind: Illusion and Truth on the Psychoanalytic Stage*, she writes about the purpose and the possibilities of the psychoanalytic experience:

> Under optimal conditions the psychoanalytic adventure allows each I to bring forth its own Jekyll and Hyde and its own Faust and Mephistopheles, split-off yet vitally necessary parts of every self. Thus love and hate may be reconciled, enabling the subject finally to sign the treaty of many years' silent warfare, which otherwise might lead to exhaustion and death. (McDougall 1982, p.15)

A person in therapy or analysis may be horrified to discover that, far from having one problem, they have several, and that their search for a single solution leads to a quagmire of possibilities. I believe that such a discovery, as in the writing of imaginative fiction, is the key to creativity and creative expression of the human condition. On the analyst's couch patients have no other material than their own self, with all its complexities and in all of its many manifestations. This is the mainstay and substance of their therapy. So, too, in creative writing the first and foremost generating and inspirational source is the writer him- or herself. When the self can be looked at and known in all its guises and permutations, it becomes the generous provider of endless fictional possibilities.

References

Freud, S. (1959) 'Creative writers and day-dreaming.' In *The Standard Edition of the Complete Psychological Works of Sigmund Freud, Vol. 9*. London: Hogarth Press and The Institute of Psycho-Analysis.

MacCaig, N. (1990) 'Aunt Julia.' In Norman MacCaig *Collected Poems*. London: Chatto & Windus.

McDougall, J. (1982) *Theatres of the Mind: Illusion and Truth on the Psychoanalytic Stage*. London: Free Association Books.

Shelley, M. (1818) *Frankenstein*. Oxford: Oxford University Press.

Stevenson, R.L. (1979) 'The strange case of Dr Jekyll and Mr Hyde.' In Robert Louis Stevenson *Dr Jekyll and Mr Hyde and Other Stories*. London: Penguin Books.

Further Reading

Berne, E. (1972) *Games People Play: The Psychology of Human Relationships.* London: Penguin Books.

Freud, S. (1962) *Two Short Accounts of Psycho-Analysis.* London: Pelican Books.

Jung, C.G. (ed) (1964) *Man and His Symbols.* London: Aldus Books.

Laing, R.D. (1969) *The Divided Self.* London: Penguin Books.

Partnow, E. (ed) (1992) *The New Quotable Woman: From Eve to the Present Day.* London: Headline Book Publishing.

Winnicott, D.W. (1990) 'Ego distortion in terms of true and false self.' In D.W. Winnicott *The Maturational Processes and the Facilitating Environment.* London: Karnac Books.

Woolf, V. (1977) *A Room of One's Own.* St. Albans: Granada Publishing.

CHAPTER 3

The Web of Words
Collaborative Writing and Mental Health

Graham Hartill[1]

In their origins, the words 'poetry' and 'healing' have a lot in common: 'poetry' comes from the Greek and means to compose, to pull things together, to shape, to create, to make; less well known is the etymology of 'healing', which derives from the ancient Germanic *khailaz*, through Anglo-Saxon *hoelan*, which also means to make whole. With today's reappraisals of the influence of psychic states on physical illness, we are again getting used to the notion of healing as the making whole of the body and mind together, rather than a state of war on some invading disease or rebellious organ or limb. Such a renewed emphasis is particularly pertinent and challenging when we are forced to consider a severe or terminal illness, either of ourselves or another, or some permanent condition or disability. We say that we must learn to 'come to terms' with both the illness and the new way of life it imposes upon us, where 'come to terms' implies a negotiation, a kind of barter with our body, our minds and whatever gods we think may have handed down such punishment to us.

Some of us may have been lucky enough to have known people who have actually found in their illness a source of strength and power, who have located the means to integrate themselves, disease and all, into new and more developed personal constellations. We feel fortunate and often profoundly moved when we encounter someone who, refusing the role of victim, has grown in character through the cancer, say, or an extreme emotional misfortune. Indeed, the case has long been made that in the illnesses and

1 My thanks are due to Angela Morton for permission to quote from her poem and interview; also to Suzy Jones, Daphne Rodenhurst and Mary Smith for permission to use their written material produced at a 'Web of Words' workshop, which forms the basis of the fictional workshop discussed in this paper.

wounds of life lie the very wellsprings of creativity. To make ourselves whole involves not just the curing of a specific condition, whether physical or psychic, but the integration of the meaning of the illness for our life. My emphasis in this chapter is not on 'illness', then, so much as on 'wholeness'; and we shall not be considering the work solely as it pertains to any specific portion of society, to whit the 'mentally ill', but to anyone concerned with using the verbal arts to benefit their psychic well-being.

Within the field of the arts and mental health there burns a continuing debate about creativity, empowerment and therapy. This is unfortunate but understandable; many artists (in whatever medium) who have experienced mental distress in their lives feel themselves to have been disempowered by the health care system (one friend of mine calls it the 'psychiatric gulag'); any artist should be free to make art from their experience of life without it being reduced to a symptom of illness, by which they may be interpreted and manipulated. However, I often hear contradictions; many who dismiss the noun 'therapy' seem happy enough with the adjective, acknowledging that writing can have 'therapeutic' benefits, whether one is working alone or in a workshop situation.

As a tutor of creative writing in adult education, I was always aware that a 'good' workshop was often 'good *for*' people, myself included. The benefits may be as various as the people attending, but an increase in self-esteem, self-confidence and, yes, empowerment, would be commonly recognised, as well as the sheer enjoyment of working with others in a supportive situation of occasionally profound intimacy; in the reading out and discussion of participants' work there is a close attention to language and feeling, to the life and presence of the person and to that person's story, poem or making, that is hard to find elsewhere in everyday life. Only when I began to work in a psychiatric hospital as part of a district council writer's residency did my attention begin to shift away from purely literary to more personal concerns; not that literary standards were jettisoned, far from it, but the chemistry of the workshop as a writing activity in itself began to assert a new paradigm for me and to challenge received notions of literary value. Actually, of course, the paradigm is the most ancient of all, and pre-dates 'literature' itself.

By 'poetry', then, I don't just mean a genre or specific technique of writing, but something in the essence of all expressive language, whether written down in blocks of prose, scattered syllables across a page or even colourful talk; it is the power we feel in language by means of its shape, its metaphors, its imagery and its music. Wherever interesting language can be found, there poetry is, whether in the chip-shop queue and on the front page of the *Sun*; it's really nothing special. Also, we won't be talking about 'therapy' as such, as a specialised discipline, but in acknowledging that individual and collective writing processes can have therapeutic value, we find ourselves challenging some conventional notions about what therapy is, or can be.

Central to the entire discussion is the belief that change is not only possible but inevitable in our lives, and that poetics can help us acknowledge this truth and engage with it in a helpful way. We talk about being 'moved' by a poem, but this movement must lie also at the heart of all philosophy of healing. I draw my inspiration here from the philosophy of the Tao and the archetypal psychology of Jung and post-Jungian practitioners such as James Hillman; human suffering is often born of getting stuck or blocked, fixated on some idea, or lack of idea, rather than responding to the reality of our actual experience. All mythology, every fairy tale, expresses the truth of transformation and change – and that therein lies the chance of our own renewal, our making new.

An interview

In this extract from a series of interviews with the poet Angela Morton, we are given an example of how metaphorical working with life, through the materials of art, can come about, and the renewal of creative activity that can grow from it.

Angela: The first period of depression was about four months, the second about seven months. The first was 10, 12 years ago. I actually gave up work and the depression lifted quite quickly after that. You're in an immense no-win situation when you've got depression and an anxiety-laden job: if you get better, you've got to go back to a set of circumstances that bring you down. It's not very easy.

Graham: You're absorbing so many other people's distress and difficulties, let alone the difficulties of the job itself.

Angela: My last depression was over 18 months, which is very scary.

Graham: And you didn't write anything over that period?

A: Nothing. A friend of mine was writing every week and I couldn't even write 'Dear Alison, thank you for your postcard'.

G: It seems as if it's really something to do with a breaking through; it's as if it hardens into a concrete wall and you couldn't even write a few words because that first chink, that first blow of the hammer, if you like, through that wall is the hardest of them all. Does that make sense?

A: Oh yes.

G: You said that whenever you wrote you felt there was a process of self-healing going on, however you want to define that.

A: I think so. There might be little dark undercurrents somewhere, or a sense of mortality might creep in, but a poem might be just about enjoying really noticing what nasturtiums look like through the window or trying to describe what a tree looks like in leaf. And I think just the act of doing it is like a meditation, something that acknowledges that spring itself is healing. We do need to look at the dark and painful things sometimes, but we don't always have to do that.

G: A good place for us to start would be to look at that Lazarus poem. So this poem was written for our evening class. Was there a particular stimulus that led to its being written?

A: Yes, you showed us a poem where every line began with 'Because...' and asked us to write something with the same recurring word or words at the beginning of each line, like a refrain. I'm aware sometimes of my mind going on a search. I got to 'And only when' and at the same time I had this image from Epstein's sculpture of Lazarus.

G: You said you hadn't written anything for 18 months prior to that, and you'd been to two or three of our evening sessions and hadn't produced anything new. Did you feel you were coming out of your depression when you started coming?

A: Oh, I must have been quite well out of it, to come at all. I think it passed quite rapidly, though I had this period of highness which lasted about a week. I was feeling much better but I wasn't writing. I was hoping to write.

G: Would you like to read the poem?

A: And only when I'd lain in severing heat:
     and only when I'd lain alone in binding ice:
     and only when all my life and love had lain eclipsed:
     and only when my sisters' tears had lain dissolving in my hair:
     and only when their linen had been bound about my bones:
     and only when bones and blood had sealed as alabaster:
     and only when I had been borne along the one way path
     and only when the stone had sealed the tomb:

     and only when all binding cloth unwound:

     and only when I was made whole again; and by the river,
     unremembering,
     I'd walked again; had walked among birdsong and perfumed
     flowers,
     had walked in the valley among spikenard and jasmine:

     only then, Lord, did I hear you call my name.

G: Needless to say, the image of Lazarus is to do with coming back to life, and you use a lot of very sensual imagery, particularly olfactory – flowers, the smell of flowers, odours, the most elusive of the senses. It's also the sense that's most associated for me with involuntary memory – we can't control it – we can close our eyes and ears, but suddenly catching a smell can take you back to a time that you can't even remember, and to that extent it's very quickening isn't it? And then in contrast there's imagery to do with the lack of sensual life. It's almost like Dante's inferno, isn't it – 'severing heat and binding ice' – you know, the various circles of hell, and 'eclipse', the blocking out of light or salvation. When you wrote this, were you at all aware of this comparison I'm making with your coming out of depression and this reclamation in the poem of sensual life? I mean, which came first, the imagery of Lazarus or the desire to write a poem about coming back from depression?

A: No, no. I don't think I said I'm going to write a poem about that. As soon as the Epstein image came I knew I'd got Lazarus in there, but one or two lines were very near the surface. It was a different way of writing from the way I was writing before I was ill. My most usual way of writing would be to shut off the critical side of my brain and try to write uncritically and then pick out from that, whereas these lines just came out, line by line. There was very little work I had to do on them. It has been strange.

This conversation is about the genesis of a single poem, but 'Spikenard and Jasmine' turned out to be only the first of a series of more than 20 poems generated from Angela's personal experience by the imagery of the Lazarus story. As Lazarus returns from the grave, so the poet recovers from depressive illness. The metaphor is large indeed, turning on the pivot of life and death, which is sense and senselessness, love and absolute loneliness, utterance and silence. Yet, like the garden in the poem, the piece is also embroidered with detail; we recognise that archetypal imagery (such as that of resurrection) is not just a generalisation, but an explosion of personal, specific and pregnant resonances.

Here is Russell Lockhart on the life of words:

> Often words fail us, verbal therapies fail us, talking together fails us. But it is my conviction that we need not abandon the word in seeking fruitful roads to soul... Words have everywhere become suspect, and we turn away from the word to seek other sources of nourishment. We are likely to find that these other things will not satisfy soul's deepest hunger, because that is satisfied only when soul is given voice, only when soul hears and is heard. In nearly all mythologies the Gods speak things into existence; the world is ensouled through the word. Instead of abandoning the word, perhaps it is time we return to the word in a different spirit. Perhaps it is we who have failed the word, we who have lost contact with the imaginal realm beneath and beyond the exterior of the word, we who have lost the capacity to connect to the interiority of the word, to the living substance in the word that is at once our most available but least known source of archetypal reality. (Lockhart 1987, p.89)

In writing 'Spikenard and Jasmine', Angela was engaging (and the metaphor is at least doubly apt) in a process which James Hillman, borrowing a phrase from Keats, calls 'soul-making':

> I've been straining for decades to push psychology over into art, to recognise psychology as an art form rather than a science or a medicine or an education, because the soul is inherently imaginative. The primary function of the human being is to imagine, not to stand up straight, not to make tools and fire, not to build communities or hunt and till and tame, but to imagine all these other possibilities...I am working toward a psychology of the soul that is based on a psychology of image. Here I am suggesting both a poetic basis of mind and a psychology that starts neither in the physiology of the brain, the structure of language, the

organisation of society, nor the analysis of behaviour, but in the processes of imagination. (Hillman and Ventura 1992, p.154)

This idea of 'soul-making' has profoundly deepened the creative response of myself and many others who work in the therapeutic arts; by it we recognise that our words and images tap into wellsprings of significance that we can never fully comprehend or manage, and that they not only describe the world according to the narrow range of our everyday, and sometimes frightened or confused, perceptions, but rather carry the world within them. When we write creatively, we are lowering a bucket into a bottomless well of meaning, paradox and metaphor. When we make a poem, we make something of ourselves, and the world, anew.

Ambiguity, and the inevitably metaphorical implications of words, are the very fuel of poetry. Lazarus, jasmine, ice, tears, alabaster, stone, cloth, name – all metaphors. 'Webs' are also metaphors, also 'keys', both images central to our purpose today, and that we shall now put to work.

The 'Web of Words' workshop

From now on, I want us to imagine that we are attending a verbal arts workshop called 'The Web of Words'; it employs an approach I have developed over the last five years, whereby 'soul' can be made in a collective endeavour and primary material can be woven into aesthetic coherence through a simple system of mutual attention. Potential topics for our exercise are endless, but today we shall focus on 'keys' – the subject is both intimate and archetypal, commonplace and symbolic, and, as we have implied, has metaphorical implications for the process itself.

Some members of our group already know one another, but most are meeting for the first time; all are interested in using writing as a means of self-exploration and some have come with an experience of illness. What follows is based on several specific writings and several different actual workshops.

Among our number are Joanne, Harriet and Bernard. Joanne is in her 40s, a wife and mother but now confined to a wheelchair through an advancing disease. Bernard, an unemployed man in his early 30s, has a history of mental distress; he was once diagnosed as schizophrenic but is now usually regarded as manic-depressive. Harriet has no particular illness but has had her share of sadnesses, including the death of her husband a year or so ago. She is an ex-civil servant.

Introductions

Everybody comes to a writing workshop with presumptions, expectations and reservations; we should never forget that in any group there is probably going to be someone who may be quite terrified about what awaits them: perhaps they've never done anything like this before; perhaps they've written but have never shown their writings, let alone read them out, to anyone else; perhaps they've never written anything. There will be those who don't know anyone else in the room and think that they are the only ones in this situation, imagining that everyone else knows exactly what's going on and feels completely at ease. Some people are far more extrovert than others and look forward to talking; for others, just to articulate a response even in a small group can be a huge challenge. They are nervous at the outset because they don't know how much of themselves they are going to be asked to 'expose'.

The simplest form of introduction is simply to go around in a circle and ask each person to say their name and a bit about themselves, including what brought them to the session and what, if any, their expectations might be. In my experience, flicking across the circle, either in the introductory stage or later in the readings, has its drawbacks in that it can put participants on edge, not knowing when their turn will come. One of your major tasks as facilitator is to minimise nervousness and maximise security and enjoyment, so informality and humour are essential. Some introductions will be very brief, a name-and-number kind of response, so a little gentle goading might be appropriate. There is a tremendous mystique about the role of the writer, the most popular notion, of course, being that you have no right to wear the spurs at all until you've been published. In our 'Web of Words' we allow and encourage the writing self in all of us to be free, without criticism or evaluation (which have their place, but elsewhere). Here, everyone stands for a while on an equal footing, even the silent ones, as we challenge a couple of paradigms integral to the arts in our culture: that some people have it and others don't, and that writing is an individual rather than a collective activity. For us it is both individual and collective simultaneously, and while some people do have a facility for verbal expression, our aim for now is to acknowledge the inherent capabilities of each. Implicit in the structure of our working process is the principle that everyone has an equal right to say what they want to say and to be listened to; that includes the facilitator who introduces himself or herself just like the others, will do the writing and speaking just like the others and may therefore feel every bit as 'exposed'.

Introducing the Web of Keys

You, as facilitator, say that we're going to do some writing, and quite a lot of talking together, and at the end of the session we're going to weave it together into a whole. Everyone's contribution is equally valid and whatever we write or say is valuable. We are all going to write and everyone will be asked to read out what they've written; this may be scary if you've never done it before, but nobody's here today with a critic's hat on or a teacher's hat; you can write whatever you want to. But here's a vital proviso: if you've written something you feel quite vulnerable about, which raises difficult and painful feelings, and you don't want to read it out, just say 'pass'. That's perfectly acceptable. But ask yourself whether it's just timidity, and if the answer's yes, then it's best to go for it. It may be daunting at first but really, it just gets easier. You'll get a buzz from it, and gain in confidence every time you do it.

Listening is every bit as important as writing. Ask the group to pay as much attention to one another as they would like to have paid to themselves. After the writing time, ask them to turn over their pieces so they can no longer scribble additions or amendments. When people are reading their pieces, everyone's attention should be on them.

Keys

Everyone fishes out a key or a bunch of keys; if anyone doesn't have one, ask them to remember or even to invent one. Delving in pockets and handbags, everyone rattles and clinks their keys. You go around the group and ask each person to say something briefly about their keys. There will be keys to cars, houses and offices. Sometimes the answers may be quite uninspiring, such as 'This is the key to my car. Every day I go to work in it. A Ford Fiesta. That's it'. But then you can ask what they do for a living and (keeping it brief, we are only just beginning to turn our key) how they feel about their work and why they do it; what it says, or doesn't say, about themselves. Houses are about where people live, their family, their social life, or perhaps their loneliness. People are talking about their past and future, but with the safety of the metaphor to support them. They can say as much or as little as they like, reveal as much or as little as they like; about themselves, their hopes and fears, delights and disappointments.

Do a brainstorm then on keys; get the wrists moving. Write words or phrases to do with keys in just two minutes; time it, and stop them on the dot. The group has fun with the gaminess of it, which is then played up further by asking each person in turn to read out a word from their list, 'gonging' them out if they repeat anything already said. Thus in a couple of minutes, the group has used the key to open up an enormous word-hoard of associations. Meanwhile, you'll have jotted down a few words you've heard and you ask about them. One or two people might end up reading out their lists:

So what does 'key' mean?

lock	wind up
box	prison
keystone	prison warder
keyword	jingle
keyhole	jangle
treasure chest	keen
map key	keep
car key	keel
key of dreams	sleep
my mother's bakelite box	peep
my father's shed	work
sausages	hate
trinkets	porch
turnkey	wellies
Billy Cotton's Bandshow	John and Mary
E flat major	latchkey
music-box	21 - the key of the door
toy-box	silver key
train set	wedding
key event	gardenias
key phrase	Morcombe

In the open conversation that ensues, the keys begin to open boxes. Some people pick up on the fact that keys both open and close things, release and imprison. I tell the group about the time I brought up the subject of keys in a prison writers' group (a loaded metaphor if ever there was one!). I was struck in the prisoners' writing by the emphasis on the sound of keys – none of the prisoners possessed any keys but they heard them all the time, rattling and jangling up and down the corridors by night and day. 'People think prison is a quiet place,' said one, 'it isn't, it's the noisiest place on earth. Some of the officers are considerate and wear thick-soled shoes at night, but others like to make some noise to wind you up, and walk up and down and rattle their keys.'

Also in the mix are all sorts of social and cultural connotations, such as those to do with weddings, or coming of age, which might also have powerful personal meanings. There are some suggestions that seem opaque, springing from purely subjective experience. Bernie says: 'My Dad always used to work in his shed on Sunday mornings and we used to listen to *Billy Cotton's Bandshow* on the radio after lunch. Every Sunday was the same routine, at least, that's the way I remember it now. 'Wakey wakey!' And my mother used to have this brown bakelite box in her bedroom and there was a little silver key to open it, and when I was very little I remember her holding me and I opened the box with this little key and I remember her lifting the lid. Freud would probably have a field day with this, wouldn't he? [laughter]. I opened the lid and there were these pink envelopes inside. I don't know who they were from, maybe love-letters from Dad or from her to Dad during the war. Who knows? They were pink and scented. Anyway, it might not have happened at all, had it? I mean, I'm sure I can remember things that could never have actually happened in reality. Perhaps I dreamed them.'

So the conversation goes around. Participants can be asked if there are any particular words they remember from others' lists, or if they have any questions they might like to ask another, or to mention any of their own associations that were sparked off. The group will probably become quite animated and talkative, dredging up words from their own personal treasure chest. And what about this treasure chest? Some may have read *Treasure Island* as a child, or have seen the film. For others, the image might connote their own toy-box as a child, or Pandora's Box, or spark off dreams of winning the lottery. What might we each find in our treasure chest, once we've opened it? What secrets might we uncover? What kind of treasure might it hold? What is *your* idea of treasure anyway? Do you need a map to find this magic box?

The Writing

Ask participants to choose a single word or phrase from their list, or any one they've heard in the conversation that resonated strongly for them, and to write from it for three, five or ten minutes, as time permits. Let them know that it's the writing that's important, not the thinking about the writing; say don't worry about what's going to come out, no one expects literary masterpieces or is even concerned about whether it's any 'good' or not; just put the pen to paper and get it moving. Write freely, whatever comes to mind. Don't worry about consistency or continuity, for often the most interesting things emerge from the fractures, when the mind changes tack or dries up momentarily but has to push itself on. Just keep the keyword in your mind and write.

Everybody, or nearly everybody, scribbles. Perhaps some people are a bit slow to start but, in full flow, some people find it hard to stop, so a minute's warning helps. Meanwhile you've been doing something different.

The Chorus

After listening to the brainstorm, you've been writing down phrases that strike you. Your job now is to weave together a chorus to bind the web, that you will read in between each person's contribution. My own approach is to use recurring refrains or motifs but to play with them, vary them, each time. It's your job to start and finish proceedings, having lent flow and power to the whole. The best way to make this clear is by example, so in a moment we'll look at a possible snippet from a completed web.

Each person is now asked to read out their piece, given the provisos mentioned earlier. No one should apologise for their piece, either before or after they read it. There's no need.

An excerpt from a 'Web of Keys'

What follows is an extract from an imaginary web; it illustrates something of the feeling of both the process and the completed event. I have run such exercises with groups of anything from 4 to 22 people, in time periods from an hour to two days; the longer workshops, of course, allow a much more thorough exploration of the material at hand, and the actual web itself can serve as a way of concluding things, by pulling the threads of your concerns together. Longer pieces can be edited down to form the individual contributions. All these matters of timing must be left to the facilitator to develop on his or her initiative, depending on the specific situation.

Chorus: This is our web of keys.
            The web is both open and closed.
            We are caught in it. Yet we are free of it.

In weaving this web of words, we can help release one another.

Fred: We were staying over the coast for the weekend. Dad had rented a chalet. We had to pick up the keys from a woman down the road. I sat in the car while he got the keys. There was your sadness, Dad, there was always your sadness, never more so than when we stood there, silently staring from the clifftops as the waves came crashing in below to cover the jagged rocks with a rush of foam. Look aloft and see the gulls swooping, soaring, jerked like puppets on an upward rush of wind. We are between the devil and the deep blue sea, Dad. You can be the devil, eh? And I can drown in the sea.

Chorus: This is our web of words,
our web of keys.
We weave this web ourselves from our common language.
A web of sheds and boxes and cars and letters.

Joanne: I am a woman who is having a physical breakdown. My mind rages and ranges over all the spaces. I have no leg to stand on, yet I see and hear so much, my own and others' raw patches. Dependent body, independent mind. I won't let it be a prison. Do I have control? Letting go of 'Lasagne, Pizza and Yorkshire Pudding Woman' really hurts! Jack's pleasure in taking all that stuff on kills me. But now I come to think of it, I always hated cooking!

Chorus: This is a sticky web!
Woven out of memories and futures,
yet it is here now, blowing and waving.
What's caught in our web today?

Bernie: The first thing for me is my very own KEY in peace that I may be freedom wish that when I want to go to church to pray it lock when I want to throw the key away that God know I love him with all my heart World of heavens I feel sad when I have to lock the door and see your key again.

Chorus: This is our very own key
which we have made from words.

Edith: When I was little we lived in a big old farmhouse the other side of the Bwlch and Grandad used to get up in the morning about five o'clock to feed the pigs and the sheep and he used to wake us up sometimes with his keys jangling loudly. 'Come on, beauties!', he'd shout and we were never sure whether he meant the pigs or us, because although he was supposed to be feeding the animals, I'm sure he thought that because he was up out of bed, everybody else should be as well, and he jangled his keys and he shouted as loud as he could to make sure we could all hear.

Chorus: This is our web of keys.
It is both open and closed.
We are caught in it,
yet it is of our making
and thus we are free of it.
In writing our web we can help to release one another,
like turning a key.

Harriet: I am travelling a long road, a lonely road, across burning deserts and snow-capped mountains, putting my best foot forward, one foot after the other. On my way I meet fellow travellers. What shall we say to each other? We share what we have, some words of comfort and encouragement, perhaps a drink and something to eat. How little we know one another, but sometimes it's as if we have a key that we can open up each other's hearts and look right into the centre of each other, like looking through a keyhole, and we can see what really goes on in the hearts of one another. On the journey of life I undergo many difficulties and hardships. I also see many beautiful things. 'Know thyself,' says the oracle. But we know ourselves through understanding one another. And vice versa.

Chorus: A web of shreds and words and jewels and memories.
This is our web of keys
that open room after room
and box within box
where our futures can be found.

Over the last few years I have run many writing workshops for people who have experienced mental health problems, in a variety of settings, from smoke-filled morning drop-ins to pleasantly scented weekend self-development centres. As the *I Ching* says, 'the place may change, but the well remains ever the same'. Words, both written and spoken, are keys to the soul, and whenever a secure and enjoyable group can be established, fears and secrets may also find some release. We all inhabit the social world of language, yet strive to tell a private tale, 'make sense' of our extraordinary common life. I try to help in making a kind of creative space where, if only for an hour or two, the gates of the soul may be opened a little, even in the middle of a busy, indifferent city or on the clanging wing of a prison.

I have received many positive comments from people who have taken part in the 'Web of Words': some have even spoken of a 'breakthrough' in their ability to express their feelings in writing, and of gaining a new insight into the role writing may have in their lives as a way forward. The processes of what Jung called 'active imagination', of creative response to symbolic images within an egalitarian process, permits personal interpretation without threat. Our web is inherently social and interactive, the weaving itself a metaphor of the inner and outer explorations whereby any writer's realisations take their place in the world. Each individual's contributions, written 'hot', are primary expressions, the web as such a holding space for their psychic and emotional content which also provides an integrative aesthetic experience in which each contribution is an essential ingredient, whatever its own literary merits.

I've outlined a method, but the skills of the facilitator in managing the material and holding the dynamics of the group are another, essential, story, as is the whole topic of the relationship between therapeutic value and aesthetic quality. No doubt this brief outline has thrown up many questions in your mind, which may find responses elsewhere in this book. I myself remain intrigued by the broader cultural consequences of our paradigm, whereby a circle of people, discarding for a while their differences of writing skill *per se*, sit down to weave both wide and deep, claiming a right to their experience, their memory and their own imaginative life, and thereby gain some further insight into their own well-being.

References

Hillman, J. and Ventura, M. (1992) *We've Had A Hundred Years of Psychotherapy And The World's Getting Worse.* New York: HarperCollins.

Lockhart, R. (1987) *Words As Eggs.* Dallas: Spring Publications.

Further Reading

Goldberg, N. (1986) *Writing Down the Bones.* London: Shambala.

Goldberg, N. (1990) *Wild Mind.* London: Shambala.

Hillman, J. (1990) *A Blue Fire: The Essential James Hillman.* London: Routledge.

Jamison, K. (1993) *Touched With Fire: Manic-Depressive Illness and the Artistic Temperament.* New York: Free Press Inc.

Lerner, A. (1981) 'Poetry therapy.' In R.J. Corsini (ed) *Handbook of Innovative Psychotherapies.* New York: Wiley & Sons.

Morrison, M. (ed) (1987) *Poetry As Therapy.* New York: Human Sciences Press.

CHAPTER 4

'Men Wearing Pyjamas'
Using Creative Writing with People with Learning Disabilities

Fiona Sampson

Men wearing pyjamas:
On their heads they wear bathing hats.
Jump into the swimming pool
And all the water comes out!

(5 February 1989)[1]

For 18 months from April 1988, Caroline, the author of this short poem, attended a weekly writing group at St Cross House, a day centre for people with learning disabilities then run by the Isle of Wight District Health Authority (DHA). She was an extrovert, literate and emotional woman in her early 40s whose learning disabilities had been caused by Down's Syndrome. Her family had chosen not to send her to live in the island's large psychiatric hospital, which in 1988 was just beginning to close down. Instead she lived at home with elderly parents, attending the Special Needs Unit at the local college of further education as well as St Cross House, and developing interests in drama, music and cooking.

Caroline's superficially straightforward poem illustrates several of the most important roles writing can play for people with learning disabilities. In

1   Although clients' names have been changed, copyright of this and all the following extracts remains with the individual authors, whom I would like to thank for permission to reproduce their work.

this comic piece she layers her characteristic sense of the ridiculous between fillings that might equally be political, feminist or the half-understood stuff of personal nightmare. This kind of light touch – permitting exploration rather than necessitating statement – is something creative writing offers participants who need opportunities to discuss what's troubling them. Its very obliquity makes discussion possible.

'Men wearing pyjamas', Caroline begins, not cluttering her line with action or adjective. The image must stand by itself. And sure enough, there is something inherently absurd about pyjamas. They seem incompatible with the exercise of authority. Small wonder that they have often been used as prison uniform – and indeed as a form of hospital discipline. Caroline's first line lets us in on her experience of 'men' as authority figures on whom pyjamas might be amusing.

Moreover, 'On their heads they wear bathing hats'. More incongruity. Bathing hats are worn by ladies of a certain age and not by men in pyjamas. Not only are they unaesthetic but in covering the hair they have the slightly unsettling ability to dehumanise the wearer. Thus by the time Caroline pushes her ridiculous men into a swimming pool in her third line they have become slightly alienated. Motiveless. And they must 'jump' rather than proceed with dignified caution. When 'all the water comes out', everything is displaced. There are men in pyjamas in the (empty) swimming pool, the water is outside it.

Caroline could be notating a sketch for *Monty Python*. Instead she's made a poem which she writes down and memorises. Later she performs it at readings, on BBC Radio 4 and on local television. Each time, she uses an accelerating sing-song in which she tries to hold on to the rhythm – with its subversive missing foot in the last line – but wants to get to the punch-line before she starts laughing too much. Why does Caroline find this last line so funny? Perhaps because it's at this moment that she dreams up a major transgression. Noise, mess and someone else to blame: she subverts the rhythm of her poem and our expectations of adult behaviour.

I suggest that something else is going on here, too. Caroline wrote this poem unaided. Unlike nearly everything else she had produced during the ten months we'd been working together, it was a poem she composed without prompts and questions, without suggestions from the rest of the group of which she was a member, and without relying on me to transcribe it. In this sense it was itself transgressing the limits of our expectations of her.

After she had written this poem, Caroline's relationship to writing – poetry in particular – began to change. She started to write and draw in her own time, sometimes bringing what she'd written to show the group. Often she seemed to have written hastily: as if ownership of the poem were more important than the piece itself. This can be seen clearly in a poem which was a gift at F's leaving party:

> There is someone dear to us
> Who we've got to know and love
> So much. It is F the best
> Of all. We all thank you for
> All you have done for us.
> We want you to stay do not
> Go.
> For we love you that's all.

(13 September 1989)

The rhythmic buoyancy of her opening couplet breaks down in the dilemma over 'so much': should it be assonantal on line two or preserve the rhythm in line three? A series of enjambments in-spite-of-themselves fail to catch the poem as it falls on to 'Go' and only the chiming repetition of 'all' holds the piece together. But it's not surprising that someone accustomed to certain exclusions from discursive participation – who is never going to vote, marry or have right of attorney, for example – should privilege her opportunity to participate an authoritative discourse in general over the particular content of her interventions. For not only the St Cross House group but the wider culture in which she lived had made Caroline aware that poetry was perceived as a complex, high-status discourse. She transcribed favourite poems and hymns into a diary. On the writing group's monthly trips to the public library she selected poetry books, though she didn't necessarily enjoy reading them. She collected the autographs of visiting writers and was keen to show off her own skills.

Before she wrote 'Men Wearing Pyjamas' Caroline was an enthusiastic group member, but her commitment to writing ended with each weekly session. She was one of four women, aged from 24 to 50, whom I met weekly at the day centre they attended. Although all four had some degree of literacy none of them had done any original imaginative writing. Although I had literature skills, I had never worked on a writing project with people with learning disabilities. I set up the original 18 month St Cross House group as part of my brief to 'develop uses for writing and literature in health care' delivered by the Isle of Wight DHA; and I was to work with the day centre for over three years. During this time we developed individual skills and professional methodologies. In particular we discovered a rudimentary aim and objectives which have informed my own subsequent work, as well as that of the day centre with other writers:

Aim:

- To facilitate a 'broad-spectrum' individuation through self-expression, participation in the written and public verbal life of the community, writing and verbal skills and increased confidence.

Objectives:

- To devise practice which complements the care context in which it is delivered. Although individuation may counter the legacy of institutionalisation, work which is delivered within a care context cannot responsibly subvert the aims, and especially the ethical concerns, which vulnerable individuals expect from this setting. The writer is not a professional carer and cannot make decisions about care. Partnerships with professional carers can be fruitful for all concerned.

- To provide activities of specifically literary quality, including skill-sharing. Participants may already have meaningful informal verbal interaction but lack skills and opportunities to participate in high-status discourses such as the production of 'literary' – published or conspicuously sophisticated – texts. Work which is insufficiently challenging only reifies this exclusion. People with learning disabilities have as much right as, say, evening class students to a genuinely literary experience from their 'writing group'.

- To facilitate access to writing and literature through the development of a wide range of appropriate activities, in particular dictation of group and individual work to a facilitating writer.

- To celebrate the participant's ownership of their own writing. The individual with learning difficulties is the writer of their work, to which the facilitator stands in the same relation as an editor, proof reader or agent, for example.

In the rest of this chapter I'd like to look at ways of working to meet these objectives. My examples are drawn primarily from the work of the original St Cross House group.

Complementing the care context

Perhaps the most significant and insidious obstacle to genuine opportunities for individuation by participating writers is that this work goes on in a care context. Although my role and skills are not those of a clinician, I was working at St Cross House as a writer-in-residence for a DHA; and in subsequent projects with people with learning disabilities I have worked for social services and voluntary sector agencies. Funding patterns and the way the lives of people with learning disabilities are organised make it likely that their access to creative writing projects will be in a care setting.

That work with people with learning disabilities is carried out in a health care context is itself a discursive souvenir: a legacy of nineteenth century diagnostic techniques which confined people with mental health problems and people with learning disabilities alike to large asylums. These may have 'protected' other citizens as much as their inmates from the encounter between society and the unusual individual. Foucault's analysis, in *Madness and Civilisation*, of the construction of social order might be regarded as more empirical than radical by today's community care professionals and user groups (Foucault 1965). Yet traces of this defensive discourse remain in contemporary media 'scares' about possible physical dangers posed by people with mental health problems who have been released into the community.

In this context it's not surprising that the distinction between mental health problems and learning disabilities is still susceptible to popular confusion. The individual with learning disabilities is not ill and does not need health care for his condition, except when his learning disabilities are caused by a clinical condition or have such a condition linked to them. For example, someone with learning disabilities might have epilepsy or suffer from recurrent meningitis, or could have impaired musculature because their learning disabilities confine them to a wheelchair.

The individual with learning disabilities is not particularly likely to be in that heightened state of emotion popularly associated with mental illness. In fact, because of a history of institutionalisation and a lack of opportunities to develop independence, she is more likely to exhibit a subdued and limited range of responses to any situation. Many adults with learning disabilities, who may suffer from low self-esteem and lack of confidence, respond to their carers with a degree of compliance which can seem uncomfortably close to obedience.

Therefore the aims of community health and social care for people with a learning disability are broadly palliative and remedial. Provision includes physical care where necessary. Sometimes this entails the work of feeding and toileting which nurses would perform for clients of acute health care. At others, it means identifying or joint-funding accommodation in group homes or with what are sometimes known as 'sympathetic landladies', so that individuals who would find it difficult to provide these things for themselves receive food, shelter and the chance to keep clean and healthy. Sometimes remedial training in self-care (classes in cooking and shopping, for example) ensures the future physical well-being of individuals who, at the time of writing, may have spent the majority of their lives unlearning these skills in institutions.

Small wonder that it was so important to Jane, a woman in her early 50s who had spent her adult life in care, to excavate her 'own' identity. For 18 months from October 1992, Jane attended a weekly writing group in the group home from which she had recently moved and which she still regarded as home.[2] In the following untitled poem, the modesty of her claims keeps the lines as short as those of the archaeological poems of Seamus Heaney's *Wintering Out* (Heaney 1972):

> I can read and write
> tell the time
> go shopping
> cooking, washing up, clean the bathroom, hoovering, dusting:
> I'm good with people
> and at looking after people.
> Sometimes I can tell:
> what the weather's going to do
> what mood people are in.
> I can tell right from wrong and I can
> look after myself.
>
> (7 January 1993)

2   Glamis Court, East Cowes, Isle of Wight, was run by Islecare for Isle of Wight Social Services and the Isle of Wight DHA.

Community care also tries to palliate the effects of their learning disability on the mental well-being of individuals. While resources are directed towards trying to integrate people with learning disabilities into the community – for example, by helping them to find mainstream jobs washing up or collecting supermarket trolleys – the prejudices of that community and the difficulty for such individuals of finding a meaningful way of life in it are acknowledged by the way in which care provides alternative foci for life. Day care, and with it the whole range of remedial and palliative activities, from literacy programmes to parties, are therefore at least identified and in many cases bought-in or provided.

Activities with a specifically literary quality

It's often as part of this day care that writing activities are made available to people with learning disabilities. The activity is seen as developing verbal, intellectual and imaginative skills but also as a form of advocacy work, since it facilitates self-expression by participants. More than this, however, it allows participants to excel. There is no 'correct' way of writing creatively and, just like anybody else, people with a learning disability succeed or fail only on their own terms when they make a poem or a story. These terms may include 'Isn't it embarrassing?' or 'Wait till I show x!'.

There are other terms on which this writing is judged, of course: those of the reader without a learning disability. The facilitating writer may be the first of these. The enduring twentieth century interest in 'outsider art', work by untrained makers which happens to meet modernist criteria of successful art, must serve as some kind of warning to the facilitator who particularly values the unconventionality of the writing participants produce. Though a text whose unconventional style or content indicates that it is the work of someone with a learning disability may afford the reader privileged experiences, and may be evidence of a relatively unmediated process of composition, conventions of unconventionality can easily generate the lack of respect for the individual author which is a mark of the treatment of exotica.

Ted Hughes makes the point, of children's writing, that:

> …it is not simply adult writing in the larval stage. It is a separate literature of its own, to be judged…by the highest artistic standards. [...] Children's sensibility, and children's writing, have much to teach adults. Something in the way of a corrective, a reminder. Theirs is not just a

miniature world of naïve novelties and limited reality – it is also very much the process of naked apprehension, far less conditioned than ours, far more fluid and alert, far closer to the real laws of its real nature. (Hughes 1994, p.29)

The usefulness of this passage lies not in potentially infantilising the person with a learning disability, but in its idea of a 'separate literature' with as much merit as any other; one which we must see as setting its *own* 'highest artistic standards'.

Appropriate forms of access

Orality is served and celebrated by dictation which, with its reification of the process of writing and its opportunities for revision, ensures sessions are not merely transcriptions of conversations, but have all the elements of choice, ownership and conscious status implied by authorship. But facilitation entails more than bald transcription, even of the developed text. Writing sessions are a chance for group members to be exposed to a range of forms for what they have to say – and even to a range of things to talk about. This is how the St Cross House group describe researching, writing and illustrating *Kids' Guide To Newport*, a town trail published by the Isle of Wight Tourist Board (St Cross House Writing Group 1989):

> We went out and went around the old places. We stopped at each one and we had to think of various things about each place.
>
> By writing letters – which Caroline did actually. St Cross House, the prison and the hospital. Library books.
>
> Fiona asked us to mention all the things the right way and she wrote them down. Take photos of them and pictures from the library books – which Jill drew.
>
> We learnt about the history of the various places. Caroline came in one morning and told us about the Blue School.
>
> (27 September 1989)

As the ambition of this project suggests, challenging opportunities are particularly useful for long-running groups whose members have built up confidence. Encouraging participants to try new skills and to excel themselves runs against the grain of any residual institutionalisation and allows individuals a sense of achievement and of being listened to which in some cases may be wholly new to them.

This 'broad-spectrum' individuation is evident in the work. Someone with a learning disability may not have explored their power to observe and characterise the world around them. The following poem by Teresa shows us a reflective sensibility beyond the gossip she was known as. We encounter someone with strong spatial awareness who handles synaesthesia – and metaphor in general – easily, and who has a linguistic sensibility which allows her to reappropriate cliché through a punning sense of its literal meaning:

The Sky
Blue.
Feels heavy.
If you put your hand up in the sky and stirred
it would be like water.
If you ate it, it would be
solid
nice: a nice person.
Flowers are the same blue as the sky,
the bags are blue,
butterflies.
Only to look up: if I look up at the sun
I scrimp my eyes up.
The sky's the limit.

(18 July 1989)

Like Caroline, Teresa, who was in her late 30s, lived with elderly parents. Like Caroline she could be noisy and boisterous. But her vocabulary was limited in ways which belied her ability to think and learn. This poem, typical of her solo work, was dictated slowly and questioningly. The lateral shifts in the piece – do bags 'go' with butterflies and flowers? – are characteristic of Teresa's search for the appropriate in language. 'Scrimp' for 'squint, screw' is another such casting around: not a malapropism but a neologism, since Teresa has seized on something onomatopoeic in the word to allow herself to use it here.

This kind of work with description can be useful for orientation exercises. Orientation is a developing practice in the care of people with dementia. It works in various media to help individuals live with the effects of confusion by strengthening their grasp on what they do know. Institutionalisation can exaggerate the confusion felt by some people with severe learning disabilities as well as the effects of dementia; and care staff work to remind these clients of their individuality. Because orientation lays stress on simplifying and repeating what is familiar – so that certain words or ideas become touchstones with which the client can continue to steer herself through the world – there is no body of expertise in orientation among community arts practitioners analogous to that in reminiscence work with older people. Orientation resists the synthesis and elaboration characteristic of creativity. However, dictated writing, with its stress on working towards exactly what the participant wants to say and on reinforcing the participant's own forms of experience, has more in common with the aims of orientation than the term 'creative' suggests. Every writing session with someone with severe learning disabilities is likely to include elements of orientation. Although the individual writer is their own expert witness, the facilitator who lets inconsistency stand, for example, colludes in a 'loop' of confusion in the writer's mind. They also help to produce a text which misrepresents the writer.

Like anyone else, the individual with learning disabilities needs access to metaphor or narratives which he can appropriate for his own experiences. Advocacy finds ways for the views of people who are failed by normal forms of discursive participation to be heard. For example, in 1995–6 I ran a three month project, designed to explore what older people attending local centres wanted from a proposed reorganisation of day care, for Age Concern Thamesdown. But less overtly, during a summer project using classical myth, the original St Cross House group – a least one of whom had first-hand experience of domestic violence – produced this powerfully focused account of power relations and blame:

The Women in the Story of Orpheus

They were villains: violent as well. But in our lives it's men that are violent, not the women. Men are fakes: they try to be nice to you but they're just using you for an excuse. They can be sent to court for assault or violence. Men are supposed to be nice to their girlfriends, but sometimes men beat their wives up.

What should a wife do? She should go and report it to the police. It's not enough to hit him back, because he's big and strong. Men should not hit women because women are fragile. They should hit someone their own size, otherwise they're a bully and a coward. But in this story they blame it onto the women. Because if they say that women are dangerous, it's alright to be nasty to them.

We think men might be frightened of women.

(13 June 1990)

Classical myth is only one example of the challenge to which writers with learning disabilities can rise. A year earlier the same women had tackled Dylan Thomas' difficult and violent credo, 'The Green Fuse'.[2] Here are their individual responses:

> *Nature*
>
> Nature is when you get an order:
> when you're younger, you get older
> and different things happen to you:
> and that's nature.
>
> (Jill, 7 June 1989)

> *Nature*
>
> I'm going to say trees or
> river
> mountains. I think
> they stay the same.
> Climb the mountain.
> Ever so high
> green
> like grass and trees.
>
> (Teresa)

> *Nature*
>
> We are God's creation.
> We're really animals
> – until Eve came along and they created
> women.
> He created the stars and the moon and all living creatures,
> he also had the rain and the sun and the stars.
> And the best thing he made of us was love.
>
> (Caroline)

2   Dylan Thomas, 'The force that through the green fuse drives the flower' in D. Thomas (1978), p.77.

As these examples show, celebrating the individual writer means celebrating the individual text. The product, perhaps even more than the process, is what defines discursive practice and practitioner.

Celebrating ownership

For many adults dictation can make the experience of composition new. It removes the stylistic and emotional constraints – as well as those of confidence – which can be associated with creative writing in particular. Someone with learning disabilities may have particularly strong anxieties about literacy. Dictation allows her to experience her own way of using language as coherent and persuasive. Writing down – rather than taping – what she says allows her to experience her voice as carrying the discursive authority of the literary text. She can see her words turning into writing.

However, that written language is no less 'owned' than the spoken word. Though language which is written down may be reified by its materiality and durability, and by the status of the form, it is not in some way owned or appropriated by that form. Conversely, though what is being dictated is not yet visibly material, and may be subject to revision and editing, it is not in any way uninformed by intention and conscious choice.

For this reason it's important, too, to write down what is dictated *verbatim*. If what is dictated is changed by the facilitator's fancy or their inability to keep up with the client, then the transaction changes and becomes similar to other discursive experiences which the individual with learning disabilities may have encountered in care, in which what she has to say is not allowed its own terms but is 'always already' pre-empted by some local discursive authority: psychologist's diagnosis or care staff time management.

However, this is not to suggest that 'editorial' discussion or writing exercises should be omitted, any more than they would be for any other writer working with a facilitator, such as their publisher or a creative writing tutor. Editorial discussion reinforces the identity of the text being produced. It underlies its separation not only from more conversational moments in the session but also from other pieces of transcription, and facilitates 'literary' judgement.

For example, the St Cross House group were drafting some ideas for an exercise about 'Feeling Nervous'. I read back their ideas and they added second draft detail (shown here in italics):

stomach feels
light and fluttery inside
my stomach feels all tight inside
slower than usual
you forget stuff
I said to myself 'Why I went upstairs for?'
when I got downstairs I said 'Blow!'
sweaty skin *hot skin same feeling to touch as underneath (where David puts his hands)*
under your arms
cold slimy like fish
heavy eyes *watery stuffed up bright blue*
so heavy they're ready to drop out
headache
felt a bit dry *mouth need a drink smooth*
worried
need a new brain *(or a new head)*
you get the shakes *twitches*
it makes you feel sick as well
hot bottom!

(13 September 1989)

But the poem into which they put these ideas develops them appreciably
further, adding narrative, personalising the feelings and playing up their
humour:

Butterflies in the Stomach

My stomach feels light and fluttery inside.
My body's hot and sweaty like fish. Hot Bottom!
Has anyone got a new brain? – Let's have it!
– I forget stuff.
I said to myself 'Why I went upstairs for?'
when I got downstairs I said 'Blow!'
(blow the cobwebs).
My eyes are so heavy they're going to drop out;
they're stuffed up and watery.
My mouth is dry, I need a drink:
I'm feeling a bit down-in-the-mouth
and my stomach twitches up and down.

(13 September 1989)

This process of re-working and contemplating the finished product makes dictation to the facilitator more appropriate than a tape recording. The close participation of the facilitator enacts the readerly attention which is one of the main aims of the process. Thus the process of dictation allows the participant with learning disabilities to experience her own fluency, agency and the status of the finished piece of writing. The aim isn't primarily to allow her to believe in the process offered by the facilitating writer. Rather, it is to allow the participant to experience the accessibility of a form of writing whose status is empowering both within and beyond the care context. It is also to reify and give authority to what the individual has to say, especially within that context.

The final destination of the product – whether it is to be typed up and returned to the client or is to form part of some ward 'book' or exhibition, or whether instead it will be broadcast or published – will for many be an important reason for participating. For some this may be important and empowering in itself. For others, it makes sense of the experience. Making decisions about what is to be published or performed is always hard. When Healing Arts published a set of six poem posters from the work of writing clients in 1993, the contributions by people with learning disabilities were all group poems because strong individual work hadn't yet built up. After discussion, the writing groups decided they preferred to show their best work even though individual contributors weren't named.

However, confidentiality is especially important in any work with vulnerable individuals. This is particularly true with those individuals with learning disabilities who might not fully understand what they are giving assent to or might forget that they have consented to having their work reproduced, for example in an exhibition or conference paper. Taking the writing of someone with a learning disability seriously may therefore mean passing up the opportunity to publish it. It means respecting it, instead, as being as much its writer's private property as any other author's work.

Conclusion

This issue of ownership sums up the whole aim of facilitating creative writing with people with learning disabilities. Ultimately, access to the pleasures and challenges of creative writing, through the facilitator's literary skills and through rigorously ethical procedures, only occurs when participants with learning disabilities are seen as – and see themselves as – taking on the role of the writer. In so participating, these writers, whether men or women, take off the 'pyjamas' of institutionalised expectation and assume their own discursive authority instead.

References

Foucault, M. (1965) *Madness and Civilisation*. New York: Pantheon.

Heaney, S. (1972) *Wintering Out*. London: Faber & Faber.

Hughes, T. (1994) 'Concealed energies.' In *Winter Pollen*. London: Faber & Faber.

St Cross House Writing Group (1989) *Kids' Guide to Newport*. Isle of Wight: Isle of Wight Tourist Board.

Thomas, D. (1978) *The Poems*. Ed. Daniel Jones. London: J.M. Dent.

Various (1993) *Six Poem Posters*. Isle of Wight: Healing Arts.

Further reading

Levete, G. (1987) *The Creative Tree: Active Participation in the Arts for People who are Disadvantaged*. London: Michael Russell.

Miles, M. (ed) (1991) *Art and Mental Health Hospitals: Art as an Effective Element in the Care of the Mentally Ill and Mentally Handicapped*. Dundee: British Health Care Arts.

Palmer, J. and Nash, F. (1991) *The Hospital Arts Handbook*. Durham, NC: Duke University Medical Center.

Sampson, F. (1989) *Writing in Health Care*. Isle of Wight: Hospital Arts.

Sampson, F. (1997) 'Some questions of identity: what is writing in health care?' In C. Kaye and T. Blee (eds) *The Arts in Health Care: A Palette of Possibilities*. London: Jessica Kingsley Publishers.

Senior, P. and Croall, J. (1993) *Helping to Heal: The Role of the Arts in Health Care*. London: Calouste Gulbenkian Foundation.

CHAPTER 5

Writing or Pills?
Therapeutic Writing in Primary Health Care
Gillie Bolton[1]

The process of writing gets me in touch.

A GP (Bolton 1996, p.5)

Why writing at the doctors?

Writing is pretty nearly free; can be undertaken by anyone with ordinary writing skills, at any time of life, day or night; and, unlike physiotherapy or penicillin, does not need a professional to dispense or administer it. So why put it in the GP's bag? Because people don't tend to think of writing in this way without it being suggested; and because GPs, those overworked and highly respected mainstays of our lives and culture, are the authority many people turn to in times of personal stress, anxiety, depression or difficulty. Possibly people in the past had more good friends; or a much more continuous contact with parents, siblings, aunts and grannies; or parochial support from their priest. The GP seems to have taken over many of these roles, as well as being the 'curer' of sickness and disease, and the gatekeeper to the acute services in hospitals and clinics.

This chapter offers some of the findings of a research project based at the Institute of Primary Care and General Practice, Sheffield University, funded

1   Grateful thanks are offered to David Hannay, without whom the writing therapy in primary care study could not have taken place; the six GPs who so generously gave their time and enthusiasm; Marilyn Lidster for support; Anna Stanford; Peter Nelson and Jean Barton for generously allowing me to quote from their writing; all the patients in the study; and Rosie Field and Stephen Rowland for their help and encouragement.

by the Royal College of General Practitioners (RCGP) (publication pending 1998). It also reports the experience of Anna Stanford, a nurse student on a Nursing BA module on 'Writing Therapy' (Sheffield Hallam University), using writing with her community group of asthma sufferers.

Psychological distress is commonly seen by GPs, who often label it as anxiety or depression. It was to patients who presented with these kinds of symptom that the six GPs in the RCGP research study responded with writing suggestions. Many physical symptoms, such as headache, backache, sickness, and so on, can be caused by psychological distress. However much medication is taken for chronic indigestion, some patients may not be comfortable again until the underlying cause of the pain is located and attended to. Writing can help with such somatisation. As one of the GPs in the study commented: 'Dis-ease is when patients are not at ease with their bodies. Patients present with many psychological problems, which it is important not to medicalise. But *they* feel they need to present with medical symptoms, and feel embarrassed to show emotions. Writing is a way of opening this area out' (Bolton 1996, p.5).

GPs need every lifeline possible to throw to so many apparently drowning patients. Writing, with its simplicity, cheapness and availability, may be one of these. Moreover, it can have an additional benefit: if the patients choose to share their writing with their practitioner, it can offer insights difficult to elicit in seven minute consultations, at least on a physical level: 'you can't mishear what is written' (Bolton 1996, p.5).

One of the aims of a GP is to help patients to help themselves, rather than to be dependent on professional support, whether for psychological or physical problems. An advantage of writing is that it is '*for* patients and *by* them rather than being done *to* them. Too much medicine is diagnosis from the outside and having treatments done to the patient' (Bolton 1996, p.5). Patients can write on their own, in their own time, at their own pace, returning to the GP or other primary care practitioner for support when necessary.

Reflective and expressive writing is private and self-directed, and in principle available at any time to anyone with basic writing skills. Like the other arts and physical and talking therapies, it can offer access to memories, feelings and experiences. It can help to clarify and organise thoughts. It can encourage development and expansion of understanding because it forms a lasting record which may be worked on later. It can be torn up unread, or form an effective communication with chosen others. Ideas and suggestions for ways of writing are readily available from popular texts (e.g. Bolton 1998; Goldberg 1986; Jackowska 1997; Killick and Schneider 1998; Rainer 1978; Sellers 1989).

Background

The use of writing and literature in primary health care has been called for nationally (Smith and Taylor 1996; Wright 1996) and projects have been piloted elsewhere in the clinical context (e.g. Downie 1994). However, this chapter focuses on writing in the primary care context. A GP has written about two patients using writing to help them come to terms with their experience of child sexual abuse (Anonymous GP 1995). An arts project involving writing in two GP surgeries has been successfully undertaken (McDonnell 1996; Ritchie 1995).

Dr Malcolm Rigler at Withymoor Village Surgery is a pioneer of arts projects in the GP surgery:

> The arts are not the spoonful of sugar that makes the medicine go down. The way in which creative artists work with the patients at Withymoor does indeed inform but also stimulates thought and provokes individual response. This empowers patients to take a mature responsibility for their own good health, often unlocking a neglected creativity. (Rigler 1997b, p.6)

Projects have included sex education through drama, poetry and song about childbirth; an annual celebratory lantern procession; an arts project to create dynamic health posters; and creative community links with the local schools. Malcolm Rigler and his nurse practitioner, Lynda Lawley, have worked at making the surgery a creative, welcoming space for health, well-being and community.

Malcolm Rigler has also piloted a writer-in-residence project at Withymoor (Miles 1990; Rigler 1991a, 1991b, 1992, 1997b; Roberts and Bond 1993; Senior and Croall 1993). Dave Reeves, a local writer and poet, undertook a six month residency in 1991. He launched the 'prescribed reading project' – a story book with no beginning, middle and end. Patients write accounts of their sickness and health. They write for each other and the book is available for all to read in the surgery waiting room.

Withymoor is a new private housing estate: smart-looking but soulless. Few of the residents have families with whom to share their troubles or who could hand on experience. They look to the doctor and the surgery:

Prescribed reading – although in truth it is more frequently described as prescribed *writing* – continues although Dave Reeves' residency is long since over. The most recent contributions are from two teachers who write movingly about the stress of their jobs. This is a complete exercise in communication – the sharing of experience both as therapy and mutual support. (Rigler 1997b, pp.9–10)

Another project at the surgery involved Penny Wildgoose creating poetry and song after shadowing a team of midwives. 'Anyone and everyone' was invited to communicate feelings and ideas on pregnancy and childbirth.

The surgery has a feel of celebration, caring and community. Sir Kenneth Calman, in his foreword to the report on the arts activities there, says: 'the objective of the whole process is to improve quality of life for patients and the community' (Rigler 1997b).

Supporters, and Rigler himself, are aware that the medical community, with its insistence on evidence-based medicine, may be unimpressed by the informal and anecdotal evaluations. As Robin Downie, Professor of Moral Philosophy at Glasgow University, says in his preface to the report on Withymoor:

> The cynically minded might ask where the words 'funding' and 'evaluation' fit in. These too are discussed. Indeed one of the features of this report is its realism, its openness to contribution and criticism from all sections of the community. The central message of this report is that disease and ill-health cannot be eradicated by narrowly medical means; they must be tackled in a community context. Medicine needs healthy alliances and the arts are a vital ally. (Rigler 1997b, p.2)

Rigler quotes Peter Baelz, retired Professor of Moral Philosophy at Oxford

> Clearly there can be no purely 'objective' testing of the relationship between medicine and the arts. But there is already evidence coming from social psychologists...that 'happier' people tend to be 'healthier' people and it should not be beyond the wit of social science to prepare tests of the validity of what you [Malcolm Rigler] are about. (Rigler 1997b, p.14)

Therapeutic writing from Sheffield GPs

The RCGP pilot research project on 'Writing Therapy in Primary Care' involved six GPs offering 'writing therapy' to depressed and anxious patients as an addition, or an alternative, to other forms of management of their symptoms. The back-up and support of anxious or depressed patients, whatever the treatment offered, generally falls to the GP. The GPs in this study saw this kind of supportive counselling as an essential, if demanding, element of their job. An ideal would be for a range of qualified arts and complementary therapists to be available within primary care; the economic situation in primary care, however, makes this an impossibility. This study sought to explore a much more possible alternative using the skills and back-up support currently on offer within general practice. The account which follows is drawn from the research reports (1998), to which the reader should refer for more detailed data. A further, controlled, trial is being planned.

One of the practitioners in the project was Professor David Hannay (Head of the Institute of Primary Care), who was my GP adviser throughout the project. Four others were already involved in using writing to explore and express professional issues in my postgraduate continuing medical education course, 'Reflections in Writing for GPs'. On the course the GPs write stories or poems about issues in their work which are troubling them, or which they feel need further understanding.

The GPs in the study and I worked together on extending their understanding of the power of expressive and explorative writing; developing appropriate ways of suggesting writing to patients and supporting them through the process; and developing methods of incorporating this approach into habitual consulting patterns. The need to be sensitive about problems of literacy, disability and lack of confidence was stressed, as was the fact that patients were writing for themselves with no need to show the results to anyone, so that in a real sense no writing could ever be 'wrong'.

David Hannay had begun to offer therapeutic writing to his patients before the formal pilot began, and this helped us to devise a more effective formal pilot study. He led a very fruitful seminar with the group, focusing on his methods and initial findings. I wrote a simple leaflet for the GPs to give to patients (Figure 5.1). The GPs were asked to administer a general health questionnaire to each patient at the beginning and end of the trial to measure (to some extent) patients' depression and coping abilities; to keep a log of their findings; to give the patients a simple questionnaire at the end of the trial; and to have a semi-structured interview with me, also at the end of the trial. We felt it was very important for patient and doctor to enjoy a supportive, communicating relationship before they embarked on this writing adventure together.GPs have a stressful workload; it was not easy for them to fit in a new way of working with patients. At the evaluation interview, however, these were some of their comments: 'Once I'd taken the plunge with some patients, I was surprised how accepting the patients were, and how many brought back writing'. 'I got in a muddle with the paperwork to begin with. Also, once I got the wording right, saying that 'A friend and I are doing a bit of research, what do you think about giving it a try?', [patients] usually felt good about it.' 'This has great potential; the more I do it the more I can see areas where it could be useful.' Many of the GPs, and others not in the trial, still habitually suggest expressive and explorative writing to appropriate patients. They can do this much more happily now that there is no research paperwork with which to keep up.

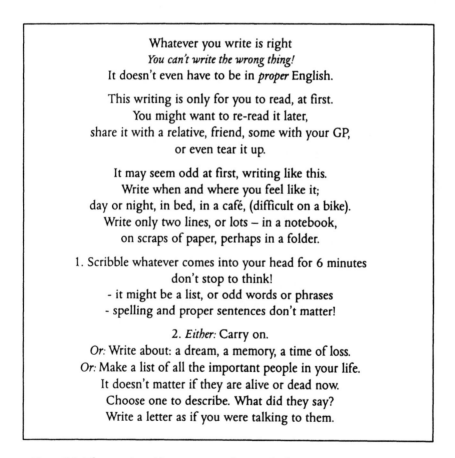

Figure 5.1: *Therapeutic writing: summary of patient leaflet*

Much of the writing was not brought for the GP to read; patients shared it with friends or relatives. This felt appropriate. Some, however, *was* brought, one practitioner commenting: 'Patients like to bring something in for the doctor. One brings chocolates, kitkats. This is a perfect gift' (Bolton 1996, p.5).

This is what some of the GPs felt about the writing they did see: 'This is a wonderful thing. It helps with diagnosis – even seeing changes in the handwriting of the person helps. It helps me communicate with patients, going into depths. It expands the time of the surgery visit, because they can present you with their thoughts. It helps to know their inner thoughts'. 'They can write *all* the things they want to say, whereas in talking they have to choose.' 'Writing helps the patient express emotion; it feels safe on paper.' 'The notes and approach were very important – they were non-threatening. It has to be quite clear it is *for them*, not that the doctor has given homework' (Bolton 1996, p.5).

Here are a few of the cases:

- An older woman who was experiencing problems with her sons had had a difficult childhood herself. She wrote about her past. This seemed to clarify a lot of things, and she felt it alleviated a severe depression and her lack of motivation. The writing revealed to her that there really were bad things in her past which had affected her, and she felt able to move forward with increased insight. However, this didn't change anything in her family. She gave the writing to her son, but he didn't read it until he heard his doctor and myself on Radio 4 talking about the work. At the time of the interview, the GP didn't know the outcome of this intervention.

- A young girl had fits at awkward moments and was often angry; she lived with her sick father. She started writing and her fits dramatically stopped within two days. She wrote about her frustration and anger. The fits restarted, but the writing helped her to see connections between her fits and her frustrated anger against her dad.

- A young woman was suffering from postnatal depression, having had a second baby after a big gap. She had a demanding career and tended to be a perfectionist. Her GP suggested she write lists and 'tick things off' them, to help herself feel more in control.

Once she put the disorder of her life on paper, things started to 'fall into place' again.

- A middle-aged woman wrote reams without knowing what she was writing or what it 'meant'. The writing seemed to 'write her', welling up without her thinking about it. On re-reading and thinking about this articulate but not consciously composed writing, she felt that she was getting in touch with past abuse which she had completely suppressed.

- A violent man began to write and put the violence on to the page. He became less violent and destructive; the GP could only attribute this change to the writing.

- A depressed teenager was living with his grandmother following his parents' separation. He commented in his evaluation: 'I wrote about my feelings for Gran, and about Dad leaving Mum...it got it out of me'. He was no longer judged to be clinically depressed at the end of the study.

- A young girl wrote many drafts of a letter to her parents. She was eventually able to send it, saying things she could never have said in person, such as 'I love you'. In this instance the writing served not as a medical intervention but as an effective form of communication.

All the patients in the study felt that therapeutic writing in general practice was a good idea. As one of them put it, 'it helped people understand themselves better'.

As was to be expected, the project threw up a number of problems and challenges. Literacy was felt to be a problem in a few cases. One doctor practising in an inner city area felt hampered by anxiety at the thought of embarrassing his patients; another, however, practising in a densely populated council estate, discovered that literacy presented far less of a problem than he might have expected.

There were two instances where the use of writing as a therapeutic intervention seems to have given rise to significant problems, and both of these offer valuable insights for future provision. One patient who already had a history of psychosis became severely psychologically ill and was hospitalised. Her GP did not know whether or not the writing had any connection with this. He felt, however, that it may have been unwise to suggest writing therapy to a patient with such a history and said that he would not do so again. This particular example highlights how important it is in using this kind of intervention to select appropriate clinical contexts, and to provide patients with adequate support.

The other instance was of a man who wrote out his grief about his first wife's death. He showed it to his new partner, as a result of which she left him. Whether or not this was a wholly negative outcome for the man concerned is unclear. However, the GP felt the message learned here was that patients needed much more careful advice about the people to whom it was appropriate to show their writing. I often include in my notes to patients/practitioners the suggestion that 'Your marriage partner may *not* be the most appropriate person with whom to share your writing'. The project helped some of the doctors to realise that they would benefit from some counselling training, which traditionally is not included in their medical training.

Peter's story

Peter Nelson presented to his GP with acute depression and physical symptoms of stress, having been unfairly dismissed from work as the live-in headteacher of a special school for severely disturbed and damaged adolescents. He began writing a diary at the GP's suggestion, taking the sections to regular consultations. He has since written between 60 and 80 closely typed pages. Peter has written out his distress about leaving his job and about the terrible tensions there before he left. He has also written about his physical symptoms, his supportive and loving wife and sons, and his childhood happiness. He has also kept a log of daily activities and habits. It became important to him to balance the difficulties of the work situation with the joys of family life, both present and during his rural childhood. His writing about the latter is lyrical, and depicts scenes and events using smells, sounds and tastes.

. Peter has written angry, unsendable letters to people at work and a questioning one to his late father, and has experimented with listening to their voices within himself by writing some of their responses. Peter wrote that he found it enormously important to choose writing materials with meticulous care; and that writing at different times and in different places affected what he wrote and his ease with, and pleasure in, writing. He was very struck by the idea which I suggested to him that access to new material can be gained when habitual writing patterns are altered. So he tried writing with fresh materials and in new places, for example by a river, which did not remind him of writing for work. Writing began to be exciting and enjoyable, so that he looked forward to being able to get back to his pad and pencil.

Peter's GP reports him to be considerably better; he has taken great pleasure and pride in his writing. Peter has found the writing to be a way of expressing himself, as well as of exploring his own emotions, thoughts, feelings and memories. Furthermore, the writing has brought about a bond between him and his GP which helps them to communicate better. The GP feels that reading the diary has been vital in effectively extending the brief consultation times: Peter does not feel frustrated that there is insufficient time to say all that he wishes to say during the consultation, and the GP feels he has access to a depth of contact with Peter through the writing which could be available in no other way.

Here are two extracts from Peter's writing. The first is about his work situation:

For Iola and I living-in meant continuous work. Hardly an evening meal would pass without the phone or doorbell ringing. The physical elements of living-in meant that I was available 24 hours a day, yes this was tiring and irksome but minor compared to the insidious psychological elements of living-in. The boys probably had little personal space, Iola and I none. Our flat door opened onto the pupil's dormitory corridor, our flat windows overlooked the front and rear access to school. Our central heating was part of the school system so every time a pupil decided to send an annoyance to his neighbour's bedroom by rattling his radiator the reverberations reached the flat – always late in the evening. The solid floors of the unit ensured that every footstep...was transmitted to the flat. The oppressive nature of being confined within the same building for days at a time did not strike me until the effects were biting into my stability. I could move between my flat and my office without touching fresh air. What I did touch on those journeys were staff and pupils wanting a response from me. Day after day of no freedom and no personal space became part of everyday living and again I was blind, certainly to the personal needs of Iola and I.

Living-in is one thing, but to do so with professional commitment means that your physical self is handed over along with every ounce of your emotional self. To do this continually with a group of damaged and challenging teenagers is plain dangerous. However, whilst there I did not take cognisance of the danger. Having left I can see the dangers in neon lights. No I could not go back to the emotional open tap that had to be turned on when dealing with 6 foot of raging teenager. Taking the brunt of the physical lashings of a 14-year-old was hard at 21, extremely hard at a tired and burnt out 49.

This piece of writing is strikingly different from another which records Peter's solitary pleasures as a lad. He had been very struck by my suggestion that he focus on all the five senses in his writing, and found smell, sound and taste particularly evocative:

> A large lavender hedge separated the formal garden from the orchard. The smell was in the first instance secondary. The game was to snap off a lavender flower stalk and entice a bee onto the stalk for closer exam-ination, particularly of pollen laden legs – how did they do that? I often think of that hedge, not only when confronted with a new source of lavender scent, but when my hearing is awakened to a seemingly still shrub that is literally buzzing with the frenetic activity of countless bees.

New Mums' Writing Group in the surgery

One of the GPs in the pilot project asked me to work on two occasions with her 'New Mothers' Group'. Becoming a mother is clearly a stressful time, and this practitioner invites all the new mothers registered with her surgery to join a support group. They have a different speaker or activity each month for an hour. The sessions I did with the group were warm and moving occasions. The most touching piece of writing was about the death of a woman's father who had died at the time of the child's birth. The writer focused on the association of new life and death.

Another group member, Katie Dudley, wrote about how her toddler developed meningitis just before the birth of the new baby. This account, which she went on to have published in *Practical Parenting* (Dudley 1997), gives the story in minute detail. Writing it down and sharing it with a caring audience not only gave her support, it also gave a sense of authority to the experience. Having it published gave her the sense that she had made use of it; she had passed her experience on to others. *Practical Parenting* used the story to give mothers a first-hand account of what to look out for and what to do in cases of suspected meningitis.

In the leaflet I wrote for the mothers to take home afterwards, I made similar suggestions to those contained in the 'patient leaflet' shown in Figure 5.1. Figure 5.2 shows a few of the other ideas for the New Mums' writing group.

This writing is for you,
for the baby in the future,
for others who've been involved.

When you write at home:
write when and where you feel like it (in bed?),
make sure you are comfortable, with a cup of tea,
get a pretty notebook/folder, and a nice pen/pencil
you can't write too little or too much.

Here are some ideas for you to write about at home:
What I've been told about my own birth or little childhood.
A memory that's come to mind over the last month.
A person who's been important to me.
A dream
A fear
A joy

Figure 5.2: Leaflet for the New Mums' Writing Group

A therapeutic writing BA module for nurses

During the same period as the GP project, I ran a module on 'Writing Therapy' as part of the BA in Health Care Practice at Sheffield Hallam University. Aesthetics, the arts and a holistic view of the patient (e.g. Smyth 1996) have been called for in nursing, just as they have in medicine. The students were all nurses; they worked in hospital, GP or community settings, as Macmillan nurses or as midwives. On each of the 12 weeks we discussed a different way of writing, for example reminiscence, dreams, making lists of anxieties, unsendable letters, and so on. The nurses practised these ways of writing for their course portfolio and also used writing with appropriate patients.

Anna Stanford, one of the students, runs an asthma support group in the community called 'Gaspers'. She encouraged the members to write, but felt she was only successful once she had experienced writing herself: 'It has been invaluable actually to experience creative writing' (Stanford unpublished). Some of the exercises were a 'shock' to her, some 'threatening' and some 'comfortable'. She feels she is now able to offer writing with 'caution and preparation'. 'I have seen patients who have struggled for months or years trying to come to terms with their changed lifestyles take a giant step forward just by writing about how they feel about their problems' (Stanford unpublished).

Anna encouraged not only her patients to write, but also her colleagues. One took advantage of this method after considerable personal family illness, and her team are considering it for multi-disciplinary team-work.

One of Anna's patients, Jean Barton, 'found it difficult to express her feelings and fears, but her poetry has been her salvation. It has helped her come to terms with her condition and adjust her lifestyle' (Stanford unpublished). Here is one of her poems:

> *Positive Action*
>
> I may go out today
> if it doesn't rain
> the damp makes me wheezy
> so I tend not to bother
> I nearly went out yesterday
> but it was too hot
> the heat makes me cough
> so I changed my mind
> I might go out tomorrow
> if it's not too windy
> the wind makes me breathless
> so I'll probably stay in again
> Or I could try the medication
> on a regular basis
> get back in control
> go out – and get a life.

Conclusion

These qualitative pilot studies into medical and nursing practice indicate that therapeutic writing has strong potential within these professions. Popular response to media reports of these and other projects suggests there are considerable numbers of patients who would like to be guided towards a self-help therapy such as writing. Distressed, anxious and depressed people do turn to their primary care practitioners in the absence of strong traditional family, neighbourhood and religious support networks, yet it is often very hard for the GP to devise appropriate interventions. One patient wrote in the *Daily Mail*:

> If only GPs who are so quick to prescribe instant tranquillisers to silence distress would suggest the cleansing therapy of putting pen to paper

instead. It's healing in rejection, grief, heartache or despair. It can clear our heads when we're faced with choice and indecision. It doesn't make you fat, sick or wreck your liver. And since nobody can possibly know more about us than we know ourselves, [it is] infinitely superior to any psychiatrist. (Wilson 1990)

References

Anonymous GP (1995) 'Writing to ease the pain of abuse.' *Medical Monitor 15 November.*

Bolton, G. (1996) *Every poem breaks a silence which had to be overcome:* Writing Therapy in Primary Care Research Report. Unpublished.

Bolton, G. (1998) *Writing Myself: The Therapeutic Potential of Creative Writing.* London: Jessica Kingsley Publishers.

Downie, R.S. (1994) *Healing Arts.* Oxford: Oxford University Press.

Dudley, K. (1997) 'Our son had meningitis.' *Practical Parenting* July, 85–88.

Goldberg, N. (1986) *Writing Down the Bones.* London: Shambhala.

Jackowska, N. (1997) *Write for Life: How to Inspire Your Creative Writing.* Shaftsbury: Element Books.

Killick, J. and Schneider, M. (1998) *Writing for Self-Discovery.* Shaftsbury: Element Books.

McDonnell, B. (1996) *Serious Fun: The Arts in Primary Health Care.* Dewsbury: Yorkshire and Humberside Arts.

Miles, M. (1990) *Arts in Primary Health Care.* Dundee: British Health Care Arts.

Rainer, T. (1978) *The New Diary.* London: Angus and Robertson.

Rigler, M. (1991a) 'A breath of fresh air.' *Arts Education: The Magazine of the National Foundation for Arts Education.* October, 3–5.

Rigler, M. (1991b) *People to People: New Writing in the West Midlands.* February, 6.

Rigler, M. (1992) 'Are you sitting comfortably? The Withymoor surgery story.' *Artery: The Journal of Arts for Health 9*, 6.

Rigler, M. (1997a) 'The arts as medicine (a postcard from Withymoor Village Surgery).' *British Journal of General Practice 47*, 423, 684–685.

Rigler, M. (1997b) *Withymoor Village Surgery – A Health Hive.* Dudley Priority Health Trust.

Ritchie, C. (1995) *Arts Work for Health: Project Evaluation.* Barnsley: Community Operation Research Unit.

Roberts, S. and Bond, A. (1993) *Good Medicine: Arts in Health in the West Midlands.* Lincoln: Artservice.

Sellers, S. (1989) *Delighting the Heart.* London: The Women's Press.

Senior, P. and Croall, R. (1993) *Helping to Heal: The Arts in Health Care.* London: Calouste Gulbenkian.

Smith, B.H. and Taylor, R.J. (1996) 'Medicine – a healing or a dying art?' *British Journal of General Practice 46*, 405, 249–251.

Smyth, T. (1996) 'Reinstating the person in the professional: reflections on empathy and aesthetic experience.' *Journal of Advanced Nursing* 24, 932–937.

Wilson, G. (1990) *Daily Mail.* 17 October.

Wright A.F. (1996) 'Editorial – GP 2000: a general practitioner for the new millennium.' *British Journal of General Practice* January, 4–5.

CHAPTER 6

Final Fictions?

Creative Writing and Terminally Ill People

Colin Archer[1]

The ideas and examples which follow are drawn largely from my work in 1992–93 as writer-in-residence at the Princess Alice Hospice in Esher, Surrey, and in 1996–97 at the hospice unit in Weybridge Hospital, Surrey. Some, however, draw on other creative writing projects which I have undertaken over five years at hospitals and day centres in Surrey, Kent and Sussex, where I have often worked with people for whom death, albeit not quite as imminent as in a hospice, was a major issue, and where many of the same principles applied.

In the first hospice at which I worked the average in-patient stay was only 12 days. A few patients had been admitted for pain control or to allow their carers respite and returned home, but most died. This is a common pattern and might seem to give little time or scope to engage in the creative writing I had been hired to develop. Perhaps, I wondered, there would be better chances with day patients who here, as in many hospices, had a longer life expectancy, up to six months even, and who came in once or twice a week: this might not be all that different from working in hospitals or other kinds of day centre with people who also might not have very long to live.

In fact, I have since found considerable scope for – and benefits from – creative writing with dying people, both in-patients and day patients, provided the writer recognises that this facility will only be taken up by a minority of patients, and is willing both to offer a wide range of approaches

---

1   In preparing this contribution I owe a great deal not only to those patients whose work is discussed, but also to those scores of other patients with whom I worked and who taught me so much about creativity – and life.

and to ensure that the patient is always in charge. Imminent death can concentrate the mind on profound issues, but patients remain free not to reflect on life in the slightest if that is their choice.

All the examples in this chapter are taken from my own experience although, in the interests of confidentiality, patients' names have been changed, except when I refer to their published work.

Barriers: real and imagined

During one induction period which was provided for me to absorb the culture of a particular hospice, I spent a session as 'assistant' to a physiotherapist which became, literally, a hands-on experience. Supporting part of a patient's body, a leg, which felt in its immobility and terrible iciness as good as dead, while simultaneously talking with the very alive person to whom it belonged, acted as a powerful metaphor for the central hospice philosophy that dying patients are living people. It is this philosophy, and the belief that living people are, potentially at **least**, creative, which lies behind the growing number of invitations to artists, including writers, to work in hospices and the acceptance of such invitations. Yet some hospice staff prove in practice to be less sure of such projects once they start, and can set up various barriers, perhaps because 'in terminal care there is a tendency to underestimate the ability of the dying patient to *give*' (Stedeford 1983, p.207).

It is certainly not easy for dying patients to give time and attention, largely because of their physical condition. Most of those I have worked with on wards have been too weak to hold a pen. This is no barrier: I can, with their permission, become their pen by recording their words on an unobtrusive tape-deck and printing them out for the patients to check and keep; even day-care patients often choose this method, especially if their life has not involved much writing. Provided patients retain sufficient mental alertness, a way can usually be found, and I was impressed by the skill with which massive doses of necessary painkilling drugs could often be administered without unduly affecting mental alertness.

Other patients confront barriers of communication. Many suffer hearing loss, which need not preclude recording and writing given the time – which is sadly not always available. Mike suffered from motor neurone disease and could only communicate through a light-writing machine, an exchange of three or four short sentences taking over half an hour. Jennie did not want to be included or even to talk much, but did not want to 'upset' me: 'You see, dear', she managed, 'I'm on these drugs which disconnect my brain from my tongue'. Julia forgot that she had recorded any work at all or had even met me.

I have sometimes been warned by hospice staff not to believe all I am told by patients: they might be hallucinating, confused by reduced oxygen supply to the brain, or affected by morphine or other drugs. But whether I believe patients has never been an issue. Whatever creative writing might be, it is not a search for 'the truth'. Yet fear by some staff that patients may not be rational enough to join in can lead them to 'protect' such patients by effectively excluding them from involvement. I was advised on these grounds to avoid Brian but somehow bumped into him, and what he wrote with me eventually proved very helpful, both to him and to his family.

However, the most serious barrier to creative writing with in-patients remains time. The writer needs time to get to know the patient; the patient needs time to trust the writer. Often work will be planned but not started, or started but not finished. Jean died before she could even begin on the letter she wanted to leave for her soon-to-be-born grandchild's eighteenth birthday, but did at least complete the baby shawl she was knitting as we talked. Much rich work is lost, but the process involved can still be of value.

Individual work and group work

I launched my hospice activities at the Princess Alice Hospice in Esher with one-to-one work with individual patients. This reflected the very impressive hospice attention to the individual needs of each patient confronting his or her unique death. It recognised the reality of life on the ward, where sustained interaction between such sick patients was seldom possible. Moreover, it assumed that anything as final as a last piece of recording/writing would be an essentially individual act.

The exclusive use of individual work was simply assumed by staff, volunteers, patients – and me – and it was not until my second and third hospice projects that I ventured to explore the potential of group writing, at least with day patients, a method of working which I have found rewarding in many other types of project, notably with users of mental health services.

Initially I introduced group methods with hospice day patients as shared reminiscences around themes such as the war or shopping or holidays. We talked a lot; patients, even of different generations – enriched and leavened by a few volunteers – started responding to each others' memories; the level of interaction gradually increased. At first I made no attempt at recording:

oral story-telling has much deeper roots than anything written: I pictured cave dwellers talking around a fire, aware of the dark forces outside.

Gradually I introduced recording, sometimes on tape. Gradually, too, I was able to move beyond reminiscence, the group experience often proving particularly good at sparking the most lively imagination, even in the most ravaged bodies. At this stage the recording typically involved my kneeling in the centre and writing patients' pooled ideas with a thick marker on an A1 sheet so all could see, comment and change.

Some of the subjects I introduced offered simply fun, such as constructing a spoof menu comprising only the most awful dishes each member of the group had ever encountered, which produced much health-ful laughter. At other times I introduced themes such as journeys, gates and light. Always it was in a way which permitted literal interpretation, such as recalling one memorable journey each of us had made. But I was always mindful of the experience of Callanan and Kelley that 'dying patients often use symbolic language' (1992, pp.17–18), for example talking, or later hallucinating, about journeys as 'clear metaphors' (1992, p.76) for the crossing to death (as in the legends of Lethe and in Tennyson's *Crossing the Bar*). As practitioners of the arts of symbolic language, writers can perhaps be extra alert for examples in hospices.

At another time we shared – and made a group poem with – lists of things we have lost, starting with umbrellas, earrings and pens, and moving (for those ready to do so) to less tangible yet more important losses such as confidence, energy and even faith (Archer 1997, pp.6–7). Such group work often opens up difficult subjects – even the imminent loss of *everything* – for subsequent individual work, sometimes with me (which may or may not lead to writing) or with others. The 'self' may not be on the page, but – to the extent that the individual is prepared to go – may be 'on the line'.

Meanwhile there are, I believe, benefits simply from being a member, however temporarily and cautiously, of such a group. It may be an unusual group, one which meets only briefly, loses and gains members with great rapidity, and comprises people of all ages and backgrounds with little in common except, crucially, their humanity and imminent death. To create and nurture such a group as both caring and creative is a difficult (but often possible) task which the writer cannot evade but can reasonably expect to share with hospice staff, given that patients who do join in are continuing the common *living* activity of connecting with others.

Kinds of writing and kinds of benefit

The range of writing undertaken by hospice patients in the 1990s is evident from some of the anthologies which have been published (Alexander 1990; Archer 1994; Fontana and Hodgson 1996; Gittins 1991), and the benefits are almost as various as that range. Many of the benefits are similar to those which other art forms would rightly claim, or to those which creative writing can achieve in other settings. Most are modest. Many simply reinforce the work of nursing staff and other professionals. But an attempt at a preliminary identification based on practical experience may help to establish realistic expectations for future creative writing projects, not only in hospices but also wherever death is on the horizon, for ultimately, write Corr and Corr, 'hospice is a philosophy, not a facility' (1983, p.xi).

Diversion

At the very least writing can offer patients something to do, just one more option to add to jigsaw puzzles, light reading, games, television and so on. For many people in society at large, reading 'escapist' books is a way of blocking out some of the pain of living; maybe 'escapist' writing can help in some measure with the pain of dying.

Jimmy dictated a crazy story about raiding the Bank of England. 'I promise it will be a good read,' he said. Yet even this piece of fiction is permeated by Jimmy's impending death. 'The Judge won't be able to do a thing,' he wrote. 'They couldn't put me in prison, not with me like this. I'll be a free man...The only problem is what to do with all the money...I'll soon be in the cemetery. You can't spend it there' (Meaney 1994, p.14). The 'self' of this writer – the Irish story-teller and defiant joker, whiskey-drinker and greyhound-owner – is reflected on the page more fully than in many a supposedly more serious piece.

But the value of such pieces of work does not, in the end, depend on what one may read into them about the originator and his deeper concerns, or even perhaps on the contribution the activity itself might have made to pain control.[2] Did the individual concerned find the act of writing *enjoyable*? The

---

2   Le Shan claims that 'work, occupational therapy, relating to others – these things do much more than just "pass the time". They also diminish the pain'(Le Shan 1983, p.29).

answer, from people who have little to be joyful about, is quite often 'yes'. And that, perhaps, is benefit enough for now.

Living fully

Nurses working with dying patients, comment Callanan and Kelley, have an opportunity 'to help a patient cherish the final chapter of her life' (1992, p.129). Creative writing can sometimes reinforce this, helping a patient to 'cherish' and capture something precious here and now and, in the words of the seventeenth century poet Thomas Traherne, 'to retain a glorious sense of the world'.

Ivy did not need my help to do this. She spent hours by her hospice window watching the comings and goings of a kingfisher which few others had noticed. Later I helped her to capture the scene in writing (Miles 1994, p.6). This not only opened the eyes of other patients to something wonderful still within sight, but also helped to preserve the experience for Ivy herself when, for a while, she returned home. Maybe even Wordsworth's daffodils flashed upon his inner eye more readily once they had been put into words.

As a creative writing tutor in adult education, I try to share with students ways of capturing the world more accurately and sharply, and some of this can be adapted for hospice patients both individually and in groups. Even inviting the members of a group to draw attention to something in a hospice day room which others may not have noticed can sometimes produce delightful results.

The playwright Dennis Potter, in his last television interview, said that as he faced imminent death the '*now*-ness' of everything about him had become 'absolutely wondrous'.

Opening communication

Some patients and their loved ones, sitting together in those last days, often do not know what to say to each other, yet seem unable to achieve a comfortable silence. Sometimes a piece which the patient, perhaps unknown to the visitors, has recorded with me and which is now professionally printed and in a pristine plastic sleeve on the bedside locker, gives an opening regardless of its content. George had written a short piece of recent family events. His daughter spotted this and thought it lovely. She then caught sight of me and congratulated me on my writing. I protested that it wasn't 'my' writing. 'That was your Dad,' I said. He lay there and glowed a little. I left them talking happily about the events which he had recorded. Insofar as writing can help open up communication, the beneficiary is no longer the patient alone, and this sits well with the hospice aim of supporting not only the patient but also the wider family.

Sometimes the communication with relatives which is opened up is particularly important but may not be known about at the time. In a piece ironically titled 'Have a Nice Day', Helen found exactly the right words to describe what, to her, cancer was like, concluding 'cancer is HELL' (Poole 1994, p.24). Helen's student daughter wrote later to thank me for helping her mother to come out and express in writing what she really felt. Helen had been reluctant to talk about it directly to her young daughter who, in the light of this writing, now felt she understood a little more.

Finished pieces strategically left on lockers also attract the attention of staff and volunteers and can open up a much wider discussion.

Highlights from a life story

I encountered among a number of hospice patients an urge to write autobiography – to record, in effect, 'this is what it was like to be me'. But with time so short such patients must be even more selective than most autobiographers, and this led many to focus on particularly vivid moments or proud achievements. Capturing a few of these on the page may not give immortality much of a chance, but at least doing so enables some patients themselves to delight in them afresh. Typical titles for such pieces were 'The Happiest Day of my Life' and 'The Day I Went to See the King'.

But some of the moments captured were extremely bad ones. One patient recounted fleeing from the Nazis; another recalled being hunted down by the Japanese in the Burmese jungle; two others at different hospices worked on remarkably similar pieces about the terrors of taking part in the 1944 D-Day Invasion.

Some at least of the records of such moments were clearly treasured by relatives. As for the patients themselves, there were hints – no more – that recapturing past delights helped some to accept their present predicament, and that recalling past terrors which had been survived may have helped others to put death in some perspective.

Life 'manifestos'

A different approach to autobiography came from those who focused not on particular moments but on key themes, declaring what, from their point of view, most mattered in life. For some this was their religious faith, for others the family, for one his art. All were important attempts, pursued with various degrees of commitment and success, to reflect on life and to find some shape and meaning in having lived.

Most implied that what was identified was not only what mattered to the individual who wrote it but also what ultimately matters in 'Life', and this led me later to encourage wider reflection in a group situation. What would we do if, as a group, we were put in charge of the whole world with the power to do absolutely anything? The only rules for this exercise were that any suggestion was ruled out if even one person opposed it, but that mere impossibility (such as one of the first and most telling suggestions: 'change human nature') was not a valid reason for excluding anything! The resultant 12-point 'manifesto' was as imaginative, idealistic, unselfish and environmentally aware as the 'manifestos' emerging from other groups (including adolescents) with which I have used this exercise, although what mattered, of course, was less the product than the process, the reflection on life itself.

Self-presentation

A third dimension of autobiography – beyond highlights or overarching themes – is the account some chose to give of the final 'self', the one here and now, facing imminent death.

Mary entitled her piece 'Don't Let This Thing Beat You'. As she recorded it she joked that everything had started when she had been sent for an 'autopsy', giving a mischievous smile before correcting her deliberate mistake to 'biopsy'. Writing only a few weeks before she died, Mary concluded 'I'm not frightened' (Roberts 1994, p.11).

I have encountered many similar brave statements. Some may be totally true; some may be voiced to see if they feel 'comfortable' enough to the speaker, a stance they can live with to the end; some may be a mask for quite different feelings. It is not my task to enquire which might be which. Whatever the answer in individual cases, there does seem to be a value to the patient in the verbal or written self-presentation involved, 'how I say I cope' being another way of saying 'I still *am*' and 'this is *who* I am'. And it would be unreasonable to expect those whose death is imminent to present themselves more truthfully than those of us who hope it is rather more distant.

In Renaissance England one of the most highly prized qualities of noble self-expression was '*sprezzatura*', the ability to speak bravely, pithily and wittily on the scaffold. In my work with dying people I have sometimes gained the impression that *sprezzatura* remains alive and well in the late twentieth century.

Handing things on

Some patients decide to record things to pass on to future generations at large. It may not always be better to give than to receive, but in this work there is certainly some benefit both to givers (who may often feel that they have nothing much else worth giving) and to receivers.

One patient contributed a recipe which helped me to recognise recipes as a rich means by which knowledge – and love – can be passed in writing from generation to generation.

Sometimes what is passed on is social history. The older patients at least have experienced and survived tremendous turbulence, about which they sometimes possess aspects of the truth not always found in official accounts. Writings from hospices – as from many other community settings – have included first-hand accounts of severe poverty and hardship, of radically changing employment practices, and of both the heroic and unheroic sides of war. One patient's war story was seized by his grandsons for a school history project and subsequently lodged in London's War Museum.

Sometimes what has been passed on is more akin to folklore. They may not be pearls of wisdom but the rest of us are not too good at producing these either. I am slowly building up a collection of sayings from different parts of the country which are new to me at least. In one group we shared old wives tales that we had heard from our grandmothers, recognised that between us we had failed to heed their advice, and constructed a group poem celebrating the fact.

Catharsis

Elizabeth Kübler-Ross, in her seminal work *On Death and Dying*, wrote that those patients 'do best' – in terms of meeting as 'good' an end as reasonably possible for that individual – 'who have been encouraged to express their rage, to cry in preparatory grief, and to tell their fears and fantasies to someone who can quietly sit and listen' (Kübler-Ross 1970, p.105). This concept of catharsis, now a commonplace of much therapy, originated of course in art.

Hospice patients do not express such emotions exclusively to nurses. All who work in such places – domestic staff and even writers – are likely to encounter them from time to time (although not always in dramatic form), simply through getting to know the patients. However, the process of writing itself can sometimes stimulate such catharsis. This may be in the patient's struggle to decide what to write or how to express it; it may even come from looking back on what has been written.

Sarah was another of the patients who wrote 'bravely' about her cancer, proud to record that she had refused to shed tears over it. When, two days after I had delivered the printed draft, I returned, Sarah said that the draft was fine, just fine. I stayed by her bedside and we were quiet for a while. Then she said she had read through it carefully, three times. I held the silence (writers, every bit as much as counsellors, knowing the importance of the white spaces between the words). Then Sarah spoke again: 'The third time I read it I cried my heart out'. For the first time, she said, these had been real, deep tears. Perhaps she thought I would be upset, because she went on to assure me that she had felt much better afterwards.

'How do I know what I think until I see what I say?' wrote E.M. Forster. And how, I add, do I know what I *feel* until I see what I *try* saying?

Other benefits

Some patients can glean other benefits from creative writing in hospices: the sense of achievement, of having left one more tiny mark upon the world, of having 'signed-off' properly (several pieces being read at funerals), even of having cheated death for a few more days. This latter benefit is what I came to think of as the Scheherazade Technique, where patients start a long piece, but break off in mid-sentence day after day, as if that will guarantee another night's reprieve.

Rating of benefits

At this early stage in the development of creative writing as a purposeful therapeutic activity with dying people – and maybe in the longer term too – I resist the temptation to ascribe higher status to some benefits (such as catharsis) than to others (such as diversion). In the related but well-developed profession of art therapy, many argue that room must remain not just for art psychotherapy but also for art as a naturally healing activity. In the world of words I can still – at different times and in different ways – find *reading* 'therapy' in both Richmal Crompton's *William the Outlaw* and James Joyce's *Finnegan's Wake*. And in creative *writing* I leave each patient to decide what he or she will put into, and get out of, the activity.

Above and beyond the range of benefits already suggested is that which comes from the attention given to the life experience and voice of each individual (whether that attention is given in or outside a group). What better evidence that your 'last words' – the final fictions or the final facts – are being listened to attentively than to have someone to help you put them down in black and white? And this benefit is gained even if, as in most cases, the full expression is not completed, or even started, before that ultimate editorial deadline.

References

Alexander, L. (ed) (1990) *Now I Can Tell.* London: Macmillan.

Archer, C. (ed) (1994) *To Talk of Many Things.* Esher, Surrey: Princess Alice Hospice.

Archer, C. (ed) (1997) *Somewhere and Beyond.* Tunbridge Wells, Kent: Artability.

Callanan, M. and Kelley, P. (1992) *Final Gifts.* London: Hodder and Stoughton.

Corr, A. and Corr, D. (eds) (1983) *Hospice Care: Principles and Practice.* London: Faber and Faber.

Fontana, J. and Hodgson, H. (eds) (1996) *Blowing a Lapwing's Egg.* Tunbridge Wells, Kent: Artability.

Gittins, C. (ed) (1991) *Somebody Said That Word.* Todmorden, Lancs: Littlewood Arc.

Kübler-Ross, E. (1970) *On Death and Dying.* London: Tavistock Publications.

Le Shan, L. (1983) 'The world of the patient in severe pain of long duration.' In A. Corr and D. Corr (eds) *Hospice Care: Principles and Practice.* London: Faber and Faber.

Meaney, J. (1994) 'The great bank robbery.' In C. Archer (ed) *To Talk of Many Things.* Esher, Surrey: Princess Alice Hospice.

Miles, I. (1994) 'The kingfisher.' In C. Archer (ed) *To Talk of Many Things.* Esher, Surrey: Princess Alice Hospice.

Poole, H. (1994) 'Have a nice day?' In C. Archer (ed) *To Talk of Many Things.* Esher, Surrey: Princess Alice Hospice.

Roberts, M. (1994) 'Don't let this thing beat you.' In C. Archer (ed) *To Talk of Many Things.* Esher, Surrey: Princess Alice Hospice.

Stedeford, A. (1983) 'Psychotherapy of the dying patient.' In A. Corr and D. Corr (eds) *Hospice Care: Principles and Practice.* London: Faber and Faber.

CHAPTER 7

A Matter of the Life
and Death of the Mind
Creative Writing and Dementia Sufferers

John Killick

I

Have you got the first date when people asked me who I was and where I was? Write to a newspaper and say 'Please help me. I am bothered. I don't know who I am or where I am, and how long I shall be that person. If you know the answer to these questions please write and let me know'.

Are you a person who could swing it for me with the authorities? I want you to ask them a question for me: would you please give me back my personality?[1]

How is a writer to respond to such requests? Bernard and Alice are part of a growing number of elderly people (and some younger ones) who cannot remember their lives and are forced by their dementias into a crisis of identity. They are frustrated, even despairing, about their condition, yet the prognosis for them is bleak – all I can do is to befriend them, hope that they remember me on subsequent visits, and share for a while their concern over the deterioration in their mental processes.

---

[1]   Unless otherwise indicated, quotations in this chapter are the words of some of the 400 dementia sufferers with whom I have worked since 1993. Sessions were on a one-to-one basis and took place in people's own homes, in day centres and hospitals and, most commonly, in nursing homes throughout Britain. All names have been changed. I am very grateful to all those who words are quoted here.

> I can't place this place at all – isn't that terrible? What street is this, what town? I can't find that label with my address. Find me, please tell me where I am! I wish to God God would do something!

This is Annie speaking. I am the helpless listener and scribe. Often I feel I am also the voyeur of an interior conflict which I know to be unresolvable. Some, like Edward, have given up the struggle. They have accepted that no further progress is possible and have abandoned any illusions they may have had of their own significance in the human process: 'Altogether you won't find much to-ing and fro-ing with me. I never carry as full as you do. I just drift about. I think that's what I usually do. I'm a kind of quiet nobody'.

In some Alzheimer patients the speech patterns seem naturally to express their condition and to assume a coherence directly communicative and affecting:

> When I think about the old days, goshee gosh it was good!
> When I think about the old days, ah memories, memories!
> Memories that bless and burn!
> When I think about the old days, oh goshee gosh!
> Time goes by and I am still here.

Nancy is at an earlier stage of deterioration than many; however, a transcript of Elsie's conversations, whilst undeniably lively, shows the beginnings of dislocation:

> You won't find me as one as goes deliberately missing. You won't find me as one that swanks with half-a-dozen in my hand to keep them sweet.
> I remember the playground rhymes:
>> *Where will you run to?*
>> *Up Bell Lane.*
>> *I'll tell the teacher*
>> *And you'll get the cane.*
> I have a book in my room full of innuendoes.
> Bell Lane is still there. We'd push our prams up it. I could go with you straight, and I don't think we'd have a gate to climb. Of course in them days they were staunch and would never tell where you'd gone.
> I'm not a day early, but I know when I have it marked down not to come.
> They say we're a gormless lot, but they're not from round here.
> I'm off now, because I'm on duty – there's nobody at home. On second thoughts, can I stick to you, I don't know who I am at the moment?

Elsie, in common with others quoted here, on the geographical plane is going nowhere: they are all residents of a nursing home. There is one word in her piece which is premonitory of the next level of decline she may suffer: 'innuendoes'. As the cognitive processes break down so does the person's control of language. Just as time-scales become mixed, so sentences, even words, become scrambled, as in this passage from Fred's life story:

> That lad I brought home from the patriarch is quick as lightning.
> Would you like my pocket-money? You get nervy inside here.
> That's a lovely glass case. I suppose it's got another name rather than its shape.
> I've got a marvellous young lady who looks after me. Is she authentic?
> This story you're writing – it might not be a complete book.
> In this place they're very keen on buying pads. What is a learned man?
> They don't always know about cutting nails and cutting corn.
> That's about half-way surgeon. They never seem to cancel themselves in the wall.
> We had an interesting spirit on Friday. It stopped then. We got some blanks after that.

There are parts of this which make immediate sense, and others where our minds make the leap to what seems intended. Even in the final two paragraphs, where intelligibility is hardest to come by, the sentences are constructed confidently enough – it is just that certain words or concepts seem to have been transposed from elsewhere.

The question might be raised as to how conscious my subjects are of the process of composition which is taking place. Using Fred as an example, the answer I would have to give is that he seems very aware of his own role as author and mine as amanuensis. At the beginning of the session he says 'Have you got your pen?' and sits on the table expectantly. His pose is upright and alert (which contrasts with the way he moves around the home which is almost bent double). He brings the session to a close with the words, 'Having regard to silence, I think it should be maintained'.

Later on, when I am writing up my notes, he re-enters the room and sits on the table. He leans across and takes the note-pad very gingerly. He turns over the pages, obviously looking for the text. Not finding it, he points to a lined but otherwise blank page. 'Please cross this line out,' he says. I carefully ink in one of the lines across the middle of the page. 'Thank you, you may continue,' he says, and leaves, having participated in the editing process.

It is when I come to hand Fred his typed piece of writing that his response is most extraordinary. He takes it from me and, quick as a flash, crumples it up and swallows it before I can intervene. He has literally eaten his own words.

II

When one reflects on experiences such as the above (and they are as representative as encounters with people who exhibit unpredictable behaviours can ever be), one is left with a series of questions which must be addressed.

The first is: to what extent is the service I am providing a therapeutic one? Clearly, as the quotations at the outset of this chapter reveal, for some people the attempt to construct a personal narrative is seen not just as helpful but as necessary, and expressed with all the urgency that they can command: it is as if it is a matter of the life and death of the mind.

It may well be that for these and many others whom I have worked with over the past four years, most of whom would have been unable to articulate their need, the process is everything and the end product is of negligible concern. I have met very few people who actively welcomed the text I have presented to them. Yet at the time of the original conversations upon which they were based, their efforts to remember, and struggles with language, were little short of heroic, as these comments attest:

> All I'm concerned with is my life's going: the truth is mine not yours!
> Oh dear, it isn't fair when your heart wants to remember!
> I'll tell you, if you can understand the language. And I'm talking, talking, talking all the time.
> With you I am putting things together. I'm blethering, but from beneath the surface.
> YOU ARE WORDS. Words can make or break you. I want to thank you for listening. You have the stillness of silence, that listens and lasts.
> Anything you can tell people about how things are for me is important.

Does the writing have a value (therapeutic or otherwise) for those in the immediate environment of the person with dementia? These people can include carers looking after relatives in their own homes, and staff who have the professional responsibility in hospitals and nursing homes. There would be a mixed set of answers here. Some relatives are deeply moved by the attempts of their loved ones to communicate. They immediately see the point of helping a person to hang on to their memories for as long as possible, and are appreciative of the fragments of reminiscence and the evidence of still-functioning imagination that emerge. Others are upset by the demonstrations of incoherence that are an inevitable element of the transcripts. As one angry carer put it: 'I don't need you to prove to me that my wife is mad!'. So one is entering an emotional minefield in attempting this work. Hurt and guilt experienced by staff are less obviously in evidence: they are more likely to seize upon insights gained from the texts to expand their understanding of the people they are looking after. It is not often that one finds oneself as a writer in a situation where one's intuitions and inter- pretations can be put to such practical use.

It seems important to add at this point that writers who use their personal qualities and professional skills in this manner are actually in the vanguard of a movement in dementia care. Until quite recently the clinical model held sway in the treatment of Alzheimer's and other dementias. It was assumed that because a physical set of diseases is progressively closing off areas of the brain, the logical and linguistic confusion that ensued rendered attempts at consulting the individual superfluous. Now there has been a sea-change, and the concept of personhood, as adumbrated by Tom Kitwood (1997), is leading to innovations in attitudes and practices. The focus that the writer brings to the relationship, the quality of listening and the unfolding of insights which this brings about, are setting an example for others to follow.

But has the writer a special contribution to make *per se*, over and above the time and dedication and empathy which are prerequisites for anyone wanting to make a contribution in this field? For me the answer is in the affirmative, and that is because of the writer's special affinity with language. Speaking for myself, I have always been fascinated by the ways in which states of mind find expression both in terms of the spoken and written word. One does not need to be a student of psycholinguistics to find oneself exploring these links in a purely intuitive and speculative manner. Because of the ways in which dementia interferes with the normal processes of intellection and memory-gathering, it provides a kind of cross-section of the mind, exposing its layers to inspection. However, the writer does not approach this task analytically, but empathetically. In this he is helped by the fact that the language of many people with dementia is unusually creative – it exploits the full range of linguistic possibilities, with particular emphasis on new combinations of words, sound patterns and figures of speech. Here are some examples:

It's a lovely day – I feel like playing with all my flaps open.
My mother is going to one of the betime worlds.
'Tis on the left down by there's my garden. There I'm turnin', turnin', turnin' all the while.
The circle of life is shot away.
My eye doesn't half bother me – it comes out as if it's going to walk through that door!
I've been playing in the House of Ages.

One can only speculate as to why such inventiveness is commonplace amongst people with dementia. I believe there may be two explanations. First of all, the disease attacks the thinking, reasoning parts of the brain, leaving the creative faculties intact. For most of adult life these have been under the control of the intellect; now they are free to be exercised as they were during early childhood, with the additional advantage of the maturity which experience has brought. Second, dementia is disinhibiting, so there is no social barrier to expressing feelings directly. Dementia thus releases the imaginative powers in partial compensation for its destruction of the intellect. One lady said to me, 'I bet you've never been so near Nature before!'.

If this idea is thought far-fetched, support for the thesis comes from an unexpected quarter. Oliver Sacks, the neurologist, in a recent book, *An Anthropologist on Mars*, makes the following assertion:

> While one may be horrified by the ravages of developmental disorder or disease, one may sometimes see them as creative too – for if they destroy particular paths, particular ways of doing things, they may force on it an unexpected growth and evolution. This other side of development or disease is something I see, potentially, in almost every patient. (Sacks 1995, p.xii)

III

A case can be made for the necessity of attempting to communicate with people with dementia, and also for the perceived need for self-expression on the part of many persons with the disease. Taken together with the instinctive feel for the more creative uses of language displayed by many, the conditions clearly exist for interventions by a writer in order to facilitate the practise of the art. What remains to be addressed is the exact nature of the role to be played. Many of those with dementia have never written before, and their capacity for creative composition has probably remained un-realised; that in itself need prove no obstacle. They have a wealth of life experience, which they may be able to access and to own, if only fitfully. The real stumbling-block lies in the shaping process to which material must be subjected. Very few people with dementia retain the capacity to write, so this must be done for them. Most have lost the ability to read, so work has to be read back to them. The majority lack the concentration which editing a transcript requires. Most crucially, they do not possess that self-consciousness which is a prerequisite for editing material. Theirs is an undiscriminating expressiveness, a stream of consciousness which, artistically, throws up the relevant and irrelevant in equal measure (as the lady said, 'blethering, but from beneath the surface'). In no other writing situation does the facilitator face such an awesome task of having to take creative decisions on behalf of another.

The way I approach this is as follows. The first transcript is a verbatim one, or a tape-recorder is employed and the text assembled afterwards.[2] I then examine the transcript to see if editing can improve the chronology, or its coherence, by grouping together similar subject matter. I decide, by the emotional or rhythmic 'feel' of the language, whether it would be better presented in a prose or poetry format. Some transcripts are untouched (and all transcripts are to be preserved in their original form, as they retain a value as psychological and linguistic documents in that form, whatever mod-ifications are made to them later).

I try to edit a text in the spirit of the original, preserving the most vivid passages and omitting those parts which do not appear to contribute to the overall effect. In this sense, what I am doing is no different from the revision to which any writer subjects the original material, only here the words are another's. It is even closer to that of the role of the active magazine or book editor. The final texts arrived at are shared with the speaker, relatives and friends, staff and, occasionally, a wider public.

I believe that I am doubly privileged – first by having the speaker's experiences vouchsafed to me, and second by being able to reflect them back to the individual concerned through his or her (or my) reading of the piece I have shaped for them. Confidentiality is a live issue, and often the most difficult decision I am faced with is whether to share a piece of writing with

2   Permission has, of course, been obtained from the individual concerned
      (and often from relatives) before any writing is embarked upon.

others in the spirit of the injunction, 'Anything you can tell people about how things are for me is important'. When I do so it is my unvarying practice to remove all personal references from the piece to preserve anonymity.

IV

By way of illustrating the practices outlined above, I shall present two complete poems and describe how they came to be written. I was spending three days in the particular nursing home where Janey was living. I was aware on the first morning that she wished to speak to me. In fact she kept interrupting and trying to draw my attention away when I was listening to other residents. I promised her a conversation after lunch.

However, when I arrived back on the unit I saw that she had a visitor, a man I took to be her husband. There was another person with him, obviously a mutual friend. On and off throughout the afternoon I observed the trio. I noted Janey's extreme distress, occasioned, as far as I could make out, by the fact that her husband and friend were talking across her all the while – I was not aware of a single example of her being included in the conversation.

The following morning Janey was waiting for me, impatient to begin the writing. The reminiscences and reactions poured from her – it was like an impassioned confessional. She asked me if I would bring her the text the following day. When I came to read through the many pages I had written, the intensity and breadth of reference suggested a dramatic monologue, and the fact that she said she had been on the stage supported this interpretation. But the play on words throughout suggested a poem, and the quotes from a popular song and a childhood rhyme were particularly poignant and demanded inclusion. In the end I pared away almost everything that was not about relationship, or seemed to be an allusive comment upon that subject. I was left with the following:

I Scream

'It's a Long Way to Tipperary' –
but I can't remember the words.

I was a very lively little girl.
I always loved jumping about.

I like children like ice-cream.
'Ice-cream, you scream, we all scream.'

'And My Heart's Right There' –
see, I've remembered another line!

My husband was a doctor.
The children rushed about calling him daddy.

I was lucky to get that husband.
I've kept the pictures, and everything.

'Goodbye, Piccadilly' –
that's another line!

I used to be on the stage when I was young.
Not singing. It was a long time ago.

I get pain now all the time.
'Ice-cream, you scream, we all scream.'

'Goodbye, Leicester Square' –
and another line!

It's a lovely ring my husband gave me,
but it's not a token of his love.

It's all finished between us.
We don't talk to each other now.

'It's a Long Way to Go' –
that's another line!

I don't know what this place is.
I don't know who these people are.

We're a nice two-lot, you and me.
I like us being with us.

'It's a Long Way to Tipperary' –
that's the line we started with!

It's nice to have a laugh.
It's nice when someone talks to you.

'Ice-cream, you scream, we all scream.'
A nice doctor. A nice barrel of fun.

'It's a Long Way to Tipperary,
It's a Long Way to Go' –

It's a long time ago –
It's a long time no go.

When I read the poem to Janey the following morning she burst into tears and threw her arms around me. It was obvious that she recognised both the words and the experience they described as being her own. What I have no way of knowing is to what extent the conversation and subsequent shaping of materials had clarified her situation for her. I have shared the poem with others because I believe it has artistic value, with the capacity to convey insights memorably.

The editorial decisions on that occasion seemed clear-cut, and I took them with comparative boldness. My approach is necessarily tentative in most instances. If I am in serious doubt I just retain the text in its original form. But very occasionally I am presented with a piece fully formed and all I have to do is arrange it on the page. There is a phenomenon which is known technically as 'spontaneous intermittent remission', where the confusion clears and the individual experiences a temporary mental coherence. It may only last minutes, but during that brief span what is said assumes great importance. This poem was spoken by Dora in a moment of reprieve from her terrible affliction, and it is all that she said. At such times I can only feel humility:

Grass

A young fella carried me
in here; it were a long way
and a long time ago.
I were lying on grass...

I don't want to stay, no
there's nothing for me
they're all very kind
but I don't want to be

inside anywhere at all
it's much too hot and bright
it just don't feel right
I've not been used

I need the fresh air
I keep calling out:
Nurse, Nurse, carry me
outside to where

I were lying on grass...

V

Because of the extreme nature of the challenge offered to a writer by working with individuals with dementia, I am aware that the methods I have outlined may appear somewhat tendentious and also highly individual. I can only claim that they have brought results. There is plenty of room for experiment in this area, and it may well be that other approaches will yield other insights.

What is certain, however, is that whoever seeks to make progress in working with people with dementia will have to come to terms with the human demands made upon them. It is not to be undertaken lightly, and should not be attempted by anybody who is not grounded as a person, by which I mean secure in their own sense of self. Tom Kitwood sums it up well:

> As we discover the person who has dementia we also discover something of ourselves, for what we ultimately have to offer is not technical expertise but ordinary faculties raised to a higher level: our power to feel, to give, to stand in the shoes (or sit in the chair) of another. (Kitwood 1993, p.17)

The human resource is half of the equation. The other half is supplied by the writer's skills, and Martha Gellhorn (1983) presents in the starkest terms the question to be addressed: 'What is the use of having lived so long, travelled so widely, listened and looked so hard, if at the end you don't know what you know?'

She is asking this of herself as she confronts the effects of ageing upon her own psyche. But this is the question posed daily by dementia to many thousands of our population. Although it is beyond the capabilities of any professional at present to give a convincing answer, I believe the writer has a role to play in helping individuals to rescue and value at least some fragments of their disintegrating world.

References

Gellhorn, M. (1983) *The View from the Crowd.* Harmondsworth: Penguin.

Kitwood, T. (1993) 'Discover the person, not the disease.' *Journal of Dementia Care 1,* i, 16–17.

Kitwood, T. (1997) *Dementia Reconsidered.* Milton Keynes: Open University Press.

Sacks, O. (1995) *An Anthropologist on Mars.* London: Picador.

Further reading

Forster, M. (1989) *Have the Men Had Enough?.* London: Chatto & Windus.

Goldsmith, M. (1996) *Hearing the Voice of People with Dementia.* London: Jessica Kingsley.

Ignatieff, M. (1993) *Scar Tissue.* London: Chatto & Windus.

Killick, J. (1994) *Please Give Me Back My Personality.* Stirling: Dementia Services Development Centre, University of Stirling.

Killick, J. (1997) *You Are Words: Dementia Poems.* London: Hawker Publications.

PART TWO

Theoretical Contexts for Creative Writing in Personal Development

The Creative Word
and the Created Life
The Cultural Context for Deep Autobiography

Peter Abbs

Introduction

Writing autobiography as a means to personal reflection, literary engagement and a means of individuation has become in the last two decades a widely accepted practice. However, in my view, the practice has often been conceived within too narrow a frame, with the result that the work has sometimes lacked any living connection with a long Western culture of introspective enquiry or any animating awareness of the field of the autobiographical genre itself. To think about autobiography and its development is to become aware of a basic principle: that of *the essential historicity of the self.* The way in which we habitually envisage the self – as being inward, with some kind of depth, with some kind of personal centre – has to be grasped as a specific cultural configuration, achieved with the greatest difficulty and in no way an inevitable part of experience. The self we cherish, if we do, is not simply given. It has been built up over centuries of cultural labour and could disappear, and possibly is now disappearing, under the impact and demands of a highly technological and highly standardising culture. There have been many societies where the self has not been conceived as inward and reflective, where it has been seen as determined by collective traditions or the dictates of omnipotent forces, or both. It is impossible in a short essay to begin to describe the intricate field of autobiography, with its deepest roots in early Greek philosophy and poetry and the early Christian Church, but it is possible to present historic moments of dramatic crystallisation when the strange quest for individuation took a new turn or a new mode or cadence of expression.

In the Western tradition before Heraclitus (c.540 BC–c.480 BC), the concept of self was essentially epic and tribal. The pre-Socratic philosopher Heraclitus marks a key stage in the emergence of our concept of the self, as does the later work of Plato and Socrates and the long tradition of the Stoics. This classical concern was then dramatically deepened by the passionate Christian quest for salvation. It was the Hebraic tradition, in confluence with the Hellenic, which gave birth to the genre of deep subjective autobiography in the form of Saint Augustine's *Confessions* (written around 397 AD), a work that was to have a profound influence on the pattern of self-figuration for centuries until Rousseau's work – also, tellingly, named *Confessions* – written in the middle of the eighteenth century, offered a different pattern of interpretation. This pattern was psychological in manner and pre-dated the work of our own psychological age by 150 years.

I want to suggest that all autobiographers, consciously or unconsciously, are part of this tradition and can only gain as writers and explorers of the life of consciousness by a fuller awareness of it. I want, in particular, to examine three moments in the story of the self. First, the birth of the notion of the self in Heraclitus; second, the birth of subjective autobiography in Saint Augustine (354–430) and, finally, the birth of a psychological hermeneutics in the sustained autobiographical enterprise of Rousseau (1712–78).

Heraclitus and the birth of the self

Heraclitus was born around 540 BC and died around 480 BC. He lived on the island of Ephesus and virtually nothing is known about his life. It is clear that he came from a royal family but that he surrendered his hereditary privilege to his brother. He is reputed to have retired often to the Temple of Artemis and to have played dice with the local children, defending himself with the remark that it was better to do so than to engage in political affairs. He is thought to have written a volume entitled *On Nature*, but all that remain, possibly from that text, are a number of aphoristic fragments, some of them highly elusive in content, nearly all of them poetic. Some of them are disputed in terms of attribution, others in terms of meaning and translation.

Taken as a whole the fragments express a high disdain for traditional answers and traditional teaching, as well as for the vast majority of people who would appear, for Heraclitus, to sleepwalk through life. Heraclitus was reputed to have surpassed all others in arrogance and disdainfulness. His attack on ancestors is particularly significant, for it indicates a desire to be free from the accepted conceptions which mark tribal cultures. Hostility makes for cultural rupture. It provokes discontinuity. It throws the light of the mind on the immediate moment, the present tense of the 'I, thinking its thoughts now', not the high past tense of epic culture and the nostalgic comfort of its formulaic expressions, always anchored in a prior period which was to be admired and emulated. It was in the present tense of philosophy – and, it must be added, in the lyrical poetry of Sappho (c.mid-seventh century BC) and other poets – that a sense of the individual self came into existence, together with a sense of its own strange, unplumbed depths, a sense of a self that could be worked on, explored and developed.

The discovery of the power of critical thought and open speculation involved a profound transformation of human experience. Heraclitus is at the very beginning of an extraordinary revolution which began to define the role of the mind in the conduct of life. There is an intoxicating element in the enterprise. With a sense of awe, consciousness discovers itself and struggles to speak its hidden and labile nature. In Heraclitus the Greek word *psyche* comes to possess a new denotation and a new set of connotations. It is no longer used – as in Homer – to denote the simple flow of breath or a general life-force but, rather, an individual soul which can only be described through the spatial metaphors of depth and inwardness. Here, then, is the origin of the modern self with interiority and hidden depths.

In Fragment 71 Heraclitus writes: 'You will not find the boundaries of psyche by travelling in any direction, so deep is the measure of it' (Burnet 1920). This famous passage depicts a self which is irreconcilable with Homer's epic world. Heraclitus is asserting that the psyche is not physical, is not the flow of breath, but rather is an indescribably deep element in individual life. Here is an emergent depth psychology with its own dynamic and dialectic. In Heraclitus psyche has its own logos or order. It is wholly apposite that one of the shortest remaining fragments of Heraclitus simply reads: 'I have sought for myself' (Burnet 1920, p.139).

In the present tense of early Greek philosophy, the formulaic epithets of the earlier Greek warrior culture were breaking down and in their place a more personal and critical orientation to experience was emerging. After Heraclitus came Socrates (469–399 BC) and Plato (c.428–c.348 BC), the former intensifying the attack on formulaic thinking; the latter offering, in Part 5, Book 4 of *The Republic*, the first dynamic typology of the self in which the psyche is divided into three, often feuding, elements: reason, the appetites and the spirit.

Out of this milieu developed the movement called Stoicism, which was to forge an array of practical strategies for the development of the reflective life, including the writing of letters and journals, the memorising of aphorisms and the emulation of exemplary figures (Heraclitus, Plato, Socrates). Yet the most dramatic development came when this classical tradition met another tradition: that of the Hebraic, especially the early Christian imperative for personal salvation, that intense existential leap out of history into the arms of a loving and listening and witnessing God. This called forth a new intensity of inwardness. It also gave birth to the first great subjective autobiography: Saint Augustine's *Confessions*. How was it that Augustine was able to write the first sustained introspective autobiography? What models was he able to draw on? And how was he able to integrate them into a new style of inner exploration?

Saint Augustine and the birth of autobiography

For all the qualifications that have been raised, scholars and literary critics agree that Augustine's 13 volumes of *Confessions*, written around 397 AD, constitute the first major spiritual autobiography in Western culture. The essentially linear narrative of the work moves from the birth of Augustine in 354 AD in Thagaste in North Africa, to his conversion to Christianity in Milan, to a mystical experience with his mother at the port of Ostia in 387.

The *Confessions* takes the form of an intimate and continuous address to God. All the active verbs in this address involve utterance: speaking, confessing, invoking, asking, saying, pleading. The context is one of urgent speaking and listening, not of writing and reading. In the opening paragraph of the work the verb 'invocare', in one form or another, is employed no less than nine times. This speaking out of experience, this pleading before the intimate God who is, at once, most secret and most present, creates a style of writing which is no longer classical.

Augustine speaks in the biblical manner, constantly employing a parataxis with the Latin '*et*' to join the flow of feelings, ideas and events. This means that instead of looking down at his feelings from an impersonal distance and soberly placing them in a system of syntactical qualifications, as was the practice of the classical rhetorical traditions, Augustine is able to re-create his emotions from within. *He emotionally participates in that which he delineates.* The method of parataxis gives him a means of speaking out of his immediate passions so that he is able to dramatise the actuality of his own fluctuating experiences. The heart is Augustine's leading metaphor and parataxis is, as it were, the syntax of the feeling heart. One of the great models for Augustine here was the *Psalms*, a work which forms a kind of sublime counterpoint running through the whole of the *Confessions*, for the *Psalms* is also a paratactic monument of praise and penitence in which the voice always sounds like intimate dramatic speech, never like written and complex composition.

At the same time, Augustine is able to draw, whenever he needs to, on the practice of classical rhetoric to dissect and conceptually analyse his interior life. He uses a rich phenomenological method deriving from Greek philosophy to understand the inner turbulence of his own feelings. It is precisely this mastery of two forms of discourse, that of Hebraic parataxis and Hellenic hypotaxis, and the agile movement between them, which enables Augustine both dramatically to narrate his own experience and to explore its nature and import, and in this way virtually to create the genre of subjective autobiography. With the disintegration of classical Latin after his death, such an achievement was rendered impossible for centuries.

Through the confessional voice, Augustine is, quite simply, able to tell the story of his own life with vivid immediacy. He is able to stop and examine whatever puzzles or perplexes him. He is free to probe whatever state of feeling haunts, torments or mystifies him: grief, love, anguish, inner paralysis, dream sexuality, mystical ecstasy. In Augustine we locate the re-creation and scrutiny of inner feeling centuries before the invention of psychoanalysis. But what made this possible? Partly the power to employ two forms of discourse – the dramatic and reflective – partly, without doubt, Augustine's own introspective power. But it is essential to notice that the format of the *Confessions* partly derives from common religious practices of Augustine's own historic period: particularly that of the confession, the conversion testimony and the growing habit of self-analysis practised by the desert fathers and the founders of the first monastic orders. Here we find in Augustine both a continuity and a transformation; he internalises all of these established practices and yet creates out of them, by his own peculiar intensity and his great literary talent, a new literary genre for the amplification of the inner life.

Perhaps most obviously the *Confessions* draws on the Christian practice of confession, where the believer brings, through the power of memory, past offences to mind, then analyses through introspection their underlying motives and finally confesses them (often through the gathered community of the early Church) to God in the hope of forgiveness and in the desire for renewal. Often, the confessional ends in a prayer of thanksgiving and of praise. The rhythm of the confessional is the quintessential rhythm of spiritual autobiography. There is a movement of the mind backwards to recall and recollect disorientating fragments of the past; there is an attempt through introspection to understand them and to bring them fully into the present through telling now how it was then; and, finally, there is a forward movement with a sense of freedom from the past, a feeling of liberation, an enhanced affirmation of what is experienced as the essential self. I have transposed the religious language of the confession into general humanist terms to bring out the autobiographical and therapeutic quality that is embedded in it. In Augustine's *Confessions* this religious practice is transmuted into the most febrile and intimate literature of autobiographical reflexivity and re-creation.

We must also bear in mind the methods for self-analysis which the hermits and early monks were developing out of their extreme ascetic lives. Saint Anthony, for example, urged believers to write down their deeds and the movements of their souls in the same manner as they would in confession. This is exactly what Augustine does. He explores the contradictory movements of his soul in a desire to understand them. It would seem almost certain, then, that the long systematic analysis of his spiritual condition towards the end of Book X – where he takes each of his senses in turn and then adds to the analysis mental curiosity and vanity – derived from emerging practices of introspection within the Christian Church of his time, though these, in turn, owed much to the tradition of Stoicism. Here, then, was the cultural and spiritual matrix which fostered the development of the inner self through the act of writing.

But there was one further practice which had a direct influence on Augustine's writing: the evangelical testimony. Here Saint Paul – such a crucial figure in the life and conversion of Augustine – is the exemplar. The testimony is an intimate oral narrative in which the protagonist tells the story of his life, often from childhood to the point of conversion, in order to praise God, to cleanse the soul and to invite others to participate in the good news. This existential testimony, this telling of a life from the perspective of a momentous conversion, was to exert a profound influence on the Western imagination, not only in theology (as it developed into the theory of grace and predestination) but also on romantic and spiritual autobiography, on Rousseau, for example, as much as on Bunyan. The manner of the oral testimony provided a structured narrative with two overt intentions: to tell the speaker's own remarkable story and to influence and convert the listener.

It was part of Augustine's achievement to make this oral voice – the voice of testimony, the voice of confession – a literary voice, and in his 'talking' to make fully concrete the life and the feelings he had experienced. By talking about his own existence as dramatic experience, he was able to establish the literary principle of autobiography and to extend enormously the range of self-consciousness and the possibilities for self-narration and self-figuration.

Augustine's confessional idiom, then, derived in part from congregational confessions, monastic introspection and the act of giving public testimony of one's own religious beliefs; brought into literature it involved a preoccupation with the minutiae of the inward life, with the hidden life beneath the visible ordinary life which had not existed previously, certainly not on such a scale or with such subtlety. For Augustine God lies at the centre of the *Confessions*, not the self. Yet his belief in God allows, and indeed compels, an active exploration into the nature of self. If God is the therapist, the patient can only reach him through stammering out of his own existence, and this is what Augustine does. His belief in God releases a remarkable courage to delineate inner and often contradictory states of consciousness. Like no writer before him, Augustine possessed a piercing perception into the depth of the irrational, the power of the daemonic and the limitation of the conscious mind either to check or to understand it. His belief in God gave Augustine a kind of strength to define the unstable and destructive elements of his own existence. It also guaranteed a kind of truth-telling. In this way he is able to chart the bewildering and contradictory aspects of his own identity and, at a more general level, to act as a kind of cartographer of inward space, creating a distinctly different philosophy and psychology from that offered by the classical world.

Thus it is that the *Confessions* represents an extraordinary objectification of subjectivity. This was not to recur in Western literature until the Renaissance and, in confessional writing, not until Rousseau began to write his equally long and labyrinthine story in 1766. But the aims that Rousseau set himself were to change the form of the literary genre. There was to be a certain continuity, but also a remarkable transformation. What was the nature of the continuity? What was the nature of the radical change?

Rousseau and the birth of psychological analysis

Rousseau's autobiographical work, like Augustine's, is vast, extravagant, contradictory and profound. All his life Rousseau was preoccupied with his own self, with his own image, his own inner meaning and with his own deep and ever-deepening sense of dislocation from others and from society in general. This preoccupation became virtually obsessional during the last 15 years of his life. Haunted by his isolation and persecution in 1766 on his visit to England, staying at Wooton Hall in Staffordshire, he began the serious composition of his *Confessions*. The 12 books took 4 years to complete and, although he gave readings from them, they were not published in his life-time.

In a sketch originally intended to form the opening of the *Confessions* and subsequently discarded, Rousseau proclaimed the originality of his work. To delineate all facets of his personality; to examine his own behaviour, the sordid and the trivial as much as the noble and the good; to demarcate an underlying pattern in that behaviour by tracing his own adult dispositions back to their sources in early definitive experience: these are the ends Rousseau consciously set himself and he presented his work as an unprecedented enquiry, requiring a new language:

> For what I have to say it is necessary to invent a language as original as my project. For what tone, what style to take, in order to handle this immense chaos of sentiments so diverse, so contradictory, often so vile and sometimes so sublime, by which I am perpetually agitated? What trivialities, what miseries will it not be necessary for me to expose? In what revolting details, indecent, puerile, and often ridiculous, must I not enter in order to follow the thread of my secret dispositions to show how each impression which has made a mark on my soul entered there for the first time? (Rousseau 1959, Vol 1, p.1148; author's translation)

Yet, ironically, the very same sketch moves on to evoke and apply a traditional paradigm which is central to the mode of its narration. Rousseau himself reveals that his literary creation has a cultural source and that this source was the sacrament of confession:

> I will fulfil rigorously my title and never the most fearful nun will make a more rigorous examination of conscience than I prepare for myself. Never will she reveal more scrupulously to her confessor all the innermost recesses of her soul than I am going to display to the public...I am saying here things about myself which are very odious and of which I have a horror of wishing to excuse myself but also it is the most secret history of my soul. These are my Confessions in the full sense of that word. It is just that the reputation which will follow the work will expiate the sins which the desire to conserve my earlier reputation had made me commit. I wait for public discussion, for the severity of judgements

pronounced on high and I submit myself to them... (p.1148; author's translation)

The writing amply demonstrates that the explicit and tacit conventions of the confession are in full operation. There is the expectation that the person who is confessing will speak the truth; there is the expectation, furthermore, that he will speak from the heart, that he will narrate his mortal sins as well as the venial, that he will accept the judgement conferred upon him and that he will seek expiation. All of these expectations are present in Rousseau's text; at the same time there is also a highly significant secular shift in the convention: Rousseau is addressing his 'odious' actions neither to his confessor nor, as with Augustine, directly to the god who created him, but *to the public*. His reader becomes his intimate audience and it is the reader who is given the onerous responsibility of casting judgement. The reader takes on the burden of the priest's office.

In the first volume of the *Confessions*, the major 'sins' confessed with difficulty and anguish are, in chronological order, the sexual pleasure derived from Mademoiselle Lambercier's smacking, the theft of the ribbon and his accusation that Marion had stolen it, and the insensitive abandonment of his travelling companion, le Maître, when he is suffering from an epileptic fit. In the second volume the major sin, which haunts Rousseau's conscience, is the abandonment of his own children, against the wishes of their mother, to the Foundling Hospital. The confession of one offence makes it easier to relate another and thus, by degrees, Rousseau in his self-portrait paints the dark and perverse side of his personality.

More than any writer before him, Rousseau endeavours to narrate his own weaknesses, his failings, his foibles, his neuroses, his questionable and perverse proclivities. He informs his readers of his pathological shyness, of his habits of masturbating, his occasional bouts of kleptomania, his visit to prostitutes, his act of sexual self-exposure, his complex urinary problems, his exhibitionism, his masochistic streaks. What is distinctive in all this self-disclosure is the author's desire to represent himself faithfully and to do so in the language of psychology rather than the language of Christian piety or theology. Here again one discerns a major modulation of the confessional form, for Rousseau tends towards an understanding of himself in terms of culture and society. To understand the foundations of his personality, he looks to early formative experience, to a complex reciprocal play between natural impulses and shaping environment.

It is in the application of this psychological understanding that the confessional paradigm takes another turn. Rousseau's confession is deeply psychological in its mode of self-analysis and self-revelation. What Rousseau is attempting to do is to understand the complex forces which shape human identity; these forces are no longer seen in theological terms but through cultural ones and, furthermore, they are located not in the present moment but in the hidden tangle of past experience.

The analysis is in-depth and retrospective. Rousseau offers two remarkable pieces of such self-analysis: one concerns his beating by Mademoiselle Lambercier, the other concerns his premature reading. Both are courageous acts of introspection. No one before Rousseau had taken intimate childhood experiences and delineated with precision and objectivity their remote and permanent consequences on the life of the suffering, dislocated adult. If in Augustine there is a psychoanalysis of feeling, in Rousseau there exist, for the very first time, the very methods of psychoanalysis.

Rousseau's accounts speak eloquently for themselves. Here I shall consider only the first account. At the age of eight, for some minor offence Rousseau is punished by Mademoiselle Lambercier. At first he is threatened and, then, finally beaten:

> For some time she was content with threats, and this threat of pun-ishment that was quite new to me appeared very terrible; but, after it had been carried out, I found the reality less terrible than the expectation; and what was still more strange, this chastisement made me still more devoted to her who had inflicted it. It needed all the strength of this devotion and all my natural docility to keep myself from doing some-thing which would have deservedly brought upon me a repetition of it; for I had found in the pain, even in the disgrace, a mixture of sensuality which had made me less afraid than desirous of experiencing it again from the same hand. No doubt, some precocious sexual instinct was mingled with this feeling, for the same chastisement inflicted by her brother would not have seemed to me at all pleasant. (Rousseau pp.12–13)

Having described the experience and the kind of pleasure it yielded, Rousseau continues by delineating its subsequent and indelible effects. In a comparatively trivial event he sees that a major propensity has been established in his own personality for the rest of his life:

Who would believe that this childish punishment, inflicted upon me when only eight years old by a young woman of thirty, disposed of my tastes, my desires, my passions and my own self for the remainder of my life and that in a manner exactly contrary to that which should have been the natural result. When my feelings were once inflamed, my desires so went astray that, limited to what I had already felt, they did not trouble themselves to look for anything else. In spite of my hot blood, which has been inflamed with sensuality almost from my birth, I kept myself free from every taint until the age when the coldest and most sluggish temperaments begin to develop. In torments for a long time, without knowing why, I devoured with burning glances all the pretty women I met; my imagination unceasingly recalled them to me, only to make use of them in my own fashion, and to make of them so many Mlles Lambercier. (Rousseau, pp.12–13)

The experience is seen as simultaneously formative and 'deformative'. This is also the case in Rousseau's examination of the effect of early reading upon his life. These acute and detailed descriptions of childhood from the *locus classicus* of confessional writing become introspective and deeply psychological. Given Rousseau's premise that our individual characteristics are largely shaped by early experiences, the art of the autobiographer is not, as in the confessional, to examine the motives as much as to examine the influences of the specific and contingent circumstances on natural impulses. In this way the individual, once he has confessed his sins (we would now say 'traumas'), seeks to understand the pattern of social action which brought them about. The autobiographer, to use one of Rousseau's favourite images, was to become a kind of botanist who introspectively examines the phenomena of his own behaviour and, without judgement, attempts to describe and classify it. Here Rousseau's work boldly prefigures the dangerous and difficult self-analytical journeys of Nietzsche, Freud and Jung, and forms a bridge from the eighteenth century into our own time.

After Rousseau, the genre of autobiography came of age. Significantly, the actual term 'autobiography' was coined in 1807. Augustine's quest for salvation had modulated, for the most part, into the quest for individuation. In the nineteenth century, many of the great writers wrote autobiographies following the linear form set up by Augustine and Rousseau. In the twentieth century this chronological narrative was to shift as life became more fluid and fractured and as many authors sought a greater closeness to the elusive rhythms of memory, but the quest for the understanding and amplification of experience remained. Most of us who now write autobiography, who keep introspective journals and diaries or who generally develop a deeply reflective disposition towards our own experience, belong to this tradition. It has forged the very language we use. We are part of its development, even if we turn critically on its methods and many of its assumptions. We can only deepen our reflective practices by envisaging our individual lives as a part of the same adventure, of that always unfinished project for human understanding and fulfilment, however broken and uncertain it may now seem.

Note on translations

For the translation of Heraclitus I have relied upon those given in Burnet (1920). For the translations from the early sketch of Rousseau's *Confessions* I am indebted to Judith Keyston. They have been translated from Rousseau (1959). The quotations from *The Confessions* have been taken from Rousseau (1953).

References

Augustine (1961) *Confessions*. Trans. R.S. Pine-Coffin. London: Penguin Classics.

Burnet, J. (1920) *Early Greek Philosophy*. London: A&C Black.

Rousseau, J.-J. (1953) *The Confessions*. Trans. J.M. Cohen. London: Penguin Classics.

Rousseau, J.-J. (1959) *Oeuvres Complètes: Les Confessions, Autres Textes Autobiographiques*. Paris: Éditions Gallimard.

Further reading

Abbs, P. (1996) *The Polemics of Imagination: Selected Essays on Art, Culture and Society*. London: Skoob Books.

Taylor, Charles (1989) *Sources of the Self: The Making of the Modern Identity*. Cambridge: Cambridge University Press.

Weintraub, K. (1978) *The Value of the Individual: Self and Circumstance in Autobiography*. Chicago: University of Chicago Press.

CHAPTER 9

Thinking about Language as a Way through the World
Some Sources for a Model

Fiona Sampson

Patricia says, 'It comes back Ibiza before it was all spoilt the top is Moorish Coudella where the nightingales sang in the woods at midday and Yugoslavia Muscana Tiacava the acacia avenue in full bloom and the hotel built around a courtyard right by the sea'.

Or perhaps, since she inflects in the normal way, what she says is:

It Comes Back

Ibiza. Before it was all spoilt.
The top is Moorish.
Coudella
where the nightingales sang
in the woods at midday.
And Yugoslavia.
Muscana Tiacava
the acacia avenue in full bloom,
and the hotel built around a courtyard
right by the sea.
And the Italian Lakes.
I think I liked Como the best.
We went by boat
to see where the mountains were snowcapped.
There was an old chapel. Monks.
They were mowing the grass by hand with scythes.
It was dark in the chapel.
There was a couple getting married
and I remember – I can still see her –

she carried a single red rose.
We went across to Belagio.
I always wanted to go there
– it was linked with a story I read –
and we went, in May.
I wanted to see the chestnut trees:
I remember the orange groves. Terraces.
The garden looking down on the Lakes.
I can talk about it
because I can see it all.
I remember that walk in Yugoslavia,
the fig trees growing in the sand.
And I can almost smell those acacia trees.
And the sea was indigo.
Our minds are a ragbag
of memories![1]

I write down what Patricia says *verbatim*. Or rather, since she is sitting with her husband, to whom she frequently breaks off to refer, I write down what she dictates *verbatim*. Patricia can see me writing down what she has to say and she shapes it accordingly. I am, as it were, the secretary who can be trusted to punctuate appropriately. Or perhaps I write down what I hear: like a playwright who marks up his script with pauses and other stage directions. When I type up the poem for an exhibition, I am like a photo-journalist framing and cropping the image that will make tomorrow's front page.

Or perhaps I resemble a cultural tourist stealing the soul of the person I photograph. Patricia says to me, 'Aren't you clever, you've written all that'. 'You wrote it,' I say, 'They're your words. Listen.' But Patricia finds it hard to believe that what she said has a literary shape or even a textual one. Her dictation was intentional, but she hadn't seen herself as an author. Authors evoke places such as 'Belagio' so powerfully that you want to visit them. They furnish your 'ragbag of memories' just as your own experiences do. In short, they have *authority*.

We say we 'hang on every word' of the writer or politician to whom we give authority. Yet for all the richness that dialect and technical language add to English, for example, it is from an essentially familiar and communal

---

[1]   Cherwell Age Arts Project, Southern Artlink, Summer 1991. Copyright of this and all subsequent material remains with individual authors. Patricia and her husband were residents of Glebe House, Kidlington, Oxfordshire, a social services residential home for the elderly.

vocabulary that the books and speeches that move and impress are made. It isn't necessary to subscribe to Wittgenstein's austerely transactional view of language to accept a rather looser premise that language-users proceed as if a language, like other elements of the material world, possesses sufficient stability to be a common object of experience (Wittgenstein 1953). And the elements of a language are necessarily shared among its users.

And yet – from my own mother's 'Time to get on' to the perhaps apocryphal 'Absolutely fabulous!' – catchphrases seize our attention as manifestations of the personal element which underlies the life of language. We can say that the way the individual uses language is as personal as the way he moves; indeed, that it is determined by a similar mixture of the taught, aspiration and unconscious material. Within the constraints of shared perceptions of comprehensibility – grammatical norms or a common vocabulary – every individual uses language in a way that is recognisably his own.

A good way to see this is in transcriptions of language use by someone you know very well. In 1993 I met weekly for several months with Brian, a former engineer suffering from Alzheimer's Disease, whose wife brought him to a unit for the Elderly Severely Mentally Ill (ESMI) for day care. Both Brian's illness and his lifelong ruminative style so strongly characterised the texts we produced together that they became important markers of his continuing presence for his wife. She was proud of his aphoristic pieces and, despite issues of culture and of confidentiality, was happy for them to form part of an inter-agency campaign raising awareness of issues facing older people.[2] It was as if in restoring his voice they restored the plausibility of his terrible new expertise and even extended its range beyond that experience: for example, in this extract from Brian's piece on 'The Old Ways and the New':

> There's been this rather old-fashioned idea about living among things, rather than at high speed and in the modern way. But people who don't think in this way don't understand because it's so opposite. And it would take a long long time to explain this: because if you can ride past but you can't see the whole strange pattern of the world, you can't understand the idea. (Healing Arts/Isle of Wight Social Services 1993)

2   *Speak Up for Your Age*, Isle of Wight Community Centre, Summer 1993. Brian attended Shackleton House ESMI Unit, Ryde, Isle of Wight.

But Brian's case isn't unusual. Since 1988, in my work as a writer in health and community care, I have become increasingly aware of the significance of such personal ways of using language. This is particularly the case for project participants who do not see themselves as authoritative writers or even speakers. To put it another way, facilitating writers – whether in a prison or on an Arvon Foundation course – cannot only think about imaginative or literary writing as *product* in the way that editors or reviewers may. Nevertheless, to concentrate exclusively on *process* is to embrace a kind of false consciousness about the role of 'writing'. Writing and creative writing generate text – which may or may not attract a readership. In practice, to exclude the community participant from the product implicit in writing practice is insulting and dis-enabling. For theory, this oscillation between process and product which characterises what we call 'writing' is a particularly good example of the relationship between the way an individual uses language and its effect. In other words, I suggest that we can use thinking about the individual's relationship with language to think about the role of creative writing – as both product and process – in a care setting.

I want to avoid the temptations of pseudo-science that lurk in big epistemological questions about language as a medium – such as whether we can have an experience without the language with which to articulate it, or of the necessarily private nature of language use – and instead propose to borrow the authority of some existing ideas about language, and about its links with the infant's experience of individuation, to model this idea of the significance of an individual's own way of using language in writing. Next I'll briefly outline its relevance for areas of discursive conflict and use the example of poetry to suggest that creative writing participates in this conflict. Finally, I'll link this to writing in a care setting.

Making a link between writing and individuation

In 'The Thinker as Poet', Heidegger says that 'singing and thinking are the stems/ neighbour to poetry. / They grow out of Being and reach into/ its truth' (Heidegger 1975, p.13). Heidegger's Being isn't a metaphysical universal but Being-*there*. *Dasein*. It is the individual's being in the world in his own 'authentic' way. In a late essay, the title of which, 'Poetically Man Dwells' is taken from a late poem by Hölderlin, Heidegger uses the term 'dwelling' ('*wohnen'*) to show how the individual's way of being is a form of relationship with the world of his experience. To 'dwell' is to be at home in the world (Heidegger 1975, pp.213–229).

In both these pieces Heidegger makes a link between 'authentic' forms of life and poetry: 'Poetry, as the authentic gauging of the dimension of dwelling, is the primal form of building' (p.227). This link springs from a Cartesian identification of the primacy of the individual's forms of experience as well as from what he identifies as poetry's refusal of the defensive fantasy of objectivity, of 'a furious excess of frantic measuring and calculating' (p.228). However, Heidegger challenges the notion of any discourse's representing 'authentic' life-experience. To name something is to introduce a system of naming between the individual and experience. So for Heidegger, language is authentic when – as does poetry – it presents its own inability to reproduce the world of the writer's experience.

Adorno counters that to claim some ways of using language are 'authentic' is to use language in an ideological way: from a non-neutral standpoint (Adorno 1973). But Heidegger's claim that the realm of experience is laden with certain values isn't a claim for something 'ontologically queer' unless we are sure we can claim the realm isn't value-laden at all. And that is unverifiable. Of course, the idea that some values are naturally occurring can lead, as it did Heidegger, to the excesses of fascism and racism. If what is unverifiable has the status of 'fact', it's immune to challenge. But a belief in the importance of the individual's speaking the forms of her experience in her own terms can also lead to increased discursive democratisation.

Some Marxisms and the feminist linguistics of Dale Spender argue that language is a determining part of individual experience. Language is material and its use culturally material. Dialect and jargon are telling instantiations of cultural context. However, this begs the analogous question of how that individual could be constituted outside such a context. (Rejecting cultural history as decisive, through theories of the writing body, Luce Irigaray and Hélène Cixous shift the pointer of determinacy from cultural materialism to the material of the body (Irigaray 1985; Cixons 1986).)

This possibility that language creates experience in its own image does, however, remove the burdensome and unverifiable concept of 'authenticity'. In psychoanalytic no less than in political narratives, it's with the acquisition of the symbolic register that the human individual 'creates' himself. In the Kleinian account, the infant realises that its self isn't co-extensive with the world when parts of that world – specifically, of its mother – fail to respond to its will. The anxiety that accompanies this discovery leads the child to its own version of its experiences. According to Julia Kristeva, the infant's separation from its mother is the first articulation in the world of its experience (Kristeva 1980). Lacan's mirror stage marks the necessary simultaneity of the ability to symbolise and of self-awareness (Lacan 1977, pp.1–7).

Not surprisingly, philosophers and writers have frequently espoused this kind of connection between – mental – forms of experience and identity.

For Plato, the real entity exists as an idea and not as any material instantiation of that idea. It is the universal template or recipe by which we recognise the particular instance of rain, for example. Any discourse which is to be precise, as well as of universal relevance, must have recourse to these ideas. The Philosopher Kings of the ideal *Republic* are qualified to rule by their reluctance to leave the 'upper' world of 'purely intellectual pursuits' in order to 'return again to the prisoners' in the earthly 'cave' of the material world (Plato 1955, pp.278–86). Pure reasoning, uncompromised by circumstance, allows the potential philosopher to reach ideal understanding. This picture of true understanding is very far removed from the intimacy of Heideggerian 'dwelling': as is Plato's view of poetry as a merely 'mimetic' hindrance to the personal development of his republicans, who might develop over-emotional behaviour in repeating and imitating it. Nevertheless, both philosophers agree on the defining role played by what we might call the 'inner life' and on the importance of living it appropriately.

Likewise Wordsworth's poet, while he finds the real nature of things mapped on his predisposed sensibilities, must nevertheless also 'have thought long and deeply'. In his 'Preface' to the 1802 edition of *Lyrical Ballads*, Wordsworth uses the famous phrase 'emotion recollected in tranquillity' to identify the poet's work as a form of sentimental confession. He sees the poet's inner perspective as mapping both the general human condition – of which the poet is the ideal exemplar – and 'the goings-on of the universe' which echo those of the poet's own 'soul'. The poet authenticates not only his own predisposition to generate poetry, but also – as do Plato's Philosopher Kings – a social hierarchy of sensibility which is naturalised by begging its own question: 'He must have a very faint perception of [the human mind's] beauty and dignity who does not know…that one being is elevated above another, in proportion as he possesses this capability' (Wordsworth 1973, pp.592–611).

These ideas suggest the work of the writer or thinker as embedded in a social role. As we've already noted, Wittgenstein points out that the medium of language, whatever its potential for individual use, is necessarily societal. Although neologism may be 'carried' by existing languages, a truly private language – not a translation of one already in existence – would be unusable because there would be no way for the individual responsible for it to fix rules in place.

Wordsworth and his fellow Lakeland Romantics would have been unable to move towards the confessional note in their work were it not for the work of Jean-Jacques Rousseau, whose *Confessions* of 1766 redefines the link between individual and social experience.[3] From its second sentence, 'My purpose is to display to my kind a portrait in every way true to nature, and the man I shall portray will be myself', the *Confessions* represents autobiography as scientific observation (Rousseau 1953, p.17). Rousseau examines the nature of one human individual – unique, but like other scientific samples illustrative nevertheless of some general truths about such natures – in order to 'display' the starting point and purposes of individual and social activity.

A model of discursive conflict

As Rousseau had realised when he proposed an uncompromised 'state of nature' which might precede and legitimate the putative *Social Contract* (1762), the problem any developed notion of the primacy of individual experience must encounter is what happens when individualisms conflict (Rousseau 1973, pp.190–93). This is no less true of conceptual than of material territory. Scarcity of resources makes the desires of the 'noble savage' in us all incompatible with those of his neighbour. In the same way, according to twentieth century thinkers, different discourses – ways of experiencing and articulating according to specific rules and viewpoints – compete for discursive territory.

The Italian philosopher Gemma Corradi Fiumara prefaces her examination, in *The Other Side of Language*, of what she calls 'discursive violence' with a quote from Canetti: 'The sciences bite off pieces of life, and life shrouds itself in grief and pain'. In Corradi Fiumara's thesis:

> Everything that is sufficiently and suitably enunciated is in practice accepted as an enunciation of knowledge...any knowledge that is sufficiently and suitably expressed (deployed) has a progressive tendency to establish itself as the only knowledge there is. And any discourse

3   Peter Abbs identifies the part played by the *Confessions* in the historical cultural context for writing and personal development in Chapter 8 of this volume.

initiated outside the dominant body of knowledge turns out to be so very difficult to think and articulate that it almost seems unheard-of, simply because it is unhearable. (Corradi Fiumara 1990, p.55)

The struggle between discourses is a struggle for discursive survival. A good example of this is that way of processing experience we call 'common sense', the prohibitions of which are sanctioned by the analytical-philosophical term 'counter-intuitive'. The appeal to 'common sense' is effective precisely because it is that to which appeal is commonly made. Catherine Belsey discusses this relationship between common sense and ideology in her *Critical Practice* (Belsey 1980).

Another picture of discursive struggle, by Laclau and Mouffe, proposes that the concept of 'hegemony' filled the place of discredited belief in 'historical necessity' in Marxist thought during the Second International. The development of this – powerful – idea of powerful discursive structures with their own mechanisms and necessities was therefore 'not the majestic unfolding of an identity but the response to a crisis' (Laclau and Mouffe 1985, p.7). The idea of hegemony, they suggest, is nevertheless useful in an era of 'radical democracy' in which multiple and overlapping challenges to prevailing ideas are being mounted.

I suggest that literary and imaginative writing takes part in this struggle as consciously as – if less brutally than – the most authoritarian political doctrine. That is to say, such discourses do situate themselves in relation to others.

Poetry affords particularly good examples of this. Almost from the outset of its life in modern academic criticism, poetry has positioned its ground in relation to that of other discourses. Matthew Arnold characterises its content in terms of the relative absence of what we would call 'spiritual values' in contemporary culture: 'Our religion has materialised itself in the fact... But for poetry the idea is everything' (Arnold 1970, p.340). He also characterises poetic diction in relation to prose: 'The poetical gift...[is] to utter a thing with the most limpid plainness and clearness' (pp.91–3).

Poetic discourse – the whole discursive field which poetry founds, from critical studies to promotional blurb – characterises its narrative personae and teleologies, in relation to the prosaic, as figuring the 'negative capability' of a John Keats or a Cyrano de Bergerac. Poetry positions itself on the page in ways which differentiate it from other kinds of text. It marks out certain media, such as – among 'literary' practices – oral transmission, as almost peculiarly its own; and it marks out its territory within those media: for example, in specific aural structures.

Kristeva situates poetry at the border of language, where it breaks down into involuntary aporia. Poetry may gasp exclamation, fail to make it across the page's dangerous width. Involuntary connections may bubble up in pun and allusion. Moreover, for Kristeva the music of poetry is a psychotic return to the babble of the infant who doesn't yet differentiate between herself and the rest of the world: the free play of unsignificant pleasure. Poetry gambles and gambols with fragmentation on the brink of that aporia which Seamus Heaney describes, in his eponymous poem, as a 'Personal Helicon' (Heaney 1990, p.9).

For Heaney, wells and springs encountered and played beside in childhood are not only sources of contemporary daydream, but are figuratively revisited in the adult explorations of poetry-making. As the closing stanza of Heaney's poem tells us, however resonant a poem may be with the unconscious, the matter of childhood, it is not in fact a tumble back into that 'soft mulch' but rather a conscious and 'adult' appropriation of the 'long roots' of individual identity. This is a project closely analogous to valuing the individual's own way of using language as part of their identity.

Writing as reification: the individual in a care setting

If we return to Heidegger's idea of poetry as refusing the false consciousness of objectivity, we can see ways in which the discursive role of creative writing in general allows the individual to play with what is personal, irrational or imaginary. The following examples of that potential at work in a care setting reflect the not unsignificant preponderance of poetry among creative writing produced in these contexts.

Creative writing affords the chance to juxtapose humour and reflection, the personal with the abstract. The following group poem approaches the universal by way of the individual experience. It was dictated by a group of women residents of a sheltered housing unit during a summer project:

Nostalgia

Nostalgia's something you remember happily surely,
and regret's something you wish you hadn't done.
I don't know whether I have any regrets but I'm nostalgic.
Nostalgia's something you enjoyed that you can look back on
like the handsome man you danced with

...but he went home.
That's nostalgia, followed by regret!

(Gore Grange, New Milton, Hampshire, June 1994)

Poetry affords the chance to mix up discourses, as where this young woman with learning disabilities appropriates a descriptive exercise to explore her preoccupations:

Waving in the Woods

Trees – green woods
– don't know who's about –
green grass – tall – sometimes short
deer moving fast
different shape leaves
swishing
shaking
in the wind.
I waved in a strong wind
to my grandmother
when she was alive.
My grandmother's dying
slowly:
she won't be around for ever.
It's scary in the woods
at evening
it must be getting dark.

(Glamis Court Group Home, East Cowes, Isle of Wight: Winter 1992)

In this poem Jane, who had recently been moved out of a small family-run house, links the trees which surrounded and isolated her new home, assaults on women which had recently taken place in the area, and the loss of her grandmother to terminal illness. Within this extended metaphor poem, the picture of waving to her grandmother in a strong wind is a particularly powerful image of bereavement. But it also records an experience which is not fully worked out. Is the strong wind also carrying ideas about the excitement associated with seeing her grandmother, or about her grandmother's character? Does it indicate distance or is it 'in your face'? Both at once? This kind of human complexity could not be fully articulated by any explanation of our feelings that we might offer to, for example, a doctor or a social worker but the poem has allowed Jane to explore them as far as she wishes or is presently able to.

The creative writer can also hide behind metaphor as behind a liberating mask. For example, Shelley, a professional woman in her late 30s who attended a day hospital for treatment for depression following the break-up of her marriage, wrote about a reservoir in west Wales:

The Chapel Bell

For whom does the chapel bell toll now?
Not for the living to summon them to prayer.
It rings now muffled
As the ghostly hand still keeps the beat.
The well-worn path lies submerged
Under the calm rippling water
That flows to bring new light
To chase away the ghosts of the past.

(The Cedars, Ryde, Isle of Wight: September 1993)

This poem, with its symbols of depression, loss and renewal, was written for an exchange project and touring exhibition which used artwork and creative writing by clients of mental health day care, in widely separated but somewhat analogous communities in west Wales and the Isle of Wight, to communicate and celebrate the participants' individuality.[4] Shelley was proud of this poem's form and style but she did not address its content during sessions at the hospital.

Reified as text, literary and imaginative writing by people receiving health or social care has a higher status than whatever they might say in conversation with their regular ambulance driver or the nurse bathing them, for example. Idiosyncratic turns of phrase can be 'seen' as strikingly insightful instead of merely 'incorrect'. Their creative writing can move, astonish or entertain. It can be published and broadcast, performed and quoted. Because poetry and fiction have high discursive status it can counter the hegemony of 'authoritative' discourses which position these individuals as discursive objects or at best as listeners. An example of this would be the clinical practice of referring to an individual as a 'case', or the more informal term 'bed-blocker'. However, not all care discourses enact such a hegemony. Rather, the idea that creative writing enables discursive participation is born out of my experience that, for a significant proportion of participants in health- or social care-based projects, what seems important may be not what they say but participation in the practice of writing itself. A text which was

---

4   *In Our Place.* Healing Arts, Isle of Wight and The Gables Day Hospital, East Dyfed Health Authority: September 1993–94.

written without much apparent time for reflection may nevertheless become an object of display.[5]

The implications of all this for writing in health care are significant. A conversation turns into dictation, which evolves into a text, which acquires an audience through publication. This process, as outlined at the start of this chapter, bears concrete witness to the reification of the individual in their ways of using language.

In other words, the link between writing and personal development is not only dependent on the fluidity of narrative personae, on the possibility of imagining other selves or on particular powers of perception, for example. The text may act as a mask behind which the writer can experiment with the possible and the actual. This is as true of facilitated texts as of those which have been produced independently. But paradoxically it may also fix the authorial perspective in ways which allow recognition, revision or acclaim to follow.

In this chapter I have been preoccupied with the role any text plays in its writer's way of life, rather than with valuing certain forms of textual content. In part this is because my work on writing in care settings has meant involvement with texts which may be the first of their authors' adult lives. This often means that they are as much markers of writing's potential, and of discursive intervention for its own sake, as opportunities for particular reflexive projects.

I have therefore tried to excavate a particular model of the importance of individual language use from the work of Heidegger, Plato and Wordsworth; and of the value of reifying that language use in high-status, individualist forms from ideas of discursive violence and about the discursive status of poetry. This process of discursive reification which writing carries out is also, of course, a process in which identity and authority become elided. And for the individual in a care setting, such a reinforcement of her individuality with authority holds the potential for every other kind of work with that self.

References

Adorno, T. (1973) *The Jargon of Authenticity*. Trans. K. Tarnowski and F. Will. London: Routledge.

---

5   For an example of this relationship between writer and text see Chapter 4 in this volume.

Arnold, M. (1970) *Essays in Criticism: Second Series* and 'On translating Homer: last words.' In P.J. Keating (ed) *Selected Prose*. Harmondsworth: Penguin.

Belsey, C. (1980) *Critical Practice*.

Cixons, H. (1986) 'Sorties: out and out: attacks/ways out/forays.' In trans. B. Wing, Cixons, H. And Clément, C. *The Newly Born Woman*. Manchester: Manchester University Press.

Corradi Fiumara, G. (1990) *The Other Side of Language: A Philosophy of Listening*. London: Routledge.

Healing Arts/Isle of Wight Social Services (1993) *Speak Up For Your Age*. Isle of Wight: Healing Arts/Isle of Wight Social Services.

Heaney, S. (1990) *New Selected Poems 1966–1987*. London: Faber and Faber.

Heidegger, M. (1975) *Poetry, Language, Thought*. Trans. A. Hofstadter. New York: Harper Colophon.

Irigaray, L. (1985) *Speculum of the Other Woman*. Trans. G.C. Gill. Ithaca, New York: Cornell University Press.

Kristeva, J. (1980) *Pouvoirs de l'horreur*. Paris: Éditions du Seuil.

Lacan, J. (1977) *Écrits: A Selection*. Trans. A. Sheridan. London: Tavistock Publications.

Mugerauer, R. (1988) *Heidegger's Language and Thinking*. Atlantic Highlands, New Jersey: Humanities Press Int.

Laclau, E. and Mouffe, C. (1985) *Hegemony and Socialist Strategy*. London: Verso.

Plato (1955) *The Republic*. Trans. H.D.P. Lee. Harmondsworth: Penguin.

Rousseau, J.-J. (1953) *The Confessions*. Trans. J.M. Cohen. Harmondsworth: Penguin.

Rousseau, J.-J. (1973) *The Social Contract and Discourses*. Trans. G.D.H. Cole *et al*. London: Dent.

Wittgenstein, L. (1953) *Philosophical Investigations*. Trans. G.E.M. Anscombe. Oxford: Basil Blackwell.

Wordsworth, W. (1973) Preface to *Lyrical Ballads*. In F. Kermode *et al*. (eds) *The Oxford Anthology of English Literature, Volume II*. New York: Oxford University Press.

Further reading

Cameron, D. (ed) (1990) *The Feminist Critique of Language*. London: Routledge.

Heidegger, M. (1966) *Discourse on Thinking*. Trans. J.M. Anderson and E.H. Freund. New York: Harper and Row.

Heidegger, M. (1974) *The Question of Being*. Trans. W. Kluback and J.T. Wilde. London: Vision Press.

Klein, M. (1986) 'The importance of symbol formation in the development of the ego.' In J. Mitchell (ed) *The Selected Melanie Klein*. London: Peregrine.

Sampson, F. (1997) 'Poetry and the position of weakness: some challenges of writing in health care.' In V. Bertram (ed) *Kicking Daffodils: Twentieth-Century Women Poets*. Edinburgh: Edinburgh University Press.

Spender, D. (1980) *Man Made Language*. London: Routledge and Kegan Paul.

CHAPTER 10

Writing, the Self
and the Social Process

Mary Stuart

This chapter will discuss the process of establishing self-identity through interactive social processes. It will examine the development of theories of symbolic interactionism, from Mead (1934), through Plummer (1995) to Scheff (1990, 1996) and the social psychological theories of Goffman (1959) and Lewis (1971). It will argue that self-development is an on-going process and that particular encounters challenge or affirm our 'self'. It will argue that the process of writing is an encounter in itself (Ivanic 1993) and offer a social explanation for the use of writing as a way of offering individuals or groups either shame or esteem. The chapter concludes with an examination of the social forces that create writer anxiety. I begin with a discussion of the development of a socially constructed theory of self.

Social definitions of the self

Theories of self-development abound. Several of these theories are discussed elsewhere in this book. This chapter focuses on a sociological perspective that highlights the 'social management' of self. It is concerned with conscious and unconscious mechanisms that shape our development, not just in childhood but throughout life. It starts from the premise that individuals exist within groups and cultures and that through a process of interacting with 'others', individuals come to 'identify' as a 'self'. It argues that language, and writing as an integral part of language, influences the development of these selves. This is not only as a form of individual encounter with the wider society, but also because language and writing carry the weight of social and cultural meanings.

Within the social sciences there has been much debate about the significance of 'society' in shaping individual identity. Structuralist writers such as Louis Althusser (1977) emphasised the role of 'subjects' as determined by class position before birth. Michel Foucault, the influential French philosopher, highlighted this process by pointing out that through the development of restrictive legal practices, the 'construction' of particular marginalised identities became possible during the nineteenth century (Foucault 1977). However, Foucault was pushing the boundaries of structuralism. He argued against Althusser, in particular, highlighting the inherent dichotomy between truth and falsity posited by structuralism which saw the capitalist mode of production as a determining edifice. Foucault also provided a fresh examination of the process of 'confinement', the move to institutionalise large numbers of people labelled as suffering from 'mental illness' and other disabilities. In the process of creating new categories of people, new identities were being developed. In other words, Foucault suggested that social constructions such as medical definitions created new identities for people, or as Paul Rabinow summarises the argument:

> In this process of social objectification and categorisation, human beings are given both a social and a personal identity. Essentially 'dividing practices' are modes of manipulation that combine the mediation of a science (or pseudo-science) and the practice of exclusion – usually in a spatial sense, but always in a social one. (Rabinow 1987, p.8)

In the 1990s structuralism is seen to be too deterministic to account for the complexity of identities, and the emphasis on social definitions has now moved to the construction of self rather than the determination of self. Roz Ivanic neatly expresses this shift by saying:

> The individual is not socially determined but socially constructed. Individuals do have a role in this construction process: after all individuals are themselves what constitute the social fabric. However social conditions restrict the building materials (including, mainly language) they have available. (Ivanic 1993, p.73)

As well as 'restricting' the building materials, society 'creates' the available 'building materials'. By that I mean that society's part in the process is not only a negative one, but one that creates the potential for 'ways of seeing ourselves'. As Anthony Giddens says:

> In the post-traditional order of modernity, and against the backdrop of new forms of mediated experience, self-identity becomes a reflexively

organised endeavour. The reflexive project of the self, which consists in the sustaining of coherent, yet continuously revised, biographical narratives, takes place in the context of multiple choice. (Giddens 1991, p.5)

In other words, there are possibilities for creating and, importantly, re-creating ourselves within the context of social forces. The significance of re-creating the self is that our identities are not fixed but are constantly being shaped and re-formed in a process of interaction with other individuals and groups. This theory of the self has become known as 'symbolic interactionism' and has been highly influential in the social sciences since its development in the 1930s.

The next section will examine the development of symbolic interactionism and explain these theorists' explanations for 'self-management'.

Developing a theory of social selves through interaction

The father of symbolic interactionism is taken to be George Herbert Mead, a social psychologist working in America during the 1930s. In fact he had several influences, including Cooley (1922) and Pierce (1955). However, it was Mead who drew a range of thinking together and produced a coherent theory that explained the development of self.

Mead suggested that the self is divided into two parts, the 'I' and the 'me', effectively the conscious and unconscious selves. The conscious interacts with the world and comes to understand itself in relation to that interaction. The unconscious self has an impact on this interaction by creating a sense of uncertainty about self-identity through dialogue with the conscious self. Mead indicated that we could never fully understand how we came to be our/selves. He wrote in 1934: 'The 'I' of this moment is present in the 'me' of the next moment. There again I cannot turn around quick enough to catch myself' (Mead 1934, p.174).

As well as highlighting the interplay between 'I' and 'me', Mead examined the social world in which the self is interacting. He suggested that our encounters with the world could be divided into encounters with 'others': either a 'generalised other' or 'significant others' (Mead 1934). The 'generalised other' was the weight of society and social forces and 'significant others' were individuals and groups who mediated the social forces. For Mead, through these encounters individuals came to see themselves through the eyes of 'others' and to 'symbolise', or 'imagine', their self.

Building on the concept of initial self-development, Erving Goffman (1959) explored the on-going process of self-management, highlighting the importance of face-to-face encounters and conscious and unconscious attempts to avoid embarrassment. Goffman saw the role of day-to-day interactions as a process of affirming or challenging an individual's sense of place within the social fabric. If it is interaction that shaped self-identity, it is necessary to understand its processes in detail. Goffman conducted a range of studies in different settings, including detailed studies in long-stay mental hospitals in America, examining the behaviour of both patients and staff. He looked for small clues, almost imperceptible but understood by individuals, sometimes without being aware of the process, such as facework, examples of demeanour, deference between people, and so on. He wrote in 1959:

> ...an individual does move into a new position in society and obtain a new part to perform, he is not likely to be told in full detail how to conduct himself, nor will the facts of his new situation press sufficiently on him from the start to determine his conduct without his giving further thought to it. Ordinarily he will be given a few clues, hints and stage directions, and it will be assumed that he already has in his repertoire a large number of bits and pieces of performance that will be required in the new setting. (Goffman 1959, p.63)

There are several interesting aspects to his ideas in this paragraph. The first is an emphasis on voluntarism. It is quite clear that Goffman sees individuals making choices about how to present self in social situations. It is also clear that he blurs the lines between the presentation of self and self as such. This blurring highlights an on-going debate about truth, multiplicity of selves and authenticity. I shall examine some current thinking in this field later in this chapter, but it is important to indicate at this stage that the debate in this area is keen and unresolved. Goffman also uses the metaphor of the individual as 'performer'. For Goffman social interactions were performances, usually impromptu, where the actor is thinking on her/his feet, but where actors have a wealth of scripts, costumes, gestures and props to draw on. Choosing the right combination determines one's success in the acting environment. However, these 'props' and so on that we collect over time are dependent on the social environment which we inhabit. In other words, our social world shapes and creates our possibilities or, as Ivanic states: '...the cultural conditions of twentieth century western society affect the way in which people see themselves…and boundaries and difference between social groups play an important role in the process of establishing an identity' (Ivanic 1993, p.75).

More recently the notion of interactions shaping individual identity has been developed by Thomas Scheff (1990, 1996), who developed the study of the process of interaction drawing on the work of social psychologist Helen Lewis (1971). Rather than the avoidance of embarrassment, Lewis saw the on-going development of self working within a cycle of interactions shaped by encounters that either offered esteem or shame. Lewis argued that shame is often not recognised in our society but is a major influence in the process of shaping identities. From her studies she suggested that shaming often goes unacknowledged and is bypassed. Later the shame is returned to by individuals on other occasions, setting up a cycle of shaming and creating a downward spiral of low self-esteem. Thomas Scheff explained the significance of this theory by saying:

> Shame is crucial in social interaction because it ties together the individual and social aspects of human activity as part and whole. As an emotion within individuals it plays a central role in consciousness of feeling and mortality. But it also functions as signal of distance between persons, allowing us to regulate how close or far we are from others. (Scheff 1996, p.4)

Scheff also suggested that offering esteem to individuals can create a reverse process, enabling individuals to see themselves positively through interaction and to develop healthy identities.

This section has focused on the development of a social theory of self through daily interaction. It has examined a range of work that highlights the significance of micro-interactions and emotional connection. The theories emphasise voluntarism but see this voluntarism within the constraints of social forces. They suggest that there is no rigid self, but a flow between the external and the internal, a constant critique, a shuttling back and forth between imagination and perception, between induction and deduction, between 'I' and 'me', creating a fragile and multi-faceted self which we represent to the world. In the next section I shall explore the relationship between the theory of symbolic interactionism and writing.

The role of language, narrative and writing

Within linguistics little attention has been paid to writer identity despite its obvious importance to the discipline (Ivanic 1993). I have argued that self-identity does not develop independently but is constructed in relation to a social and cultural environment, or, as Ivanic argues: 'The self should not be conceived of as something to be studied in isolation, but as something which manifests itself in discourse' (Ivanic 1993, p.79).

'Discourse' is an over-used word. In debates about the modern or post-modern era, discourse is a common concept. However, it does contain important elements and is useful for a symbolic interactionist understanding of self. In the context of this chapter, Foucault's construction of 'discourse' suggests that it is a framework within which individuals are able to function. Discourse is therefore a notion related to the social. However, as an idea discourse is slightly different from social forces because it suggests a semi-organised, semi-connected set of ideas. Discourse is not disparate but loosely contained within itself. Foucault suggested that a range of identities were developed by particular scientific or medical discourses: the Malthusian couple, the masturbatory child, and so on. It is through the process of being 'named' and 'classified' that self is created or, as Jean Francois Lyotard, the post-modern French philosopher, says:

> As a child or immigrant, one enters culture through an apprenticeship in proper names. One must learn the names...names are not learnt by themselves – they are lodged in little stories... In reciting its narratives, the community reassures itself of the permanence and legitimacy of its world of names through the recurrence of this world in its stories. (Lyotard 1992, p.43)

There are several interesting ideas in Lyotard's comments. He begins by emphasising the importance of the social 'rite of passage' into society and/or culture. Like Foucault, he sees the naming or classification process as vital to the ordering of culture and the development of self. However, he places the classification or naming process in the context of narrative – a context that places individuals within culture within a story. For our/selves to find a 'place' in society through a story, language becomes crucial. I have focused the discussion of the development of self in relation to 'face-to-face' encounters. However, face-to-face encounters and distanced encounters should not be usefully seen as dichotomous. Ivanic emphasises this: '...the varieties of spoken and written language cannot be neatly separated...spoken language [is equated] with face-to-face encounters and written language with communication which is separated in time and space' (Ivanic 1993, p.49).

The development of self is significantly influenced by language, whether this is spoken language, written language or other languages, such as gesture, expression, clothing, and so on. Encountering a text or writing a text is as much about presentation of self and interaction as is talking to another individual in the street. The significance of narrative is that it is more contained than a loosely ordered discourse. As Ken Plummer, a leading symbolic interactionist, says: 'Many social movements and therapies are engaged in the very task of providing cultural accounts of history, coherence and identity which themselves create an essence' (Plummer 1995, p.173).

Narrative can provide the 'vocabulary that enables people to cope with inadequacy, to manage failure and to gain a sense of esteem' (Plummer 1995, p.173). However, as with debates about face-to-face encounters, there is contention about where the 'real' language lies in creating narrative. Within linguistics there is a tendency to see spoken language as more 'true'. Jacques Derrida outlines this argument:

> It has sometimes been contested that speech clothed thought...but has it
> ever been doubted that writing was the clothing of speech? For Saussure
> it is even a garment of perversion and debauchery, a dress of corruption
> and disguise, a festival mask that must be exorcised...one suspects that if
> writing is image and exterior figuration, this representation is not
> innocent... (Derrida 1976, p.35)

In other words, the production of the 'true' self continues whether it is through daily encounters and 'performance' or whether it is in the 'clothing' that our 'writing' represents.

Plummer suggests that, as Derrida, Foucault and Lyotard imply, attempts at the 'essence' are as much versions of the 'truth' as more fractured presentations. He says: 'I have slowly come to believe that no story is true for all time and space: we invent our stories with a passion, they are momentarily true, we cling to them, they may become our lives and then we move on' (Plummer 1995, p.170).

Writing is no further away from 'essence' than speech or thought, nor is a form of oneself presented in a particular environment more or less oneself than any other presentation. Writing is a highly significant indicator of the construction of self. Writing is one way in which we express our/selves, and the 'signs' of writing have shaped the development of language, which provides another significant indicator of self. As Derrida suggests: 'Language is (as much) a possibility founded on the general possibility of writing' (Derrida 1976, p.52).

In this section I have argued that the on-going development of self is framed within discourse and especially narrative. This process is significantly dominated by language and writing. I have suggested that it is not necessary to agonise about where the 'essence' of self lies, as there is no one truth, no overarching narrative that explains our history. Rather, self and presentation of self become one, our presentation is our/self and that self will alter over time. In the next section I shall examine the process of interaction between reader and writer, the use of different styles of writing and the fracturing of self in relation to writing.

Constructing the writer as character

Writing is a process of social interaction. In writing we imagine our reader, we write *to* someone or something. This both constrains and creates the possibility of writing. Imagining the reader is a vital component in being able to write. As I write this, I have some notion of who 'you' are. I imagine the kind of work you are interested in, the sort of background you may come from, and so on. It is unlikely that I would use the writing style I have adopted in this piece of work if I were writing a letter to a friend. In that situation I would be drawing on a range of other imaginations and constraints. However, as with all presentations of self, the writing re-creates a self. You too will have been imagining me as you read, and I begin to see myself 'anew' as the writing develops. The interactions in writing are not only between the reader and the writer, but are enlivened by a wealth of other encounters that shape the presentation of self. For example, discussing the range of social theories of identity with you in this chapter adds a range of other selves to our encounter. The particular concerns of academic writing and debate are also very much in my mind as I write this. Equally, in developing creative writing, other genres and fashions construct the self presented. In other words, it is not just personal knowledge about your reader (or lack of it) that shapes the way you write. There are a range of constraints placed on writers as members of particular communities. We do not present ourselves as writers as isolated selves, but in interaction with others. As Ivanic says of writer identity:

> The discourses writers have available for writing have been acquired
> through specific encounters with them in actual (spoken or written) texts
> in their past experience. These intermental/intertextual encounters have
> provided the scaffolding for acquiring the discoursal repertoire available
> to them at the moment of writing. (Ivanic 1993, p.85)

Not only do we acquire a range of tools to construct our writing, but we
choose to frame our words within particular structures. In other words, it is
not an issue of 'truth' that we look for in analysis of writer identity but rather
an analysis of choice of presentation, or as Ken Plummer argues:

> [With]...symbolic interactionist analysis...concern is less directly with
> matters of truth, and more with matters of consequence: to consider the
> consequences of saying a particular story under particular circumstances.
> In this lies much of the power of story analysis. Stories help people to say
> certain things at certain times and in certain places, and likewise not to
> say them in others. (Plummer 1995, p.172)

To use my example of this chapter again, I could have chosen not to write this
section in the first person. Traditionally academic work is written in the third
person, but my choice reveals my theoretical position on the academy, which
draws on a feminist interpretation of the significance of the personal. As
Plummer says, the significance of my style is not in its inherent truth but in
my choice of presentation, or, in the development of a poem, the meanings
attached to the words are related to the choice of presentation, not to their
intrinsic truth. However, any piece of writing is only a presentation of one
self; writing also creates fractured selves that can provide a space for
experimentation and play.

As with other presentations of self, writers want to be seen as 'valuable'
people; the definition of valuable is perhaps the beginning of anxiety and can
create tensions for any writer (Ivanic 1993) through the dialogue between
the conscious and unconscious selves. Values and definitions of 'valuable'
vary, and writing has the potential for shaming and creating a sense of self
that is negative. Anxiety about writing is common in our society, where many
adults do not identify as writers or readers. The construction of identity
through education impacts significantly on many people's sense of
themselves and writing is often equated with school education. While some
linguists (Street 1984) may recognise that writing is used for diverse
purposes and is a vital aspect of encounters between people, many
individuals fear writing. In Ivanic's study of mature returners to higher

education, she found that many writers felt inadequate and angry when confronted with the constraints of writing. She says:

> At university you are under great pressure to write in a certain way which identifies you with that 'academic' community. This 'certain way' is quite like what you did at college, but it is not like the language you use at home, at work or in your social life. This is pressuring you into adding new dimensions to your identity...most of you also experience a conflict: you resist becoming this person... (Ivanic 1993, p.632)

In resisting, students are defined as 'bad' writers. As with academic writing, in learning the craft of creative writing the constraints placed by genre and style can create resistance and will impact on the social definition of the value of the work. Making choices about which character to play in the presentation of self has consequences. The interplay between shaming and esteem continues to be a significant force in developing writer identities.

This chapter has discussed the development of social theories of the self, in particular highlighting the development of symbolic interactionism. It has shown that despite the emphasis on face-to-face encounters, interaction through writing can equally be understood using the principles of symbolic interactionism. It has highlighted how post-modern debates about narrative, story-telling and writing impact on ideas of self-development. Finally, I have argued that writing is a process that often creates anxiety because of the connections between writing and the discourse of education. Writing, whether academic or creative, as a social process has, therefore, played its part in both offering some individuals self-esteem and others shame. The significance of writing to personal development is therefore contradictory and powerful, and should be recognised and analysed carefully.

References

Althusser, L. (1977) *For Marx*. London: New Left Books.

Cooley, C.H. (1922) *Human Nature and the Social Order*. New York: Scribner's.

Derrida, J. (1976) *Of Grammatology*. Baltimore: Johns Hopkins University Press.

Foucault, M. (1977) *Discipline and Punish: The Birth of the Prison*. London: Allen Lane.

Giddens, A. (1991) *Modernity and Self Identity*. Cambridge: Polity Press.

Goffman, E. (1959) *The Presentation of Self in Everyday Life*. New York: Anchor.

Ivanic, R. (1993) *The Discoursal Construction of Writer Identity: An Investigation with Eight Mature Students*. Lancaster University, unpublished DPhil thesis.

Lewis, H. (1971) *Shame and Guilt in Neurosis*. New York: International Universities Press.

Lyotard, J.F. (1992) *The Post Modern Explained to Children: Correspondence 1982–1985*. London: Turnaround.

Mead, G.H. (1934) *Mind, Self and Society*. Chicago: University of Chicago Press.

Pierce, C. (1955) 'Abduction and induction.' In J. Buchler (ed) *Philosophical Writings of Pierce*. New York: Dover.

Plummer, K. (1995) *Telling Sexual Stories: Power, Change and Social Worlds*. London: Routledge.

Rabinow, P. (1987) *The Foucault Reader*. Harmondsworth: Penguin.

Scheff, T. (1990) *Microsociology: Discourse, Emotion and Social Structure*. Chicago: University of Chicago Press.

Scheff, T. (1996) *Parts and Wholes: Integrating the Human Sciences*. Cambridge: Cambridge University Press.

Street, B. (1984) *Literacy in Theory and Practice*. Cambridge: Cambridge University Press.

CHAPTER 11

The Empty Word and the Full Word
The Emergence of Truth in Writing

Trevor Pateman

I

I am afraid that my beginning is hardly a contemporary possibility. For I imagine myself setting off with my companions on a journey of discovery and, for convention's sake, I imagine that we shall travel up the Amazon and that among our many hopes is that of discovering a tribe previously lost or unknown to those who make such journeys of discovery.

It is within our power to plan our journey and equip ourselves with everything needful within the limits of current technologies. But there are things which may befall us on the way, such as disease and attacks by less than friendly natives, which we may foresee as possibilities but which it is not within our power to control. Some things we can do, but some things just happen to us.

Solid preparatory research may maximise our chances of discovering a tribe, previously unknown or at some point lost to our culture, but it is not within our powers to guarantee that we achieve our goal. If we knew exactly where we were going and what we were going to find, there would be no voyage of discovery to undertake. In the end we may find a tribe, but when we do so, most likely we will congratulate ourselves on our good fortune, our luck rather than our powers to conjure human beings out of the jungle. We may even exclaim that we can't believe what is happening to us.

If we don't find a tribe, we may console ourselves by writing travel narratives, perhaps fictional ones. Lack of discovery is the mother of invention. After all, were we sponsored by a rich and curious patron, he may prefer to read a fanciful account of tribes we have invented for his pleasure than witness us return empty handed. The feelgood factor has a long history in anthropological research.

When we sit down to write fictions, we may also hope to discover something about ourselves on the way, and may even have that as an aim (courses of study exist now in therapeutic writing, for example). But we may not discover anything about ourselves, and may achieve no more than the writing of a fiction. In parallel, aiming only to write fiction, with no hope or aim other than that, we may nonetheless chance upon moments of self-discovery, as when we suddenly remember something about our lives that we had not thought about for so long that it appears to us as lost and forgotten. It is little different when reading an autobiographical fiction of childhood which evokes memories of our own past. If you are touching 50, and reading Kate Atkinson's *Behind the Scenes at the Museum* (1995), the words 'Andy Pandy', 'Bill and Ben' and 'The Coronation' are triggers to reminiscence.

Self-discovery is not something of which we can assure ourselves by careful planning and, by definition, whatever it is that is lost or unknown in ourselves cannot be known in advance of the journeys – including fictional journeys – we undertake. A discovery is a discovery is a discovery. This means, among other things, that we may be surprised by what we find – and may not like it one little bit.

But do we really make self-discoveries as anthropologists have indeed discovered lost and unknown tribes? Or is the philosophical realism that there is something In Here – something inner and true, waiting to be discovered – untenable, at least as an account of our relationship to ourselves? How can I blithely write of self-discovery when all around me I read that (really? essentially?) all we can reasonably hope for is self-invention, self-improvisation, plausible story-telling, in which the frontier between truth and fiction is not so much transgressed as abolished? (I think, for example, of how such positions influence the writings of Adam Phillips (Phillips 1993).)

This little binary opposition between self-discovery and self-invention is so neat that it really ought to arouse at least a little deconstructive suspicion, and the search for a third term.

When I sit down to write a story (I don't know about you; you may be better organised) it would be true to say that I make it up as I go along (and I want it to be *obvious* that I made up this chapter as I went along). Classical rhetoric presented three aspects of speaking and writing as if they were temporally ordered. So invention (*inventio* – having ideas) precedes organisation (*dispositio* – beginnings, middles and ends) and that precedes the actual business of speaking or writing well (*elocutio* – phrasing and sentence structure). And it is easy to let this pass. But then we have allowed ourselves to be taken in by a very misleading picture. A much better picture would have it that invention and organisation go on *in the elocution* – in the acts of speaking or writing (and analogous acts in other symbolic fields such as music and painting). There is no essential temporal ordering. The rhetorical tripartition is analytic, not a classification of an essential order of real time events.

Only in the enactment do the ideas and organisation become embodied, and disembodied they are of limited interest: nobody offers creative writing courses in the writing of *synopses* of novels. But, from the other side, this is also to say that there is not only enactment (*elocutio*). Invention and disposition are also visible (or, rather, lisible) in the enactment – obviously, a novel can be praised as inventive or commended for its plot structure.

I'm going to pin my hopes on *enactment* as a possible middle term which may help avert a rather silly war between the advocates of self-discovery and the advocates of self-invention. It may allow us to see that self-discovery is not (essentially) about introspection, and that what is often called self-invention is (actually) self-enactment. For enactment to do the job I want, I also have to draw a distinction between something which I shall call the *empty word* and something which in contrast I shall call the *full word* (see the second section for the source of this distinction).

If we are unhealthy, we may (we are told and I believe it to be true) act out unresolved psychological conflicts in our behaviour. Acting out is something to which we are *liable*, rather than something of which we are *capable* – to use a distinction I owe to the work of Rom Harré, (see, for example, Harré and Madden 1975) – and it can happen to us (and those with us) anywhere: in the living room, the bedroom, the seminar room, the consulting room. I think that in often obscure ways, we can also act out in our writing. Acting out is both full and empty. It is indeed filled up with something coming from inside us (from our mental life), but it is empty in that in it we lose ourselves as agents, as responsible beings, as individuals capable of reflexively monitored action. We are blind to what we are doing and to who we are. (The idea of reflexively monitored action comes from Giddens 1979.)

Now, there are desperate measures which individuals can take to bring acting out under (apparent) reflexive control, so that it at least begins to look like something they are doing rather than something which is happening to them and of which they are ashamed and embarrassed or for which they will be punished. We call these desperate measures by such names as rationalisation, self-deception, projection and denial. Just as the acting out is full of us, so these measures are empty of us: the very meaning of 'rationalisation' is that it is the giving of a reason which is a pseudo-reason, a false reason, an empty reason. Characteristically, when we rationalise we draw on the socially available stock of acceptable excuses for bad behaviour. In other words, we go right outside to try to make ourselves acceptable, to ourselves and to others. Lost in the original acting out we lose ourselves again in the rationalisation by means of which we try to recuperate ourselves to ourselves and integrate ourselves with others.

We move away from acting out and rationalisation to the extent that we can begin to express what we feel, say what we mean and mean what we say. We may need psychotherapy to help us achieve that, and so we can characterise the object of psychotherapy as helping us towards a full word – an enactment of self which does not leave us split from our feelings, including our oldest and most difficult feelings.

Some people are split from their feelings yet give no obvious sign of acting out. But there are such things as empty game-playing, empty story-telling, shallow inventions of self which all have a rather obvious history. The archaeology of these frivolities is always to be found in the repression of passion, of seriousness and of play. The sceptical and deconstructive turns in post-modernism are, in this sense, frivolous.

What has all this got to do with writing?

There is a craft task in writing which can be discharged more or less well, producing a more or less well crafted story. We can award marks, if we need to, for invention, disposition and elocution. Good marks mean that we are satisfied that the work is well formed. But at another level, we may be dissatisfied with a piece of work which stylistically is 'all right'. And we may find ourselves having recourse to that metaphor which transgresses the boundary between speech and writing, and enquiring whether the writer has (yet) 'found their voice'.

Now, my central claim is that the distinction between writing which lacks some factor x and writing with a found voice can be connected to the distinction between the empty and the full word.

Finding a voice is something which can only be achieved and confirmed in enactment – you don't find your voice by silently soliloquising. You find your voice by doing something with your voice. For a writer, finding a voice is about writing with feeling (see Hunt 1997), achieving a sureness of touch which allows a reader to animate the bare text with a feeling tone and to go on reading with a sense that the author-in-the-text is not going to go out of their emotional depth, even though they may lead us into waters which we find difficult and murky. A writer is also a guide. Together we are searching for lost and unknown tribes of experience, and for human beings experience is always felt experience: we don't just see the sunrise, we are elated by it; we don't just watch the sea raging, we are awed by it. (Able to mobilise such images out of nature, film is apt to evoke our strongest feelings and emotions.)

Does this emphasis on such sublime feelings as elation and awe beg a question? Why shouldn't we be looking for fictions of experience which are more inventive than I am suggesting, fictions which surf the phenomenal rather than plumb the depths?

The phenomenal is part of our experience, and close observation of it part of the talent and training of the writer as well as, for example, the painter. But the Impressionists, for example, are more than painters of the surface play of light on light-reflective surfaces. They are painters of mood and vision, and their paintings are consequently animated with a feeling tone. If they were not, they would be that much the less interesting. So it is with writers. That is why, for example, Marxist critics (beginning with Lukács (Lukács 1975)) have consolidated a distinction between realist and naturalist writing: the latter may be politically correct (as in Zola), but fails to hold us because it is too much surface and not enough depth. Given the choice between politically correct naturalism and incorrect realism (such as they find in Balzac), Lukács' vote goes to the latter (as does that of Roland Barthes (Barthes 1972)).

Inadvertently (I said I was making this up as I went along), I have in the preceding two paragraphs twice used the idea of something animated with a feeling tone. This idea comes to me from the work of Richard Wollheim and Peter Kivy (Kivy 1980; Wollheim 1987). They say that an unlearnt ability (or liability) of human beings is their capacity to see one thing in another. At one level, this is the capacity to see the Man in the Moon and the face in the fire. At another level, it is the capacity to see a landscape as melancholy, a sunflower as joyful. We are also liable to see such qualities in a work of art, not least when they are expressed there. So the music strikes us as sad or lively, the painting as gloomy, the novel as anguished. In Peter Kivy's terms, we animate the art work with a feeling tone. But when we do this, we do it (I want to say, and I am wondering if I can get beyond the standard metaphor) from inside ourselves, whether as makers of the art work or as audience for it. We reach into that vast reservoir which is our experience and all that has happened to it and all that we have made of it, connecting it and framing it.

I realise that this is rather in the form of an empirical claim, and not universal in scope. I can imagine the case in which someone, lacking the experience they need for an artistic task, reaches out to books or conversations for their material – indeed, that is a common enough aspect of writing. For example, I've written a story called *Crete* and, never having been there, used a handbook for the names and descriptions of wild flowers which I needed for the story I wanted to write. Roland Barthes, in the famous essay 'Death of the Author' (Barthes 1972), wants us to see such ways of working as at the heart of the (modern) writer's work, so that the (good) writer is really a *scriptor* who 'no longer bears with him passions, humours, feelings, impressions', but rather an 'immense dictionary from which he draws a writing that can know no halt' (p.147).

But the scriptor's strategy looks less plausible in relation to basic ways of experiencing the world – either we have those ways available to us, or at least analogues of those ways, or we are at a loss. If we have never experienced profound depression (let us say), either in ourselves or in another, I find it hard to see how from books or conversations we could do much more than mimic it in an artistic work, rather than express it fully – and that means that while an audience might catch our drift, they would not get to the point of unwilled animation of the work with its appropriate feeling tone. And to that extent, they would remain unsatisfied.

Likewise, where experience has been subject to *repression*, we are denied reflexive access to it: that's what the word implies. We can act out in ways driven by the continuing psychic efficacy of repressed material, but we cannot enact it. So the repression blocks us either creatively as writers or imaginatively as readers. It is not immediately obvious to me that the experience of reading has much to do with the undoing of repression (though I think a case could be made out for this), whereas the experience of trying to write – like that of trying to talk in a psychoanalysis – can return repressed material to consciousness. It then has to be dealt with by the person whose repressed material it is, if it is to be shaped into writing. But just as I wanted to deny that the tripartition of invention, disposition and elocution represented a necessary chronological ordering, so I want to suggest that it may be that repressed material which comes to the surface in the course of writing may be dealt with (worked through) *in the writing itself.* The working through does not have to be anterior to or exterior to the writing. This is to imply that at some points what we distinguish as the psychologically individual author or writer, on the one hand, and the implied-textual author or imagined-fictive narrator, on the other, may be operating simultaneously and in the same words. We then have two faces to the same text.

One of the things which art therapists of all kinds have discovered, following on from the diagnostic use of play in child psychoanalysis, is that repressed material can often be accessed and worked through *symbolically* – that is to say, by means of non-literal representations. In her essay 'Finding a Voice – Exploring the Self', Celia Hunt has shown how the inventive use of a metaphor of the circus, which liberates repressed or semi-repressed material in the context of fiction-writing, is then carried over by the author and becomes successfully used as an extended metaphor in talking about her own ('real') life (Hunt 1997).

The line of thinking developed in the preceding paragraphs is intended not so much to contradict 'Death of the Author' theorising, which in the past 30 years has insisted on the autonomy of the literary text in relation to its psychologically real author, but rather to make this simple point: that literary texts are double-faced.

On the one face, they are indeed works of art which have left behind their real creators: as Roland Barthes puts it, 'writing is the destruction of every voice, of every point of origin' (Barthes 1972, p.139). As such, writing possesses expressive qualities and internal properties (formal, relational properties) which we can value aesthetically. But on the other face, the words of the literary text can appear as expressive of the life of the psychologically real author, and serve as evidence for the character and opinions of that author. (This is not to deny that writing psychobiographies of novelists on the evidence of their novels may well be something not terribly worthwhile, however much such works dominate the Sunday supplement market-place.)

Nonetheless, it is quite possible to read a literary text, now from one side, now from the other; we can Gestalt-switch our mode of attention. Barthes, and the many others who have written in the same vein, could be taken as trying to show us how not to get our modes of attention mixed up.

And it remains true under this view of the literary text as double-faced, that it is a failing in a literary work of art that it obliges us to eke out a literary reading with biographical data about the author. There is, for example, poetry (such as the early poems of Louis MacNeice (see MacNeice 1988) – I owe the example to Laura Dunn) which is too 'private' in that its line-by-line meaning can only shine when we bring to bear knowledge of quite specific detail of the poet's biography. When that is the case, the poetry is rightly judged unsatisfactory.

There is, of course, nothing in my commitment to an idea of self-discovery through writing which says that you can only talk literally about yourself, and never metaphorically. That would do no more than rationalise another kind of obsessional neurosis. But our power to invent metaphors to talk about ourselves does not mean that we invent ourselves, nor does it mean that metaphor is not subject to the discipline of truth. To judge a metaphor as apt is to engage in the same kind of activity as to judge a literal statement as true. And metaphors are made to be so judged. One interesting fact about metaphors which liken life to a journey, and narratives which chronicle real and imaginary travels, is that the metaphor and the forms never become tired. They remain apt ways of expressing something important about human life.

To think as I am thinking is to be humanist about human beings and humanist about art. It is to say that human life is not (essentially) a fiction, and that fictions are (essentially) about human lives.

II

As an epigraph to Section 1 of his 1953 Rome Discourse *Fonction et Champ de la Parole et du Langage en Psychanalyse*, Jacques Lacan inscribes this prayer from *L'Internelle Consolacion*: 'Donne en ma bouche parole vraie et estable et fay de moy langue caulte' (Give me a true and stable word in my mouth and make of me a cautious tongue' – Anthony Wilden's translation in *The Language of the Self* (1967)).

Lacan uses this epigraph as a way of introducing a distinction between the empty word and the true or full word, and this in turn defines the aspiration of psychoanalysis to enable the emergence of Truth in the Real.

Empirical reality includes the rationalisations, projections, denials and disavowals which make our words empty rather than full as expressions of a personal Truth. Empirical reality is not (in Lacan's Hegelian vision) the Real, for the Real is the Rational where everything is what it ought to be.

Personal Truth (Truth in the Real) is not to be thought of as the acquisition of new knowledge (for example, theoretical knowledge couched in the language of psychoanalysis), but rather as the recognition of what we already know, but only unconsciously. As Lacan puts it, in Wilden's translation: 'The unconscious is that chapter of my history which is marked by a blank or occupied by a falsehood: it is the censored chapter. But the truth can be found again; it is most often already written down elsewhere' (Wilden 1967, p.21) – for example, written down as neurotic symptom.

Such recognition is best looked upon not as something ever fully achievable – the unconscious always slips away from us – but as a rational endeavour towards something which is only achievable asymptotically. The notion of asymptote could be rendered as *deferral*, and some connection thereby made with more recent strands of sceptical, anti-Realist thought (notably Jacques Derrida's).

Outside of psychoanalysis, twentieth century philosophers have also utilised distinctions between the empty and the full word. For example, Heidegger in *Being and Time* (1962) – a major reference point for Lacan – uses the concept of *Gerede* (idle talk) to define 'a discoursing which has lost its primary relationship-of-Being towards the existent talked about, or else has never achieved such a relationship' (cited in Wilden 1967, p.201).

What I have done in this chapter is no more than to suggest an extension and application of this kind of thinking to the processes and results of literary endeavour, suggesting that the traditional notion of 'finding one's voice' is an analogue of Lacan's full word. In turn, Lacan's full word plays the part in his thought that the idea of the True Self plays in Donald Winnicott's, and Lacan's Empty Word is Winnicott's False Self. So the connections I am making are not just to one version of psychoanalysis, but are meant to be more general in resonance.

To pursue the analogy with psychoanalysis is to say that finding a voice just is the emergence of Truth or a True Self in the Real of writing, but it is something only asymptotically achievable. Worse, writing need not carry a voice at all: it can be blank or filled up with empty signifiers. Such writing we may end up calling 'vacuous' or 'flaccid' or 'lifeless' or even 'insincere', however emphatically it may be expressed. A writer, for example, can be earnestly insincere in ways little different from those of the soulful politician or the seductive hysteric.

To wish to be a writer does not suffice to enable one to write, and to enable writing in someone else is not just a matter of offering them craft instruction. The writer must be able to write out of the fullness of his or her history, measuring choices of word and theme against or in that history. It follows that if the writer is in some measure not available to himself or herself to measure the writing, then the writing will itself be unmeasured, and judged accordingly.

In writing one is at a sort of double jeopardy: that one may find oneself blocked expressively, unable to write a full word, and blocked critically, unable to bring critical candour to what one has succeeded in putting on paper. It is usually only the former problem which receives attention; consider instead the latter.

In writing, just as in speaking, the unconscious finds a way to express itself – Freud gives examples in *The Psychopathology of Everyday Life* (Freud 1976), though obviously we have to do with much more than slips of the pen. Now, to be blocked critically is to be in the position of being unable to integrate what we have unconsciously expressed into our conscious plan of writing. But that does just mean that we are in the position of not being able critically to control our writing, which to that degree remains unmeasured. In my view, an inability to bring one's 'critical faculties' (as we call them) to bear on one's writing is just as much a writing block as the primary inability to get any words on to the blank paper before one.

There is a further possibility of blockage caused by hypertrophy of the critical faculties which leads one to reject everything one writes. Such hypertrophy is like a punitive super-ego, a vigilant censor committed to extinguishing every last flicker of self-expression.

In summary, there are at least four obstacles readily identifiable as obstacles to the emergence of Truth in Writing, to the emergence of a voice:

- primary inability to write (writer's block)

- secondary inability to find a voice in and through one's writing

- inability to bring critical judgement to bear as one writes or in reviewing what one has written

- hypertrophy of the critical faculties, slowing the flow of words or leading to their too-ready consignment to the wastepaper basket.

Put differently, what I have done is to compare the practice of writing and the conditions and nature of successful writing, to the clinical practice of psychoanalysis. The page is a blank just as the psychoanalyst is a blank, and as a blank invites the transference of the writer, in which the writer's other seeks out its other. Writing is apt as a place for the expression of need, desire, wish and demand. But if a writing is to be successful, all four – need, desire, wish, demand – have in some sense to be measured, to be compassed, by the author.

In a psychoanalysis, the analyst is paid to listen for the moments in which the Truth has a chance of emerging into the Real, and to encourage such moments. In writing, it is we who have to pay ourselves to recognise such moments and to elaborate them – and, equally, to cancel and to put into the wastepaper basket the empty words, the junk, which compete to blind us to such unknown and lost tribes of experience as it may be our good fortune to discover and rediscover on our narrative journeys.

References

Atkinson, K. (1995) *Behind the Scenes at the Museum*. London: Doubleday.

Barthes, R. (1972) 'Death of the author.' In *Image, Music, Text*. Trans. and edited S. Heath. London: Fontana.

Freud, S. (1976) *The Psychopathology of Everyday Life*. Trans. and edited A. Tyson. Harmondsworth: Penguin.

Giddens, A. (1979) *Central Problems in Social Theory*. London: Macmillan.

Harré, R. and Madden, E. (1975) *Causal Powers*. Oxford: Basil Blackwell.

Heidegger, M. (1962) *Being and Time*. Trans. J. Macquarrie and J. Robinson. London: SCM Press.

Hunt, C. (1997) 'Finding a voice – exploring the self: autobiography and the imagination in a writing apprenticeship.' In *Auto/Biography 1, 3*, 169–179.

Kivy, P. (1980) *The Corded Shell*. Princeton, NJ: Princeton University Press.

Lukács, G. (1975) *The Young Hegel*. Trans. R. Livingstone. London: The Merlin Press.

MacNeice, L. (1988) *Selected Poems*. M. Longley (ed). London: Faber and Faber.

Phillips, A. (1993) *On Kissing, Tickling and Being Bored*. London: Faber and Faber.

Wilden, A. (1967) *The Language of the Self*. Baltimore: Johns Hopkins.

Wollheim, R. (1987) *Painting as an Art*. London: Thames and Hudson.

CHAPTER 12

Transformative Reading
Reconfigurations of the Self Between Experience and the Text

Jan Campbell

Reading has perhaps traditionally been seen as a less creative enterprise than writing. This is mainly because whereas writing is regarded as active, reading is often viewed as a more passive and receptive endeavour. The pleasure of reading is therefore often understood as the pleasure of receiving the text's meaning, rather than the pleasure of constructing that meaning. Literary theory has (historically) moved away from the traditional, Leavisite humanist approach to literature, through more structuralist forms of interpretation to arrive at a contemporary emphasis on post-structuralist and post-modern approaches to the literary text.

Humanism was a-historical in its romantic and elitist promotion of great writers. Leavis' refusal of theory was grounded in a moralising empiricism that established the value of a literary text according to its closeness to 'experience' or 'life'. Structuralism, on the other hand, grounded in the linguistic theories of Ferdinand de Saussure and the anthropology of Levi-Strauss, focused on the internal linguistic system of the text and was equally closed to history (de Saussure 1974; Levi-Strauss 1968). For example, Levi-Strauss structurally analysed the Oedipal myth as a universal linguistic structure that revealed the primary structure of the human mind, and the consequent structures of social institutions, knowledge, and so on. But Roland Barthes' seminal essay 'The Death of the Author', introduced a more open post-structuralist analysis of the literary text by demonstrating how the reader is free to enter the text at will and to connect that text to meanings that go beyond and displace structural unity or the author's 'intention' (Barthes 1977).

This emphasis on reading has been taken up in contemporary reader theory in a way which does negotiate a more historical approach to studying literary theory. I want to link some narrative ideas on reading in this chapter to psychoanalysis and to argue for a narrative reading of psychoanalysis that can explore not just the creative and transformative role of reading, but how reading can transform and create ourselves.

Whereas psychoanalysis has been used in post-structuralist theory, which follows Lacan to argue both for the 'decentred subject' and the notion of an unconscious that hides as a kind of unspeakable signifying presence within the literary text, there has been a problem in historicising both the literary and the decentred subject (Lacan 1977). Part of the problem is the universalising Oedipal baseline to Lacanian theory. Lacan's work was rooted in structuralism, and the a-historical determinism of his linguistic account has led to a widespread acceptance of the notion that language is masculine, structured through the paternal law and the phallic metaphor, with the feminine located as an unconscious metonymic lack. Lacan's theory of the phallic nature of language is a linguistic restatement of Freud's Oedipal position, where social identity means identification with the father and repression of the desire for the mother's body. For Lacan, the phallus is symbolic and cannot be attributed to the physical organ. But the phallus still remains as a dominant linguistic term in his theory, designating sexual identity and the symbolic order.

The feminine is, then, the unconscious of both language and identity, representing the negative, bodily underpinning of our Western, phallic symbolic. Julia Kristeva has shown how this unconscious relation to the feminine body can disrupt language through a semiotic playfulness. The semiotic is, then, a more bodily and poetic narrative associated with the rhythm of the body which disturbs the more rational meaning of language proper, and the symbolic. More problematically, in Kristeva's account, the unconscious feminine becomes associated with a deathly psychotic or abject relation to the mother. Abjection, then, is a collapse into a bodily and psychotic relation to the mother, outside language, culture and representation. It is brought about by a refusal of the linguistic phallic signifier (Kristeva 1986). Lacanian post-structuralist theory, therefore, positions the subject as constructed through language and sexual difference. Translated into post-modernism, this linguistic subject becomes a narrative fiction, constructed through a phallic symbolic, with the real relation to the body and to history being characterised as unrepresentable. History and subjectivity are no longer perceived as real, but can only be understood in textual or fictional forms.

Conventionally, in literary theory, the notion of a real self has been bracketed off as an authentic and humanist identity that transcends historical context. Dismissal of the real as the authentic self might be seen by some, especially in the field of the creative arts, flagrantly to contest established notions of what is meant by the creative self. Often creative work has been described as an expression of the inner voice, or a journey to express some hidden core. Ted Hughes used this sort of language to describe Sylvia Plath's poetry. For him, Plath's creative genius, finally achieved in her *Ariel* poems, was the 'true' realisation, both of an authentic voice or self and of her literary greatness (Hughes 1985). A more post-modern way of perceiving the self is to see it in terms of a plurality of fictions. Creativity in the construction of subjectivity signifies not so much an access to notions of authentic real selfhood as the ability to construct more than one story or narrative.

But surely this understanding of the self as a plurality of fictions must connect to the real in some way, whether that real is located in the experiential real of the body or the literal real of history. In other words, the real does not have to mean a unitary, singular or true self; it can also point to more multiple historical selves. If the old humanist rendering of the authentic self evacuates history through notions of experiential genius and the great literary scholar, then the more post-modern emphasis on the self seems to dispel history just as easily with textual fictions that are seemingly constructed through a universal code of one Oedipal and phallic symbolic. This chapter explores a post-structuralist account of transformative reading, moving beyond Lacanian conceptions of phallic textuality to historicise the subject in a more hermeneutic and narrative way. Bringing together post-structuralist psychoanalysis and hermeneutic reader reception theory, I want to discuss how the creation and construction of subjectivity can neither be located as some experiential essence nor seen solely as a linguistic textual fiction. Instead, I want to explore how subjectivity is constructed through numerous and multiple stories; stories which mediate between bodily experience and language.

Hermeneutic reader response theory has been informed by the philosophical writings of Paul Ricoeur (1991) and Hans-Georg Gadamer (Kearney and Rainwater 1996). Ricoeur and Gadamer (in turn) were originally influenced by Heideggerian phenomenology. Reader response theory followed hermeneutic phenomenology in arguing that the subject is (both) placed in the world and therefore subject to it at the same time as projecting that world through consciousness. We are, therefore, not separate from the object of our consciousness. Meaning and thinking are situated and historical, but that historical situatedness is experienced in an unconscious and internal way. In this way readerly literary theory pronounces the text, not as some objective and delimited artefact, but as a form of meaning which is dependent on its historical interpretation or reader. By reading we establish meaning in relation to the text, which is intimately connected with our historical situation. *But this must also mean that by reading we psychically reconfigure and create ourselves in relation to the literary text.*

Paul Ricoeur has developed his hermeneutic understanding of narrative interpretation in terms of psychoanalysis, but before I discuss this, I want to look at the relation between literature and psychoanalysis in a more Lacanian, phallic post-structuralism. Traditionally, psychoanalysis and literature have, according to Peter Brooks, long been unhappy and 'mismatched bedfellows', with psychoanalysis assuming the privilege of a conceptual system which can be used to explain and understand literature. For Brooks, the importance of psychoanalysis and literature lies in the encounter and confrontation between the two: a dialogue between them, then, which does not privilege either but uses them to explain and question how we read. Following Lacan's interpretation of the unconscious through the structuralism of linguistics, we arrive at the rhetorical relationship between psychoanalysis and text where language becomes the medium of both. Brooks asks: 'What is the status of a de-authorised psychoanalytic discourse within the literary critical discourse, and what is its object? If we don't accord explanatory force to psychoanalysis, what is the point of using it at all' (Brooks 1994, p.24)?

If the earlier psychoanalytic criticism in literary studies was involved with over-psychologising the author or the characters in the text, then the more recent deconstructive versions of psychoanalysis claim it within an exclusively linguistic frame. For Brooks, this linguistic emphasis refuses to 'make the crossover between rhetoric and reference', which for him is the major reason for using psychoanalysis in the first place (Brooks 1994, p.26). Brooks makes the claim (and I have made it elsewhere – Campbell 1994, 1997) that psychoanalysis and narrative can be read as the inverse of each other. Psychoanalysis can therefore also be read as narrative, and for Brooks this is moved one step further when he argues that the structure of literature is 'in some sense' the structure of the mind. But this structure, as Brooks himself admits, is 'essentially a phallic model' (Brooks 1994, p.112). If literary narratives can be seen as somehow analogous to a narrative of psychic subjectivity, then surely it is not just the case that a phallic structure of the psyche can be used to read the text, but that literature can also be used to revise and rewrite that phallic psyche.

If literature and psychoanalysis can be read as cultural and narrative forms that revise and instruct each other, then psychoanalysis remains as contingent as literature, dependent on context; the time and place where it is historically and spatially situated. The Oedipal doesn't then become some universal theory based on phallic castration and prohibition of the maternal body. It can be seen instead as an imaginary and a story which has been culturally instituted and made law within certain languages and organisations of the symbolic. But this does not mean it is translated across time and space in a continuous and irrefutable way. Brook's narrative theory is significant in that he reads a structure of desire within Freud's text as a form which is implicit within narrative. But why, given that he accedes to the interchangeability of psychoanalytic and fictional forms, does he insist that narrative is always and universally organised within a phallic model?

Between experience and language

It seems to me that psychoanalysis remains important because it can help us to explain and understand how human subjectivity is reconfigured through narrative in relation to the world outside and to history. If the subject is indeed constructed by the fictions she or he makes, but at the same time those fictions are an imaginary potential which are always already situated at an unconscious or experiential level, then the interaction of psychic process and literature can also help us to understand the configuration of the self in relation to life and history. In Brook's view, psychoanalysis can help us realise the 'human stakes in literary form', and because the self is constructed by fictions then the 'study of human fiction making and psychic process are convergent activities and superimposable forms of analysis' (Brooks 1994, p.36). Psychoanalysis is a fiction which is constructed in the clinical space between analyst and analysand; it is a fiction which brings together the potential stories of the analysand which are transformed within the analytic encounter to give a new and different narrative of self. But what happens when those stories are not potential or failed Oedipal narratives? This does not mean that the Oedipal story does not exist, but in the case of the girl or woman it might be the dominant text which has excluded her story in relation to the mother. If she is Afro-American then the Oedipal as a colonial text has not just excluded her story *vis-à-vis* her mother, it has denied her rights (period) to any story of self. This chapter discusses psychoanalysis and literature as narrative forms which can address a cultural understanding of subjectivity. The relevance for literary studies is not just in making a case for reading psychoanalysis with literature, but also in opening up psychoanalytic interpretation to the challenge and revision of reading different stories and histories. Such a narrative reading of psychoanalysis has further significance for thinking about the practice of reading and writing and for a creative and therapeutic understanding of personal development.

In order to do this, psychoanalysis has to be understood as a narrative, but it cannot in the Lacanian sense be understood simply as a linguistic, Oedipal structure. Narrative has to be distinguished from more linguistic and structural definitions of language. As this chapter will suggest, narrative is a more fluid term that can incorporate a secondary discourse of mental representation as well as more primary, experiential stories. If psychoanalysis is to be understood as narrative, then the linguistic status of language accorded by Lacan to the unconscious has to be challenged. Although Lacan understands the unconscious to be structured like a language, (other) post-modern thinkers disagree with him. Jean Francois Lyotard argues that the unconscious is more figural, a libidinal force at the heart of language, 'of a general disposition of experience'. This figural, 'as image or as form', is not language but the force exerted to displace, or to have an effect on, language (Lyotard 1991, p.25).

For Paul Ricoeur 'the work of hermeneutics begins where linguistics stops'. Hermeneutics grasps the meeting point between rhetoric and reference, between the '(internal) configuration of the text and the (external) refiguration of a life' (Ricoeur 1991, p.432). In other words, hermeneutics understands meaning to be constructed through interpretation or reading, where the meaning of the text is constructed internally through the reader, but at the same time the reader's subjectivity is externally refigured in relation to the experiential world. A hermeneutic understanding of the relationship between psychoanalysis and narrative provides an understanding of the crossover between rhetoric and reference in a way which linguistics does not. In this trajectory, the meaning of the literary text and the construction of our narrative self is created through the act of transformative reading.

Crucial to my argument is the understanding that psychoanalysis involves both potential stories, which are the analysand's scattered fragments of the past and unconscious self-experience, and a secondary narrative between analyst and analysand which recounts and reconfigures the potential stories of the analysand into a narrative of self-understanding between two people. In Ricoeur's narrative terms this means a self-understanding between reader and text. Paul Ricoeur argues for a pre-narrative structure of experience where life 'constitutes a genuine demand for narrative'. Stories are not just recounted, they are also 'lived in the mode of the imaginary' (Ricoeur 1991, p.432). Ricoeur links the analytic encounter which features a movement from pre-narrative experience to narrative with an understanding of reading literature. In this account the analytic transference is similar to the encounter between 'the world of the reader' and 'the world of the text'; reading, like the analytic session, involves a process where the potential unspoken stories of lived experience are mediated by a secondary process of narrative, reconfiguring the self: 'Narrating is a secondary process grafted on our "being entangled in stories". Recounting, following, understanding stories is then simply the continuation of these unspoken stories. From this double analysis, it follows that fiction is an irreducible dimension of self-understanding' (Ricoeur 1991, p.435).

For Ricoeur, then, the secondary process of narrative does not reflect life, it reconfigures and transforms pre-narrative experience; but that experience, in the form of life stories, is in 'quest' for narration. These primary, pre-narrative stories are, in Ricoeur's view, a form of 'narrative intelligence which issues from creative imagination' (Ricoeur 1991, p.429). These unspoken stories are part of the creative imagination, but they are also part of the unconscious imaginary because they have not yet been reconfigured and represented within a second-order narrative thinking.

Ricoeur describes this primary structure of pre-narrative stories as experiential, as lived in the imaginary and as poetry. Poetry offers a very different landscape or representation of the unconscious from a linear linguistic structure. Whereas (linguistic) language implies an unconscious of thinking and mental representation, poetry foregrounds more painterly images, creating a more sensual narrative closer to bodily experience.

How does Ricoeur's interpretative theory of reading apply to the actual creative act of reading, and what model of psychoanalysis does this imply if, as Ricoeur states, hermeneutics begins where Lacan's linguistic Oedipal model stops? For Ricoeur, interpretative reading goes beyond an analysis of deep structures in the text because the act of reading will always bring new meaning, meaning that has hitherto been only a potential in the text. So instead of the implied reader (like the implied author) being understood within the semantic autonomy of the text, the implied reader becomes actualised in Ricoeur's account to reconfigure the meaning of the text, at the same time as refiguring the self in relation to the outside world. When we read we bring to the literary text our unspoken and experiential life stories, and it is the dialogical interchange between these stories and the second-order narrative of the text which produces new meaning. Narrative meaning is not simply there, structurally embedded in the text, but is produced through a dialogical interchange between our life stories and the text. This dialogical process of reading between narrative and referent is also the meeting place of narrative and temporality. The subject is constructed through a language which does not reflect reality but transfigures it so that meaning and self-understanding go hand in hand with new possibilities of the world in relation to the text.

Linguistics or a poetic unconscious?

Ricoeur's description of a poetic, bodily unconscious seems quite close here to Freud's notion of a primary unconscious. Other critics have used, like Ricoeur, the example of the analytic transference where the text and reader are analogous to the analysand's stories and the interpretative analyst. But instead of referring to a primary or poetic unconscious, these critics analyse narrative in Oedipal terms, using either Freud or Lacan. Shoshana Felman has argued for a mutual relationship and dialogue between literature and psychoanalysis 'as between two different bodies of language and between two different modes of knowledge' (Felman 1980, p.6). Linda Williams' more recent work has positioned psychoanalysis and literature as narrative forms which can read each other, and Peter Brooks reads plot and narrative in terms of the analytic transference (Brooks 1994; Williams 1995). For all these writers what is at stake is an Oedipal transference and phallic plot. The transferral relation between psychoanalysis and literature has been understood, therefore, in terms of what Brooks calls 'Freud's Masterplot' where narrative time and plot is understood as either 'a return to its origins or a return of the repressed' (Brooks 1994, p.288).

The reason for this is fairly straightforward. Freud's own work mainly elaborated a secondary unconscious, linked to thinking and mental representation; he did not develop his ideas on a primary unconscious associated with the pre-Oedipal maternal body. Although post-structuralism has developed the Oedipal model via the linguistics of Lacan, other schools of psychoanalysis, such as object relations, which does focus on the pre-Oedipal mother, have been relatively overlooked because there is no available theory of narrative in their writing; no explanation of how bodily desire moves into language and representation. One of the key criticisms of object relations theory from a post-structuralist perspective is that it is rooted in a positivistic empirical frame, offering up the subject as some unified and transcendental whole. Indeed this is how Winnicott's concept of the real and authentic self has been cast: as legitimating some fixed, true self, oblivious to forces either of the unconscious or of history.

Christopher Bollas, a contemporary Winnicottian analyst, reads Winnicott's true self in a different way. For Bollas the true self is merely a set of idiomatic or potential selves which seek elaboration through significant objects. Selection of objects is for Bollas a form of self-expression where 'objects, like words, are there for us to express ourself' (Bollas 1993, p.30). This true self is linked to a primary unconscious experience and can be distinguished from Freud's secondary model of the unconscious: a model of phallic repression and mental representation. Bollas theorises that early experiential relation to the mother – which is impossible to retrieve within a Lacanian/Freudian account where the relation to the mother's body is unrepresentable – *can* be narrated.

Bollas calls the early wordless experience between child and mother the 'unthought known'. This relation is known but not thought because the child cannot process it through mental representation. Distinguished from Freud's classical model of repression, this model of the unconscious refers to a 'holding' experience where the mother is identified with/as a transformational process which alters self-experience. She is perceived as an 'enviro-somatic transformer of the self'. Early ego processes of relating to the mother are not actually thought through but become instead part of the known (Bollas 1987, p.3). When this process is re-enacted within analysis the patient can use the analyst as the 'transformational object' or early mother to transform previous unthought aspects of potential selves into mental representation (Bollas 1989, p.12).

Bollas links this world of unconscious experience, the unthought known, to the action of what he calls 'psychic genera'. Psychic genera is perceived as an elaborative mode of unconscious being, linked to the mother, forming part of the 'simple' self as opposed to the complex narrative self of the secondary or Oedipal unconscious. The workings of psychic genera contribute to an unconscious and symbolic elaboration or development of the potential idiom/self and are part of what Bollas calls a 'theory of psychic reception'.

Bollas suggests that future selves arise due to an evocative transformational process, a form of self-experiencing (beginning with the mother and extending to the world) in which objects are used to bring potential parts of ourselves to life. He links this experience of symbolic elaboration to narrative through his own particular definition of our lives as a sort of narrative dreaming, projecting ourselves into an object of desire. Whether it is a piece of music, a novel or a person, we both use and are transformed by it. Projective identification of ourselves into a selected object of our choice does not have to be simply a loss of the self; it can be enriching and meaningful. Identification and transformation by the object is followed by a mutual self-experiencing between self and object, Winnicott's 'transitional space', where distinctions between self and other disappear (Bollas 1993, pp.22–7). Some people are more intuitively in touch with the objects that can generate psychic self-experience and therefore elaborate the idiom or self. For instance, the book we should read is not automatically the book we would intuitively choose and lose ourselves within.

Bollas distinguishes unconscious self-experiencing from a more representational, hermeneutic unconscious. The subject emerges from self-experiencing and can then reflect on it. Reflection takes place where the subject re-enters his or her complex self. I want to argue, alongside Ricoeur, that the relationship between secondary narrative and unconscious self-experiencing is itself a much more dialogical process. If Bollas' simple self can be seen in terms of experiential stories – Ricoeur's pre-narrative structure – then these stories in search of narrative transform the self, but they also reconfigure the narrative. In terms of reading, this would mean that a transformation of ourselves through self-experiencing goes hand in hand with the production of new meaning and interpretation of the narrative or text.

I have developed elsewhere Bollas' theory of unconscious experience, in terms of narrative and history, but in this chapter I want to compare it with Ricoeur's interpretative account of reading, because these two versions of psychic reception and reader reception are strikingly similar (Campbell 1996). For Ricoeur the act of reading is likened to the analytic transference, where the reader's (analysand's) experiential stories are elaborated in terms of the secondary text of literature (or the analyst's narrative). There is no need for us to compare this with the analytic transference, because Ricoeur has already done so. But Bollas' model of unconscious experience potentially provides a different and more dynamic hermeneutic account of reading than is usually inscribed within the parameters of a strictly Oedipal account of the unconscious. This is because Bollas describes not just how reading interprets reality, but how reading negotiates and transforms our relationship to it. Although Bollas seems to divide his experiential unconscious from a more complex narrative one, his more primary, bodily unconscious – so reminiscent of Ricoeur's poetic, pre-narrative stories – can perhaps be perceived, not as distinct from secondary narrative but dialogically in play with it.

Creative reading

Poetry also helps to define Bollas' elaborative unconscious experience. Memories tapped in the transference liberate internal generative objects that are captured by the poetic image. Transformative internal objects, characteristic of the artist's internal abstract pictures, are a 'common psychoanalytic perspective on the nature of creativity' (Bollas 1993, p.79). Perhaps one of the most famous examples of this in modern literature is the moment in Virginia Woolf's *To the Lighthouse* when Lily Briscoe experiences her artistic vision: 'with a sudden intensity, as if she saw it clear for a second, she drew a line there, in the centre. It was done; it was finished. Yes, she thought laying down her brush in extreme fatigue, I have had my vision' (Woolf 1985, p.192).

Bollas cites imagist theory and the poetry of Seamus Heaney to illustrate inner images of psychic creativity: 'I think of imagist theory, which Heaney believes yields a "sense of that which presents an intellectual and emotional complex in a moment of time". Baudelaire, Poe, Rimbaud, Pound (and one could go on) believed that the image created life in it'. Such unconscious creativity of the internal object is named by Bollas as an 'operational intelligence', again similar to Ricoeur's primary and poetic 'narrative intelligence' (Bollas 1993, p.79).

Modernist movements such as surrealism were known to influence Woolf's fiction. The idea that psychic procreativity and the inner creative image can both disrupt and transform more traditional narratives, creating new meaning, has already been developed in various ways. Less familiar is the connection between the creative act of writing and painting and the creative work of reading. Toni Morrison is a contemporary novelist and critic, writing out of the Afro-American tradition, who views both writing and reading as analogous creative acts. She describes her narrative strategy as 'a kind of literary archaeology'. The act of imagination, together with what remains of memory/history, can symbolise a move from 'image to text':

> On the basis of some information and a little guesswork you journey to a site to see what remains were left behind and reconstruct the world that these remains imply. What makes it fiction is the nature of the imaginative act: my reliance on the image – on the remains – in addition to recollection, to yield up a kind of truth.

Morrison stresses that her recollection as a writer moves from the image to the text, not from the text to the image. Her image figures as painterly and sensual, rather than a linguistic or mental representation: 'by "image" of course I don't mean "symbol"; I simply mean "picture" and the feelings that accompany the picture' (Morrison 1987, p.112).

Writing also occurs as reading. In her book of critical essays, *Playing in the Dark*, Toni Morrison describes certain kinds of reading which are for her inextricable from certain kinds of writing:

> In these readings a sense that the text has appeared to be wholly new, never before seen, is followed, almost immediately, by the sense that it was perhaps always there, that we, the readers, knew it was always there, and have always known it was as it was, though we have now for the first time recognised, become fully cognisant of our knowledge. (Morrison 1992, p.xvii)

For Morrison it is *the act of writing and reading* which constitutes an act of the imagination, transporting experience to representation within language. Imagining is not 'merely looking or looking at; nor is it taking oneself intact into the other. It is, for the purposes of the work, becoming' (Morrison 1992, p.4). In another essay, 'Unspeakable Things Unspoken: The Afro-American Presence in American Literature', Morrison talks of the writing strategies she implements to unsettle and disquiet the reader. Language, which becomes the first shared experience between the reader and the novel's population, snatches the reader just as the slaves were snatched, from one place to another, with no preparation and no defence. Morrison wants the readers to experience as much as possible being there as the characters were, 'without comfort and succour from the "author", with only imagination, intelligence and necessity available for the journey' (Morrison 1989, p.33).

The reader not only accompanies the characters on their journey, she is drawn into a participatory interaction with the text, where her experienced imaginary is reconfigured in relation to possible new worlds, through the text. As Bernard Harrison argues, literature contains the 'dangerous power to move and change us'. The signs that constitute the text shift and change so that 'not the world but our perception of the possibilities of the world changes' (Harrison 1991, p.4). Morrison's evocative prose style is linked to narrative strategies which (she says) are designed in *Beloved* (Morrison 1987b) to 'get out of the way', to pull the readers into a re-experience with the text, which combines that confrontation with the new with the always already there (Morrison 1989, p.33). Morrison talks about how her literature has to have holes and spaces in it through which the reader can come in. This kind of participation is what Ricoeur calls 'active' reading. The author writes as she reads, anticipating a response from the unknown reader, much as the reader will respond to literature, as a creative artist of that text.

My own experiences of reading Morrison's work have been transformative in a variety of ways. The novel was given to me at the birth of my daughter by a close African friend. I had historically discussed feminist issues with him, but it was through reading *Beloved*, Morrison's famous novel of slavery, that I actually had to confront a lot of my own racism as a white woman. The novel subsequently became a central book not just for me but for the whole of my MA literature group that same year at Sussex University. The way the novel moved us as readers and made us really examine our positions as critical readers of texts was lasting for many of us. Morrison's writing, as she intended, 'snatched, yanked' and threw us into territory that was new and startling. The book was shocking because we were so moved by the shared experience of being there with the novel's population but, at the same time, as white readers we were made acutely aware of our own historical culpability. The book forced us to deconstruct our whiteness.

My DPhil thesis set out to explore an alternative to the Lacanian phallus in the narrative terms of the mother–daughter plot. As I discussed at the beginning of this chapter, in the classical Oedipal model, whether this is read through Freud or Lacan, the linguistic or social law of the father determines the narrative meaningful self. The experiential stories of a more bodily unconscious remain repressed, outside culture and language. My doctoral studies turned to the analyst and philosopher Luce Irigaray to examine the historical contingency of the Oedipal myth and to explore how this myth repressed the bodily relation to the mother, along with other experiential stories; stories that could possibly reconfigure narrative in symbolic ways that are not phallic. My work at first turned to the writing and poetry of

Sylvia Plath, but I found her texts, although they were seeking an alternative to the phallic myth, ended up proving a Lacanian thesis.

It was only when I turned to Toni Morrison's work that I managed to find the alternative that I was looking for, and I used her text *Beloved* to re-write Lacan's symbolic, imaginary and real as narrative terms (Campbell 1994, 1997). In this sense I used fiction writing to read and critique theory. Of course, Morrison's work is not an isolated instance and other writers from her tradition could have been read in similar ways. What was important and transformative for me as a reader was the gradual awareness of how Morrison's work challenged and re-wrote a lot of classical and accepted psychoanalytic theory from the perspective of race. This book, therefore, is very important for me in my practice as an analytic psychotherapist and I read it to inform my work in the same way I would read philosophy or psychoanalytic theory. In fact, reading Morrison's writing has taught me the creative potential that reading literature provides or yields in my development as a therapist.

If psychoanalysis can be understood, like the act of reading, to constitute a dialogical narrative between the experiential body and the text, refiguring the self in terms of the world outside the text, then alternatives to Oedipal models of language and subjectivity can be found. Morrison's novel *Beloved* is written in a poetic lyrical form. The poetic image constantly disrupts the linear movement of narrative in this book in ways that foreground feelings and the body. Morrison's transformative bodily narrative, however, is not confined exclusively to women. Milkman in *Song of Solomon* and Paul D in *Beloved* are both examples of the different journeys male characters make that move them away from colonial and Oedipal configurations of masculinity to an identity which is more connected to black women and history. Neither is Morrison the only black woman novelist to offer alternative plot paradigms which displace universal Oedipal narratives. Writers such as Gloria Naylor, Alice Walker, Ntozake Shange and Toni Cade Barbara can be seen in different ways to explore positive and historical configurations of the mother/daughter relationship. Morrison's writing can, as an evocative object, transform us as readers in numerous ways. But the way we are moved as readers to construct textual meaning and new narrative selves is a re-negotiation of how we live and experience our bodies and our histories. Reading Morrison is not just an artistic interpretation of the literary text, it transforms us by re-figuring our situated relation to the world in which we live. For white readers, and the ethnocentric texts of psychoanalysis, the transformative effect of reading Morrison's writing is the acknowledgement, not just of new stories but of different symbolic narratives.

Conclusion

Post-structuralist literary theory has aligned the relationship between narrative and psychoanalysis in terms of Lacanian linguistic theory. As I have discussed, the Oedipal plots implicit in this theory of the unconscious and language privilege a structural organisation of the narrative text which does not allow creative licence or activity to the reader. Barthes opened up the text to the pleasures of reader reception theory, but the linguistic heritage of post-structuralist psychoanalysis has remained at odds with a more historically situated hermeneutics of reading. Object relations theory has historically been problematical for literary theory because of its designation of a real, ontologically fixed self, thereby harking back to the old humanist self who transcends both the literary text and all cultural context.

This chapter has re-read Christopher Bollas' theory of unconscious self experience in terms of a hermeneutics of reading. Ricoeur's dialogical account of reading argues for a transformative space between text and reader in which experiential selves, as bodily stories, are always already caught up in language as a pre-narrative structure and yet they continually displace and shift the secondary meaning of the text. Bollas' explanation of the psychic transformation of ourselves through significant objects can be re-framed in a narrative way, to explain our constructed selves through the interpretative act of reading. Although Bollas distinguishes between a mode of simple unconscious experience and a secondary, more representative, unconscious, I have argued for a dialogical relation between these two. Bollas' work can inform a phenomenology of reading, thereby lifting object relations theory out of its ontological rut of the real self and simultaneously re-writing (reconfiguring) the Oedipal script of post-structuralist narrative. Now, this does not correspond, in my mind, to a textual practice of psychoanalysis where the literary object exists as a primary stake and the relation to the real remains ineffable or impossible. We can avoid the twin pitfalls of a dogged structuralism negating everything but the text, and the over-psychologising of the author, by focusing on the dialogical tension that Ricoeur places between rhetoric and referent. Dialogical reading between experiential life stories and secondary narrative not only represents the experiential relation to the body, thus re-writing the text, but it also transforms and constructs our own narrative selves.

In Morrison's fiction, narrative reconfiguration of the reader's unspeakable stories entails a dialogical interplay between her/his experiential bodily self and the secondary order of symbolic narrative. Meaning is produced within the text but change also occurs within the reader. The narrative journey of the characters within these novels reflects our own transformative voyage as readers, not simply in relation to the text but to the possible worlds in negotiation with it. The interpretation of textual practice resides in this work between life stories and the secondary order of narrative; an exchange which is integral to the activity of literature and psychoanalysis. Psychoanalysis is important, then, for literary studies, not because of some master plot which reveals textual truth, or even a science of signs, but because its transference between sign and referent can help us to understand the dialogic relation between history, text and reader/critic.

As for the transformative role of reading, there is much potential both in the institution of literary studies and in the pedagogical task of teaching to recognise the therapeutic task of reading. The possibilities in terms of learning, knowledge and psychic re-creativity all make these ideas of transformative, interpretative reading a future concern for academics, teachers and therapists. Not forgetting, of course, the unspoken creative stories that reside in each of us, seeking the narratives we will read in order to elaborate our future selves.

References

Barthes, R. (1977) 'The death of the author.' In *Image, Music, Text*. Trans. S. Heath. New York: Hill & Wang and London: Fontana.

Bollas, C. (1987) *The Shadow of the Object: Psychoanalysis of the Unthought Known*. London: Free Association Press.

Bollas, C. (1989) *Forces of Destiny*. London: Free Association Press.

Bollas, C. (1993) *Being a Character: Psychoanalysis and Self Experience*. London: Routledge.

Brooks, P. (1994) *Psychoanalysis and Storytelling*. Oxford, UK and Cambridge, USA: Basil Blackwell.

Campbell, J. (1994) *The Mother as a Subject within the Writings of Psychoanalysis and Women's Literature*. DPhil Thesis, Sussex University.

Campbell, J. (1996) Images of the real: reading history and psychoanalysis in Toni Morrison's *Beloved*. *Women: A Cultural Review 7*, 2, 136–149.

Campbell, J. (1997) 'For Esme with love and squalor.' In J. Campbell and J. Harbord (ed) *Psychopolitics and Cultural Desires*. London: Taylor and Francis.

de Saussure, F. (1974) *Course in General Linguistics*. Trans. W. Baskin. London: Fontana/Collins.

Felman, S. (1980) 'To open the question.' In S. Felman (ed) *Literature and Psychoanalysis: The Question of Reading: Otherwise.* Baltimore, MD and London: Johns Hopkins University Press.

Harrison, B. (1991) *Inconvenient Fictions.* London: Yale University Press.

Hughes, T. (1985) 'Sylvia Plath and her journals.' In P. Alexander (ed) *Ariel Ascending.* New York: Harper & Row.

Kearney, R. and Rainwater, M. (eds) (1996) 'Introduction to Gadamer.' In *The Continental Philosophy Reader.* London: Routledge.

Lacan, J. (1977) *Ecrits: A Selection.* Trans. A. Sheridan. London: Tavistock.

Levi-Strauss, C. (1968) *Structural Anthropology.* Trans. C. Jacobsen and B.G. Schoepf. London: Allen Lane.

Lyotard, J.F. (1991) 'The dream-work does not think.' In A. Benjamin (ed) *The Lyotard Reader.* Basil Blackwell: Oxford.

Moi, T. (ed) (1986) *The Kristeva Reader.* Oxford: Basil Blackwell.

Morrison, T. (1987a) 'Site of memory.' In W. Zinsser (ed) *Inventing the Truth: The Art and Craft of Memoir.* Boston: Houghton-Mifflin.

Morrison, T. (1987b) *Beloved.* London: Chatto and Windus.

Morrison, T. (1989) 'Unspeakable things unspoken: the Afro-American presence in American literature.' *Michigan Quarterly Review 28*, 1, 31.

Morrison, T. (1992) *Playing in the Dark: Whiteness and the Literary Imagination.* London: Harvard University Press.

Ricoeur, P. (1991) 'Life: a story in search of a narrator.' In M.J. Valdes (ed) *A Ricoeur Reader.* London: Harvester Weatsheaf.

Williams, L.R. (1995) *Critical Desire: Psychoanalysis and the Literary Subject.* London and New York: Edward Arnold.

Woolf, V. (1985) *To the Lighthouse.* London: Grafton.

Further Reading

Brooks, P. (1995) 'Freud's master plot.' In S. Felman (ed) *Literature and Psychoanalysis: The Question of Reading: Otherwise.* Baltimore, MD and London: Johns Hopkins University Press.

CHAPTER 13

Autobiography and the Psychotherapeutic Process

Celia Hunt

Psychoanalysis is autobiography by other means.

Adam Phillips (1994)

Psychoanalysis or psychotherapy[1] are often referred to as the 'talking cure'. This chapter discusses whether autobiography can serve as the basis of what might be called a 'writing cure'.

One of the most striking similarities between the writing of autobiography and engaging in psychoanalysis is that both involve working with narratives of the self. It used to be believed that when we wrote autobiographically we were revealing or discovering the truth of the self. This belief is epitomised by Rousseau's opening resolve in his *Confessions* 'to set before my fellows the likeness of a man in all the truth of nature, and that man myself' (Rousseau 1782/1992, p.1).

In the twentieth century the idea that we can write the truth of the self has become problematical. Freud and psychoanalysis have shown us that what we take to be the truth of the self is often a lie; things we say about ourselves are often a means of diverting our own and others' attention from things we are hiding. Research into memory reveals that as much as we might strive for

---

1   In what follows I use 'psychoanalysis' and 'psychotherapy' interchangeably, on the assumption that psychotherapy is a less intense, and theoretically more catholic, version of psychoanalysis, involving fewer weekly sessions and often dispensing with the couch.

accuracy in remembering ourselves in the past, this may not be possible. As Ulric Neisser says, autobiographical remembering is a complex, many-layered procedure which involves:

> (1) actual past events and the *historical self* who participated in them; (2) those events as they were then experienced, including the individual's own *perceived self* at the time; (3) the *remembering self*, that is, the individual in the act of recalling those events on some later occasion; and (4) the *remembered self* constructed on that occasion. (Neisser 1994, p.2)

This means that: 'The self that is remembered today is not the historical self of yesterday, but only a reconstructed version', a mixture of fact and fiction, or even, on occasion, a complete fiction of our imagination (Neisser 1994, pp.6–8).

Post-structuralism has also highlighted the multiplicity of selves involved in speaking or writing about ourselves. As Roland Barthes says: '*who speaks* (in the narrative) is not *who writes* (in real life) and *who writes* is not *who is*' (Barthes 1982, p.283). Even before words are committed to the page, there is, as Derrida maintains, an essential and unbridgeable gap, *différence*, between the words we speak and the 'trace' written in the unconscious by society and history (Derrida 1978, pp.196–231). Therefore we cannot assume a mirroring of psyche and text; even when we are speaking or writing about ourselves in the present, we can only know ourselves at several removes.

Thus we are much more aware now that the moment we put pen to paper to write about ourselves, we are producing a kind of fiction. Autobiography's designation as fiction, however, does not imply that it has no validity as truth. For contemporary writers on autobiography, the autobiographical enterprise continues to be a quest for the truth of the self, but that truth is more in the nature of a subjective or personal truth rather than 'objective truth'. As Georges Gusdorf says: 'In autobiography the truth of facts is subordinate to the truth of the man' (Gusdorf 1980, p.43). And the truth of the man, and of course of the woman, will be a truth *in the present* rather than a truth in the past or a truth for all times, for the writing of autobiography is always done through the perspective of our present consciousness. As Janet Varner Gunn says: 'Autobiography, at the level of perspective, involves a certain mode of self-placing in relation to the autobiographer's past and from a particular standpoint in his or her present' (Gunn 1982, p.16). Indeed, as Paul John Eakin suggests, the present has a crucial role to play in *creating* our truth as well as in enabling us to discover it: '…autobiographical truth is not a fixed but an evolving content in an intricate process of self-discovery and self-creation' (Eakin 1985, p.3). This means that the only kind of truth which we can hope to find through autobiography is provisional and specific to the present moment, and will therefore change over time.

The idea that our truth is a kind of fluid and ever-changing fiction is also implicit in current thinking on the psychotherapeutic process. Freud himself was already aware of the possibility that many of the stories of the past which his patients told him were, in all likelihood, imaginary or fictional elaborations, and that it was these fictional elaborations which held hysterical symptoms in place. According to James Hillman, through the writing of his case studies Freud invented a new genre, somewhere between fiction writing and science (Hillman 1983, p.5), which Hillman calls the genre of 'therapeutic fictions' (p.13). These are not, however, fictions written by the patient, but the analyst's written version of the patient's story which has been created between them during the analysis: the patient and the analyst are 'two authors...collaborating in a mutual fiction of therapy, though conventionally only one of them will write it' (p.16).

The text here is literally a written document, and its content will, naturally, be more the analyst's version than the patient's. However, in current psychoanalytic thinking the idea of a written text is also used as a metaphor for the spoken content of the analytic relationship. Thus Spence: 'The patient's history is...a constantly changing story that the patient is writing and rewriting, together with the analyst, inside and outside the analytic hour' (Spence 1985, p.81). When a patient comes into therapy, she has a version of her story which she will tell the therapist. The patient is locked into a particular version of her past which is not working, so that she cannot make sense of her current life. The therapeutic process involves re-shaping or re-writing that story in collaboration with the therapist. Depending on the theoretical orientation of the therapist, whether he is Freudian, Jungian, Kleinian or whatever, he will interpret the patient's story according to the plot implicit in that orientation. For example, a Freudian will see the 'universal plot' of the Oedipus complex, and a good deal of attention will be paid to the relationship with the mother or the father. The patient may resist the therapist's version of her story; sometimes the new version will be no more healing than the original. Successful therapy 'is...a revisioning of the story into a more intelligent, more imaginative plot' (Hillman 1983, pp.17–18).

For some of those who regard psychotherapy as the revisioning of a story, the question of truth does not figure largely. For Adam Phillips, who adopts a post-structuralist approach, the 're-written' story of a patient is a more workable rather than a more true version of the one with which he came into therapy (Phillips 1993). For Peter Brooks, on the other hand, narrative truth is "true" insofar as it carries conviction' (Brooks 1994, p.60). Again, he is not talking about 'objective truth', although confusingly he uses the term 'historical truth' to denote a person's conviction that something is 'true to the *experience* of the past' though it may be 'the experience of fantasy…just as well as what we usually call fact' (emphasis added).[2] Nevertheless, for Brooks a narrative can be more true than less, and there can be 'faulty narratives' which stand in the way of self-understanding and the finding of meaning. Psychoanalysis or psychotherapy will not provide us with 'a final narrative truth…[but]…analyst and analysand work together dialogically in an effort to create…narratives that may achieve a provisional but crucial truth' (p.9).

It is clear from the above that there is a strong similarity between autobiography and psychotherapy in their central concern with fictional narratives of self and the personal or subjective nature of our own truths. There are, of course, also differences between autobiography and psychotherapy, some of which are explored by Adam Phillips in his essay 'The Telling of Selves'. Whilst acknowledging that autobiography and psychotherapy are both ways of telling the story of the self and that both deal in fictions, he concludes that they are very different, even opposite, activities. In psychoanalysis the story of the self has to be deconstructed, to become unreadable, in order to be read and interpreted. Autobiography, on the other hand, is a process of finding a shape for the story of the self, finding a beginning, a middle and an end (Phillips 1994, p.68). So whilst psychoanalysis aims at a sort of controlled fragmentation, autobiography seeks to impose order on the fragmentation. From this point of view,

---

2   Opinion is divided on what Freud meant by 'historical truth'. Freud's archaeological model (Freud 1938/1952) implied that there was a grain of truth in every memory, and psychoanalysis was seen as a 'science that retrieves genuine fragments from the past and constructs essentially valid scenarios of ancient events'(Neisser 1994, p.6). Donald Spence's book on *Narrative Truth and Historical Truth* (1982) sets out to counter Freud's idea of historical truth. Peter Brooks maintains, however, that Spence's opposition between 'historical truth' and 'narrative truth'is wrong. Referring to *Moses and Monotheism* (Freud 1937–9), Brooks says that Freud regarded historical truth as opposed to 'material truth' that is, 'truth substantiated by observable events or verifiable facts' and accorded 'historical truth' the same status as 'psychic truth', that is, 'that which is true for the subject, whether its origins be real or phantasmatic, that which belongs to his understanding of his own story' (Brooks 1994, p.74).

psychoanalysis could be seen as a prelude to autobiography – it would create the necessary conditions for the creation of a new story of the self through autobiography – but autobiography itself would not be a psychotherapeutic exercise (p.69).

Perhaps understandably, Phillips is assuming that autobiography means a published book about a person's life, written for a wide audience, whilst psychoanalysis is an unrecorded and private conversation between two people. He is also assuming that one does not set out to write autobiography with a view to curing oneself of psychological problems, whereas a person enters into psychoanalysis, if not for a cure, then at least for relief from debilitating symptoms. But is he right in these assumptions? Can one set out to write autobiographically, not primarily for publication (although this may be a by-product), but with the specific intention of trying to understand better one's psychological problems? And if so, what sort of autobiography would facilitate such an approach?

There has been, in recent years, a good deal of discussion of the possibility of incorporating the methods of psychoanalysis into the writing of autobiography, and thus making out of autobiography a means of self-analysis or 'autopsychography' (Sturrock 1993, p.258). The prevailing view, however, is that attempts to do so have not been successful. As Philippe Lejeune says: '…if the new 'psys' encourage the discovery and expression of the self…they have not, it seems, elaborated individual or collective methods that make use of writing' (Lejeune 1989, p.222). For Christine Downing, the problem lies in the conventional structure of autobiography: 'the usual chronologically ordered arrangement of outward events misses the point' (Downing 1977, p.212). For her, a psychoanalytically informed autobiography would take into account what Freud called 'primary process material', that is, the material deriving from the id, in the form of dreams, fictions and myths.

John Sturrock is also of the view that autobiography is hemmed in by the chronological model. This results, he says, in an end product which is a 'counterfeit integration of a random life into a convenient fiction' (Sturrock 1977, p.55). If autobiography is to provide a vehicle for therapeutic insight, it requires 'a revaluation less of the past than of the present, the moment of writing' (p.55). This could be done, he says, by adopting a thematic or free associative approach, and he holds up the example of Michel Leiris as 'the new model autobiographer'.

Leiris (1901–90) was an art critic, anthropologist and poet associated with the Surrealists who is best known for his autobiographies *L'Age d'homme* (1939) and *La Regle du Jeu* (1948–76). These he wrote using the technique of free association within a Freudian framework, with the aim of curing himself of problems of impotence and masochism which had not been relieved by psychoanalysis. In *L'Age d'homme* (ET *Manhood* 1992), Leiris takes as his focus a double portrait by Lucas Cranach the Elder of Lucretia and Judith, and the stories of these two women as reported by Livy and the Old Testament, respectively. Lucretia is the wife of a high-ranking Roman who is raped at knife-point by her husband's friend, a member of the Roman royal dynasty. The morning after the rape, Lucretia tells her husband and father what has happened and, overcome by the shame of it, stabs herself to death before their eyes. This act incites the Roman people to rebel against the royal dynasty, causing their downfall. Judith is a virtuous widow living in the city of Bethulia, which is under siege by the Assyrian army under the command of Holofernes. To save her people, Judith seduces Holofernes in his tent and, whilst he is in a drunken stupor, cuts off his head. With their general slaughtered, the Assyrians raise the siege and flee.

Common to these two stories is the theme of self-sacrifice in a great cause, a theme which underlies Leiris' project: in the 'great cause' of ridding himself of his emotional and sexual problems, he 'sacrifices' himself by revealing to the reader in great detail the most intimate secrets of his failed sex life and of the punishment he visits on himself for his failures, in the form of self-woundings and attempts at suicide. In line with Sturrock's call to 'revaluate the moment of writing', Leiris puts the emphasis not on past events themselves but on the language he chooses to describe them, 'concentrating on certain salient words or groups of words in the certainty that these will show themselves to be privileged points of entry into his past' (Sturrock 1977, p.58). Not only does he organise his volumes of autobiography by association of ideas (and sometimes of words) instead of by chronology, but he 'deliberately follows those networks of association which will cause him the greatest unease' (p.58).

This approach, however, fails to cure Leiris of his emotional and sexual problems. Sturrock's view is that this is because 'language is never the possession of any individual, so that to employ it is to be alienated from the self' (p.58). As language is one of the few media through which we *can* access the self, autobiography coming closest to bridging the gap, this does not make any sense as a reason for failure.

In my view there are several reasons why Leiris fails to cure himself through the autobiographical act. First, the idea of a cure is unrealistic; the more modest aim of gaining insight into his problems would have been more manageable. Second, he does not, at least in *Manhood*, take the necessary next step and analyse his writings from the psychoanalytic point of view; rather he indulges in a form of acting out. Third, if, as Sturrock suggests, the point of the exercise is to 'revaluate the present', then the psychoanalytic perspective that Leiris adopts is not the most appropriate. A strictly Freudian approach encourages a preoccupation with the past, with the *origins* of disorder rather than with trying to understand the mechanisms which hold the disorder in place in the present. It also makes sex and aggression the primary focus of exploration, which means that other relevant factors may be overlooked. Like an obedient Freudian analysand, Leiris sticks closely to the rules, showing us again and again how gruesome incidents in his innocent early life laid the foundation for his behaviour in adulthood. In so doing, he creates for himself not a way out of his dilemma, but an expression, albeit finely wrought, of his self-hate and self-disgust. As Susan Sontag says in her foreword to *Manhood*, the book is: '...a manual of abjection – anecdotes and fantasies and verbal associations and dreams set down in the tones of a man, partly anaesthetised, curiously fingering his own wounds' (Leiris 1992, p.viii).

A psychoanalytic theory which puts the emphasis on the present is that of Karen Horney (1885–1952). Whilst Freud's theory is *diachronic*, explaining the present in terms of the past, Horney's theory is *synchronic*, seeking to explain psychic phenomena in terms of their *function* within the present character structure. This does not mean that the past should be disregarded; the present character structure has evolved out of the past, but it has developed into an autonomous system with an inner logic of its own (Paris 1994, pp.120–21).

According to Horney, character disorder is the consequence, in the first instance, of difficult interpersonal relations in childhood. If conditions for healthy psychological development are in place within the family – unconditional positive regard, safety and a sense of belonging – the child will be able, through good object relations, to realise its potential, although the forms of self-realisation will be strongly influenced by the environment. More often than not, however, those conditions are not sufficiently in place and the child, feeling its individuality threatened, reacts by developing what Horney calls 'basic anxiety' and defences to cope with it. She identifies three main defences, which she calls 'moving against people', 'moving away from people' and 'moving towards people' (the pursuit of power, freedom and love). All of these defences involve a move away from self or 'alienation' from the 'real self' (Horney 1951, chapter 1).[3]

In the adult, Horney's defensive strategies become fully blown 'life solutions', of which there are three main kinds: the expansive, the resigned and the self-effacing, with the first subdividing into the narcissistic, the perfectionistic and the arrogant-vindictive solutions. Whilst all three tend to be present at any one time, one of these solutions will become dominant, thus providing a sense of identity and a modicum of security. However, the others do not disappear; they are merely repressed into the unconscious, where they continue to generate painful inner conflicts and new difficulties.

Whilst character disorder originates, according to Horney, in strategies to cope with difficult interpersonal relations in childhood, once this development is in train, intrapsychic factors become more important in terms of consolidating and integrating the chosen solution. Of central significance here is the development of what Horney calls the 'idealised image'. This she describes as 'a kind of artistic creation' which, through imagination, attributes to oneself the characteristics that are glorified by one's dominant solution (Horney 1945, p.104). The function of the idealised image is to provide a feeling of identity, as the development of an authentic sense of identity is inhibited by self-alienation and inner conflicts. It also provides substitute self-esteem, which is crucially important in view of the impossibility of generating genuine self-esteem where there is alienation from self. However, the fact that there are already inner conflicts between the life solutions arising out of the interpersonal strategies means that there will be conflicts within the idealised image, each aspect of the conflict imposing its own different demands or 'shoulds', as Horney calls them. Not only are these shoulds contradictory, they are also largely unrealistic and impossible to achieve. The failure to fulfil them results in an inner turning against oneself or, as Horney calls it, the forming of the idealised image's counterpart, the 'despised image'.

The shoulds are one aspect of what Horney calls the 'pride system', which is generated by the idealised image and its 'search for glory' (Horney 1951, chapter 1). Its other aspects are what she calls 'neurotic pride' and 'neurotic claims'. Because the idealised image is the source of substitute self-esteem,

---

3   See Hunt (1998) for a discussion of the given and created aspects of Horney's notion of 'real self'.

the drive to realise this image in reality, to become the idealised self, is very strong and generates intense pride in the characteristics of the idealised image. This pride, in turn, justifies the making of claims on others. In order to maintain the illusion that we are our idealised self, we have to live up to our shoulds and others must honour our claims. Failure to do so is likely to switch us into our despised image and the accompanying self-hate.

For Horney the task of therapy is to dismantle the pride system and to re-establish contact with the real self, thus setting healthy development in motion again. Horneyan analytic technique involves directing the patient's attention to the structure of the defence system. It aims to motivate the patient to fight the battle against the pride system by becoming aware of all the aspects of the defensive structures: '...his pride, his self-hate, his alienation from self, his conflicts, his particular solution – and the effect all these factors have on his human relations and his capacity for creative work' (Horney 1945, p.341). This is not an awareness of how these things operate in the abstract, but 'of the *specific* ways in which these factors operate within him and how *in concrete detail* they manifest themselves in his *particular* life, past and present' (p.342). This awareness is also not just intellectual knowledge but an emotional experiencing.[4]

A Horneyan approach to self-analytic autobiography would put the emphasis on using the writings to throw light on the present structure of the psyche, through increasing intellectual understanding and emotional experiencing of the defences in operation. How would one go about this? A brief consideration of the work of Bernard Paris, who for many years has been applying Horney's theory to literature, will help us to answer this question.

Paris' work is multi-faceted, but one of his main concerns is to throw light on the psychology of the author, primarily through an understanding of the author's relationship with his or her fictional characters. He focuses his attention exclusively on realist fiction, including the plays of Shakespeare and the major nineteenth century novels of writers such as Jane Austen (Paris 1978, 1991a, 1991b). Unlike many literary critics, he sees mimetic characters[5] as whole rather than partial human beings, as 'round characters'

4   This is a necessarily brief summary of Horney's theory. For further detail, see Hunt (1997a) and Paris (1994, Part V).

5   According to Scholes and Kellogg (1966), characters can be divided into 'mimetic', 'illustrative' and 'aesthetic'.

or 'creations inside a creation', as E.M. Forster called them (Paris 1997, p.8). He believes that, using Horneyan theory, they can be understood in terms of their inner motivations and defences, just as if they were real human beings with a life of their own. When they are so understood, it becomes clear that authors are faced with a dilemma. Either they have the choice of 'allowing their characters to come alive and kick the book to pieces', or of 'killing [them] by subordinating them to the main scheme of the work' (p.14). Most great realist authors, Paris says, remain true to their psychological intuitions and allow their characters to live out their lives at the expense of their creators' own intentions. However, this often leads to a conflict between character and plot, a conflict which can be particularly revealing of the author's psychology. Sometimes this conflict is discernible in the author's rhetorical treatment of the characters' experience (p.13). By rhetoric, Paris means 'the devices an author employs to influence readers' moral and intellectual responses to a character, their sympathy and antipathy, their emotional closeness or distance' (p.16). Whilst authors often have an intuitive grasp of their characters' psychology, they often misinterpret them. Horneyan analysis reveals that 'Writers tend to validate characters whose defensive strategies are similar to their own and to satirise those who have different solutions' (p.17).

Apart from conflicts between the characters and the author, Paris has also observed that there are often, in realist fiction, inconsistencies in the author's rhetoric itself. When reading Thackeray's *Vanity Fair* in the 1960s, he was puzzled by the thematic contradictions he observed there, and was reminded of a passage in Horney's *Our Inner Conflicts* which says that 'inconsistencies are as definite an indication of the presence of conflicts as a rise in body temperature is of physical disturbance' (Horney 1945, p.35; Paris 1997, p.4). By applying Horney's theory to novels such as *Vanity Fair*,[6] Paris began to see their thematic contradictions 'as parts of an intelligible structure of psychological conflict' of the author (p.5).

By interpreting psychologically both the mimetic characters themselves and the rhetoric surrounding them, Paris believes that it is possible to build up a picture of the *implied author* of an individual work and, by applying this analysis to the writer's *oeuvre* as a whole, to build up a picture of what he calls the 'authorial personality': 'When the rhetoric consistently glorifies

6   See Paris (1974) for his discussion of *Vanity Fair*

characters who embrace a particular solution while criticising those who have adopted others, it reveals the implied author's own defences, repressions and blind spots. In works where the rhetoric is inconsistent…it reveals the implied author's inner conflicts' (p.18).

Paris further believes that by psychoanalysing the implied authors of individual literary works and the authorial personality of a writer's *oeuvre*, using Horneyan theory, one can then go on to use the texts 'as a source of insight into the inner life of their creator' (p.18).[7]

The term 'implied author' was coined by Wayne Booth (Booth 1983, pp.67–77). As a writer writes, Booth says, he 'creates not simply an ideal, impersonal 'man in general' but an implied version of 'himself' that is different from the implied authors we meet in other men's work' (pp.70–71). For Booth this is an inevitable effect of fiction writing, for there is no such thing as a neutral presence in fiction. The author will always imbue the work with certain values, and the reader will create an image of the author on the basis of those values. They may not necessarily be identical with the values of the real life author. Indeed, an author may choose to imbue his work with a set of values which he specifically does not hold, for the sake of the overall effect. But it is the author who chooses these values, consciously or unconsciously, and who expresses them through the total form of the work. When we read, we 'infer [the implied author] as an ideal, literary, created version of the real man; he is the sum of his own choices' (pp.73–5). Thus the implied author of a work of fiction is not a straightforward representation of the real author; it is an expression, possibly an unconscious expression, of certain views or values of the real author which bind the work together into a completed artistic whole. Rimmon-Kenan refers to the implied author as 'a set of implicit norms' within the text, or 'the governing consciousness of the work as a whole' (Rimmon-Kenan 1983, p.86). 'Voiceless and silent,' the implied author is inferred and assembled, by the reader, as a *fictional construct* out of the components of the text (pp.87–8).

If we apply these considerations to autobiography, we could say that the implied author is a *fictional construct which embodies certain norms and values of the real author at the time of writing.* These values will not necessarily be those

---

7   There are many examples in Paris' work of how he goes about his analysis. The interested reader might usefully start with his latest book, *Imagined Human Beings* (1997).

which the author has consciously set out to express in the work, nor will they be his norms and values for all time; rather, they will be a projection, or externalisation, to use Horney's term, of aspects of the author's psyche into the text – the author's prevailing *personal fiction* containing elements of his *personal truth*.

If it is the case, as Paris suggests, that it is possible to gain insight into the inner life of the author by analysing the implied author of a work of fiction from the Horneyan point of view, then it should be similarly possible to analyse the implied author of our own autobiographical writings in order to gain insight into ourselves. For this purpose we would need to produce autobiographical writings suitable for a Horneyan analysis.

What sort of writings would these be? I would suggest that autobiographical writings most suitable for a Horneyan analysis would be more in the nature of autobiographical fiction than straightforward autobiography. We would use the techniques of mimetic fiction to create characters out of ourselves and other significant people in our lives. We would place these characters in a context, constructing short stories or a novel around them, or simply writing individual scenes.[8] In so doing, we would be looking to reveal the themes which preoccupy us in the present or which repeat themselves in our lives, the types of character whose behaviour we approve or disapprove, and the kinds of conflict which underlie our own rhetoric.

For this process of fictionalising from ourselves to be of value, it would be crucially important to allow our material to emerge as freely as possible, and our themes and characters based on ourselves to develop and take on a life of their own, even if we did not like what was emerging. In other words, we would need to make an 'agreement' with ourselves that we would try to be as 'truthful' as possible. Such an agreement would be in the nature of an 'autobiographical pact' of the kind which, according to Philippe Lejeune (1989, pp. 119–37), autobiographers implicitly make with their readers: that they are engaged in a sincere quest for truth, even though that truth may only be an approximation, or what I have called 'personal truth'. The autobiographical pact would provide us with a framework of honesty and truth-seeking, within which we would pursue our personal truth through the imagination – through primary process material, as Downing suggests –

8   One might use some such method as the 'objectifying the self' exercise discussed in Hunt (1997).

rather than through the literal facts of our lives. Having produced the writing, we would need to put it away for a period of time, in order to gain distance from it. In retrospect it is likely to be much easier to look at the writing from the more objective position of reader than of author[9], to construct our version of the implied author and the way it relates to the characters in the text, and to identify any conflicts within the rhetoric itself.

I have found the analysis from this point of view of my own (unpublished) novel *Stages* extremely useful. I have also used a Horneyan approach, in collaboration with a former student, 'Jane', to try to understand problems of identity which were interfering with her use of herself in her fiction writing (see Hunt 1998). A Horneyan approach can also work well with non-fictional writings, as Bernard Paris discovered when using it to analyse the writing of his PhD dissertation on George Eliot. When writing the dissertation, Paris believed that he had discovered in Eliot's Religion of Humanity 'the answer to the modern quest for values' and expounded her views 'with a proselytising zeal'. After completing the dissertation, however, he suddenly lost enthusiasm for this belief and could not understand why:

> Reading Karen Horney helped me to understand what had happened. Horney correlates belief systems with strategies of defence and observes that when our defences change, so does our philosophy of life. I had had great difficulty writing my dissertation, for reasons that therapy later made clear, and had frequently felt hopeless about completing the PhD. Faced with the frustration of my academic ambitions, I found George Eliot's Religion of Humanity to be exactly what I needed: we give meaning to our lives by living for others rather than for ourselves. But when I finished my dissertation and was told that it ought to be published (Paris, 1965), I could once again dream of a glorious career. Since I no longer needed to live for others in order to give meaning to my life, George Eliot's philosophy lost its appeal. In Horneyan terms, my inability to write my dissertation forced me to abandon my expansive ambitions and to become self-effacing, but on triumphantly completing it, I became expansive once more, and George Eliot's ideas left me cold. (Paris 1997, pp.3–4)[10]

---

9   There are clearly complicating questions here, which are outside the scope of this chapter, of the relationship between the reader and the text.

10   See also Rancour-Lafferiere (1994) for a discussion of self-analysis in literary study.

If Michel Leiris had reflected on *Manhood* from the Horneyan point of view, and had focused his attention on the 'philosophy of life' implicit in its pages, he might well have succeeded in increasing his self-understanding, for on close reading there is a discernible inconsistency in the rhetoric of the implied author. Whilst his stated aim is to cure himself of his obsessions, it is also clear that the 'great cause' of his writing is not cure, but self-glorification. This is strikingly demonstrated in his important 'Afterword', which reflects on the writing of the book (Leiris 1992, pp.153–64). Here, as also in the chapter on 'Lucrece' (pp.37–42), Leiris compares the autobiographer to the matador. The matador, to his mind, is a species of priest engaged in a ritual sacrifice; or he is a hero in a mythical drama who masters and kills the beast. Whilst he is the sacrificer, he is 'constantly threatened with death', which makes the sacrifice 'more valid than any strictly religious sacrifice' (p.38). Rather than being a mere '*littérateur*', Leiris wants to be like the matador 'who transforms danger into an occasion to be more brilliant than ever' (p.155). Just as the matador performs his ritualised movements, risking his life for the glory of the kill, so the autobiographer, or at least *this* autobiographer, risks his life by self-exposure, raising himself up in his imagination into a glorious being. When Leiris writes, he can feel like the bullfighter, courageous and virile, strutting his manhood in the public arena to great acclaim: he becomes his idealised, expansive self. This, however, involves the sacrifice of the impotent, tortured person he actually is, the person whom his idealised self despises. 'When I go to a bullfight,' he tells us, 'I tend to identify myself with either the bull at the moment the sword is plunged into its body, or with the matador who risks being killed (perhaps emasculated?) by a thrust of the horn at the very moment when he most clearly affirms his virility' (p.42). Leiris is both matador and bull, sacrificer and victim, virile and emasculated, his glorious imaginary self and his despised actual self. His writing is simultaneously a self-sacrifice and an act of great courage which gives him the sense of identity and self-esteem he so badly needs. This self-esteem, however, only lasts as long as he goes on writing. So write he does: as Sturrock tells us, Leiris' autobiographical quest occupied him for 50 years (Sturrock 1993, p.262). For Leiris to have gained therapeutic insight into himself from his writings, he would have had to put some distance between himself and the work and to ask himself what *function* it was fulfilling. This he could not do; for as long as the writing was providing him with a means of raising himself above his self-hate, he had a vested interest in keeping his obsessions – the raw material of his writing – in place.

A Horneyan approach to self-analytical autobiography, through an analysis of the implied author of our own writings, can help us to gain insight into our dominant defensive solutions and the way they affect our lives. This is not to suggest that on their own they can effect a cure. Like many psychoanalysts, Karen Horney was not optimistic about the possibilities for self-analysis conducted in isolation. In her book on this topic (Horney 1942) which discusses the case of Clare, a woman entrapped in an extreme form of the self-effacing solution which Horney calls 'morbid dependency'[11], she suggests that self-analysis is best undertaken *in conjunction with psychoanalysis*. After her psychoanalysis, Clare continues to work on herself through writing self-analytic reflections, and occasionally returns to see her therapist to discuss her progress. I would suggest that something of this nature, where the risks of self-exploration are contained within a therapeutic framework, might be possible using the approach I have outlined above. Alternatively, writing might be used during breaks in therapy, when, for example, the therapist or the patient is away on holiday.

It may also be possible, within the framework of an eclectic approach to psychotherapy which puts the emphasis on the present configuration of the personality rather than on retrieving the past, to suggest to patients that they engage in creative writing between sessions. The resulting work might be used as a basis for analysis between patient and therapist or for interpretation by the therapist. This would clearly not be a technique one could use with all patients, as they would need to have some knowledge of the methods of fiction writing. One would also need to bear in mind the importance of distance in gaining a useful perspective on the writing.

The above discussion, then, indicates that autobiography which involves fictionalising from self, whilst not on its own constituting a 'writing cure', can be a valuable tool in guided self-analysis or self-therapy, or within a psychoanalytic or psychotherapeutic setting, when approached from the Horneyan point of view.

11   Bernard Paris suggests that the case of 'Clare' is a disguised account of Horney's own problems (Paris 1994, p.xxiii–xxiv).

References

Barthes, R. (1982) 'An introduction to the structural analysis of narrative.' In S. Sontag (ed) *A Barthes Reader*. London: Jonathan Cape.

Booth, W. (1983) *The Rhetoric of Fiction*, 2nd edn. London: Penguin.

Brooks, P. (1994) *Psychoanalysis and Storytelling*. London: Blackwell.

Derrida, J. (1978) *Writing and Difference*. Chicago: University of Chicago Press.

Downing, C. (1977) 'Re-visioning autobiography: the bequest of Freud and Jung.' *Soundings 60*, 210–228.

Eakin, P.J. (1985) *Fictions of the Self: Studies in the Art of Self-Invention*. Princeton, NJ: Princeton University Press.

Freud, S. (1938/1952) 'Constructions in analysis.' In J. Strachey (ed) *Collected Papers of Sigmund Freud Vol. V*. London: Hogarth Press, pp.358–371.

Freud, S. (1937–9) *Moses and Monotheism: Three Essays*. J. Stratchey and A. Freud (eds) Standard Edition of Complete Psychological Works of Sigmund Freud Vol. 23. London: Hogarth Press, pp.3–137.

Gunn, J.V. (1982) *Autobiography: Toward a Poetics of Experience*. Philadelphia: University of Pennsylvania Press.

Gusdorf, G. (1980) 'The conditions and limits of autobiography.' In J. Olney (ed) *Autobiography: Essays Theoretical and Critical*. Princeton NJ: Princeton University Press.

Hillman, J. (1983) *Healing Fictions*. Woodstock, CT: Spring Publications.

Horney, K. (1942) *Self Analysis*. New York: Norton.

Horney, K. (1945) *Our Inner Conflicts*. New York: Norton.

Horney, K. (1951) *Neurosis and Human Growth: The Struggle Toward Self-Realisation*. London: Routledge and Kegan Paul.

Hunt, C. (1997) 'Finding a voice – exploring the self: autobiography and imagination in a writing apprenticeship.' *Auto/Biography 1*, 3, 169–179..

Hunt, C. (1998) 'Creative writing and problems of identity: a Horneyan perspective.' In J. Campbell and J. Harbord (eds) *Psycho-Politics and Cultural Desires*. London: Taylor and Francis.

Leiris, M. (1939) *L'Age d'Homme*. Paris: Éditions Gallimard.

Leiris, M. (1948–76) *La Regle du Jeu*. 4 Vols. Paris: Éditions Gallimard.

Leiris, M. (1992) *Manhood*. Trans. R. Howard. Chicago and London: University of Chicago Press.

Lejeune, P. (1989) *On Autobiography*. Minneapolis: University of Minnesota Press.

Neisser, U. (1994) 'Self-narratives: true and false.' In U. Neisser and R. Fivush (eds) *The Remembering Self*. Cambridge: Cambridge University Press.

Paris, B. (1965) *Experiments in Life: George Eliot's Quest for Values*. Detroit: Wayne State University Press.

Paris, B. (1974) *A Psychological Approach to Fiction: Studies in Thackeray, Stendhal, George Eliot, Dostoevsky, and Conrad*. Bloomington: Indiana University Press.

Paris, B. (1978) *Character and Conflict in Jane Austen's Novels: A Psychological Approach*. Detroit: Wayne State University Press.

Paris, B. (1991a) *Bargains with Fate: Psychological Crises and Conflicts in Shakespeare and His Plays*. New York: Plenum Press.

Paris, B. (1991b) *Character as a Subversive Force in Shakespeare: The History and Roman Plays*. Rutherford, NJ: Fairleigh Dickinson University Press.

Paris, B. (1994) *Karen Horney: A Psychoanalyst's Search for Self Understanding*. New Haven and London: Yale University Press.

Paris, B. (1997) *Imagined Human Beings: A Psychological Approach to Character and Conflict in Literature*. New York: New York University Press.

Phillips, A. (1993) *On Kissing, Tickling and Being Bored*. London: Faber and Faber.

Phillips, A. (1994) 'The telling of selves.' In *On Flirtation*. London: Faber and Faber.

Rancour-Laferriere, D. (ed) (1994) *Self-Analysis in Literary Study: Exploring Hidden Agendas*. New York: New York University Press.

Rimmon-Kenan, S. (1983) *Narrative Fiction: Contemporary Poetics*. London: Methuen.

Rousseau, J.-J. (1782/1992) *Confessions*. New York: Alfred A. Knopf.

Scholes, R. and Kellogg, R. (1966) *The Nature of Narrative*. New York: Oxford University Press.

Spence, D. (1982) *Narrative Truth and Historical Truth: Meaning and Interpretation in Psychoanalysis*. New York: Norton.

Spence, D. (1985) 'Roy Schafer: searching for the native tongue.' In J. Reppen (ed) *Beyond Freud: A Study of Modern Psychoanalytic Theorists*. Hillsdale, NJ: Analytic Press, pp.61–82.

Sturrock, J. (1977) 'The new model autobiographer.' *New Literary History 9*, 51–63.

Sturrock. J. (1993) *The Language of Autobiography: Studies in the First Person Singular*. Cambridge: Cambridge University Press.

CHAPTER 14

Towards a Writing Therapy?
Implications of Existing Practice and Theory

Fiona Sampson and Celia Hunt

The previous chapters, which have looked at existing theories and practices of creative writing and personal development, present a remarkable range of viewpoints and experiences. These include the ideas of poets and counsellors, academics and people with learning disabilities. The result has been, we hope, loosely to model the contemporary field of creative writing and personal development. Our contributors' model is rich and multi-dimensional, in part because of the diversity of current activity and in part because we have deliberately juxtaposed representative viewpoints from across the range. These mark out some of the field's present scope and potential for future developments. They also indicate some of the directions in which the field is liable to dissent and some contradictory developments.

What, then, does this contemporary model show us? We can see that writing practices linked with personal development can be carried out in a variety of contexts. They may form part of a therapeutic intervention in the writer's life, or may take place in a health or social care context, where they represent a significant opportunity for the participant to reflect on or celebrate his individuality. The link with personal development may be deliberately or accidentally made by an individual engaged in her own professional or amateur writing practice. Such links have been made by writers and philosophers since before the time of Christ; and have produced literary classics from *The Consolation of Philosophy* (Boethius 1969) to *To the Lighthouse* (Woolf 1927).

Writing and personal development is, in other words, a field of practice which is polyvalent, fluid and maleable. How, then, can we attempt to stabilise that which is not only itself discursively plural but in which – since development is always a form of change – every single constituent practical process and textual product necessarily destabilises its own set of expectations? This would suggest that it is impossible to identify any certainties from which to proceed.

One answer to this problem is of course that not every account of writing and personal development is also an *example* of it. The various discourses which observe links between writing and personal development are sufficiently stable to engage in debate with each other. For example, close critical reading – of, say, the autobiographies and novels of Janet Frame – can speak to the lengthy debate on Freud's *Interpretation of Dreams* (1976). The diary kept by a student of creative writing can cite and be cited by a Foucauldian analysis of discursive transgression and innovation. Some contributors to the present volume would embrace this potential for theoretical discursive plurality as peculiarly apt for a field in which many practices value increased participation by writers with diverse textual identities.

Others, however, would regret any theoretical appropriation of what they see as an essentially practical field in which the role of participant, as reader or more usually writer, is given unusual prominence: is indeed often enlarged to include individuals hitherto uninvolved in any writing practices. To some extent this regret also represents a struggle for clarity. Workers of all kinds in the field are understandably eager to define what it is that they are involved in.

It's here that this chapter can make a contribution. Several major questions block the way, however. Is it possible to speak of the field as a whole? Even if it is, can we predict which way the field as a whole will develop? And should we attempt to propose appropriate lines of development? Our chapter must proceed from some common denominator on which everyone in the field can agree.

Some ideas about 'benefit'

Although not all participants embrace our term 'writing and personal development', it's one we have chosen to identify the field's defining features. We should therefore start our search for the elusive common denominator by briefly unpacking this term.

By 'writing' we mean what is generally called 'creative writing', rather than, for example, report writing or clinical notes. Such 'creative writing' includes imaginative or literary writing across the genres, from drama to poetry, including literary travel writing, autobiography and *belles lettres* as well as fiction. It does not include the related practices of story-telling or reminiscence as such, though it often shares their aims. This is a field which explores the role of the personal textual artefact, primarily in its writer's life, although we shall discuss therapeutic reading practices below.

The 'and' of our definition is important too. It indicates a field composed of practices which *explicitly link* personal development with creative writing, whether in their process or their product. What, then, do we mean by 'personal development'? This familiar term is slippery from being used to designate so many disparate practices. We take it to indicate any process of beneficial self-reflexive change which an individual chooses to undertake. This does not include, for example, momentary insight, although that may subsequently give rise to change; nor does it include harmful self-reflexive changes such as those undertaken by someone in the grip of anorexia nervosa. It does include practices which develop personal confidence as well as obviously self-exploratory work. Of course, there are difficulties with this. For example, it is possible to argue that a writer might produce a best-seller in order to enhance his confidence and feelings of self-worth. And there are novels, such as Charles Dickens' *David Copperfield*, which though clearly autobiographical do not in themselves constitute proof that they have excited change in the author. However, these difficulties are overcome when we propose that any element of personal development in the writing practice must be overt rather than the object of speculation.

However, as previous chapters have demonstrated, the field of writing and personal development is not unanimous on the principle of benefit. In the work of a trained counsellor such as Cheryl Moscowitz, 'benefit' can be taken to mean a degree of clearly therapeutic transformation of the writing client's self. Jan Campbell records the beneficial insights into their own limited cultural awareness which she and members of a student seminar gained from studying Toni Morrison's *Beloved* (1994). John Killick shows how recording what people with dementia have to say can confuse or upset some participants and their families, yet be highly valued by others.

Most profoundly, the field is composed of fundamentally differing approaches to the question of benefit. We can model these as three sub-divided strands:

1. *'Literary' or product-oriented work:*

    - writing which gives rise to therapeutic gain by default rather than design, such as when a novelist rediscovers his own experiences of loss while writing on the subject

    - writing which consciously uses self-exploration to produce a literary work. Blake Morrison's *And When Did You Last See Your Father?* (1990) is a carefully constructed and powerful story of loss.

2. *'Writerly' or process-oriented work:*

    - the practice of writing *qua* art whose practice seems beneficial. An example might be the adolescent writing lyrics about unrequited love in order to 'feel better'

    - writing formulated as a therapeutic art activity, including the use of self-help writing and personal development books and, in particular, the work of facilitating writers who do not have training in personal development.

3. *Therapeutic work incorporating writing and oriented around the textuality of the self:*

    - existing counselling, therapy and care practices in which professionals, from occupational therapists to psychotherapists, use writing as one of their methods of delivering therapy

    - forms of therapy which are largely or wholly based on the literary arts: for example, poetry therapy and narrative therapy.

'Literary', product-oriented practices focus on the quality of the product. They use literary criteria – in the broadest sense, from commercial viability to formal technique – to measure benefit. Crafting is important, as is potential publication. The writing may be carried out by distinguished and unknown writers working in isolation or in the context of writers' groups and creative writing courses.

On the other hand, many of the activities which we identify as 'writerly' or process-led are facilitated by practitioners with special experience in this area. Their emphasis is on the writing process, but for many participants the facilitator's skill-sharing and/or the display or publication of an end product are important too. This balance between writing as an art and the demands of personal development can be aligned in a variety of ways. Because it entails seeing benefits as a mixture of the artistic and of personal development gains, it can lead to difficult claims, such as for an automatic link between self-revelation and style. Particularly significant here is the model of a 'therapeutic arts activity', developed by the Hospital Arts to indicate an arts activity which is led by an arts professional rather than a therapist and which is introduced into a care context specifically because it is felt to benefit clients in ways related to such care aims. These might include raising morale or contributing to a culture of self-reflection.[1]

Therapeutic arts activities differ from arts therapies, which are led by professional art, music or drama therapists (for example). Arts therapies are supported by a framework which offers firm theoretical foundations for every procedure. Characteristic too are formal interpretative agendas of the work produced. In the third strand of our model, a writing therapy on these lines would see the literary quality of the writing as purely instrumental to therapeutic benefits. Where the traditionally 'talking' therapies already use writing, it can serve as an extension of the textual nature of the therapeutic encounter. As Celia points out in her chapter on 'Autobiography and the Psychotherapeutic Process', client and therapist are engaged in 'writing' the client's story. Benefits here may include reconfiguring the client's relationship with his own self.

Despite the varied picture this tripartite model presents, the field of writing and personal development does have one common view of benefit, which is to exclude that which harms, limits or compromises the participant. In practice it isn't possible to guarantee that one writing group participant will be able to cope with another's latent competitiveness. Nor is it possible to guarantee that no one reads A. Alvarez's *The Savage God* at the point in a depression when thinking about suicide might be a final incitement to the act (Alvarez 1971). However, it *is* possible to define good practice as that which *intentionally* avoids any perceived harm to participants.

This is a common denominator of theory as well as of practice. If writing and personal development is a field which is by definition guided by the effects – the benefits – of participation, it must be a matter of moral, and also intellectual, principle for the practice to be guided by the importance of

---

1   For a brief history of the Hospital Arts movement in Britain, see Senior and Croall (1993, pp.8–15).

avoiding harm. We suggest this means that the field must adopt a *primarily* ethical approach to its practices and in its thinking. It is pre-eminently important for emerging techniques and discourses to develop within appropriate ethical frameworks.

Towards some ethical frameworks

How can practitioners identify appropriate ethical codes for practices they have not yet fully defined? There are several answers to this, all of which depend on the necessity to proceed with caution. Much writing and personal development work takes place in a health or social care context in which such codes already exist. This work must adopt the ethical framework within which it has been placed if it is not to undermine such care practice. Writers are brought in to supplement existing provision rather than to destabilise it. Most importantly, the ethical codes which govern the running of a social services day centre or an orthopaedic ward have been developed over decades by highly experienced professionals. It will be a long time before the field of writing and personal development has equivalent expertise which will allow it to press the case for variations in these codes, although research developments will be an important contributing factor here. For example, Davies (1997) indicates that writers working in mental health care place less value on having an ethical code to work to than do occupational therapists running writing groups in similar settings.

For these and other trained therapists using writing practices in their work, the necessary ethical context is already part of their professional practice. This context will differ from that of Cheryl Moscowitz's counselling work, for example. Although we don't want to pre-empt future ethical codes for writing and personal development activities, some common areas of ethical concern in care practices will plainly be relevant here. We can loosely group these around certain key areas, such as the rights, dignity and well-being of participants. They include specific issues such as confidentiality, respect for the authority of what has been written, and the client's right to receive input from workers with appropriate skills. For example, a participant has the right not to expect therapeutic claims to be made by an untrained writer.

Counsellors and therapists practising in this field have training and professional ethical guidelines which enable them to initiate such therapeutic strategies as a risky catharsis, or the recommendation that their client attend a writing session rather than a stress management course. But what training is available for the practitioner without any such transferable skills? Although some specialist training is available – for example, a Postgraduate Diploma at the University of Sussex studies the links between creative writing and personal development; and in west Wales, Artscare, a therapeutic and community arts charity, provides seminar training days for writer practitioners – these do not produce fully trained practitioners.[2] Expertise is at present a matter of thoughtful experience. Until a rich ethical code – which identifies the aims of writing and personal development practice, the rights of participants and the duties and rights of practitioners, as well as applying them in ethical procedures – has been established, practitioners will have to continue taking their ethical lead from the context in which they find themselves.

Some practices, however, take place outside both a professional care context and the context of the practitioner's own training. We aren't talking here about work undertaken by individuals working alone, where context and expectation are both transparent to the writer. Rather, we're thinking of writing and personal development practitioners working with voluntary sector groups or even setting up private courses. Here it must be important to proceed cautiously and by analogy. In the absence of professional codes of his own, we suggest that the practitioner must work with one that is borrowed. Such a code should be borrowed from an arguably analogous practice, such as occupational therapy or music therapy, although any limitations of the analogy must be borne in mind (music therapists are also highly trained).

Adopting an ethical code may mean limiting the role of the writing practitioner to responsibilities for which they have appropriate skills. But it can also enhance that role. For example, a writer working to the code of a health care unit may well find herself receiving the detailed support and debriefing which supervision provides. It's also important to remember that adopting context-appropriate ethical codes does not necessarily mean fully endorsing the contexts in which participants find themselves. A writer working in one of the former long-stay psychiatric hospitals might have

2   The Postgraduate Diploma in Creative Writing and Personal Development in the Department of Continuing Education of the University of Sussex was set up by Celia in 1996. In 1995 Graham Harthill and Fiona ran a series of training days for writers for Artscare/Gofal Celf in conjunction with Poetry and Healing Wales.

respected the referral decisions of the staff nurse on duty while privately anticipating the advent of community care. The opportunity to work with clients in ways which affirm their individual worth, and to bring that work into the central life of the care unit, is more clearly in line with the aims of writing and personal development than is displaying a – possibly ill-informed – personal attitude.

The role of research

We have linked a specific ethics of writing and personal development to the need for research into the character and benefits of writing and personal development practice. Such research is beginning to develop. In keeping with the character of the field as a whole, however, it is being carried on in an often fragmentary fashion across a series of disciplines.

Of interest for personal development which takes place in the course of producing 'literary' writing is theoretical work on the relationship between writers and their texts which calls upon issues of personal development. For example, Paul John Eakin (1985) makes a case for autobiographical writing as a necessary second stage in the creation of the self through language, the first stage being the moment of language acquisition in childhood; while Liz Stanley's highly influential work on *The Autobiographical I* (1981) helps us to think, amongst other things, about the fluid and fragmentary nature of selves and about autobiographical writings as temporary containers which encapsulate and embody these selves in the moment of writing.[3] Chandler (1990) stresses the cathartic role of form and crafting in autobiography.

Although work on life histories does not fall strictly within our field, its concerns with personal development through language – such as work by Hoar *et al.* (1994) on the links between language, education and identity – are relevant here. Relevant too are attempts to reconstruct the experience of the author from her text, such as Jacqueline Rose's *The Haunting of Sylvia Plath* (1991) in which psychoanalysis meets literary biography, or the earlier literary New Historicist movement. This kind of literary criticism

---

3   *Auto/Biography*, the journal of the Auto/Biographical Study Group of the British Sociological Association, edited by Liz Stanley, occasionally publishes articles on research into the personal development component of autobiography. (See, for example, Bastable (1995).)

problematises the writing process and authorial identity in its search for a 'truth' at the heart of the text.

The growing number of popular self-help books which link writing practices with personal development are aimed at individuals working alone, as well as suggesting techniques which may be used in writing workshops. Recent examples include Jackowska (1997) and Killick and Schneider (1998). These useful aids to thinking about writing which is carried out for personal development ends are not, however, research into the basis for such practices. Some work which attempts to theorise what goes on in these practices and why is, however, underway. Hunt (1998) explores the personal development component of a creative writing course on 'Autobiography and the Imagination', while Utting (1997) reads the processes and products of a writing class in personal development terms.

Harthill (1994) moves research in this area forward to look at principles of practice in his paper on the important regulatory mechanisms of evaluation. Since practitioners often enter this field without relevant experience or training, defining the sorts of skills which are needed and the forms which training should take will be crucial for the development of this area of practice. Davies (1997) and Sampson (1998) draw our attention to the importance of understanding the potentially fraught relationship between the writing and personal development practitioner and other professionals such as health carers and social workers.

All this though must be underpinned by a conceptual framework which will eventually be rich enough to interpret what goes on in the practice and why (Sampson 1997a, 1997b, 1998). Some quantitative and qualitative research into the benefits of creative writing, particularly poetry, in a health care context has already been carried out with a view to making a case for health service funding (Harthill and Sampson 1996; Philipp 1996). In 1996 a working party was set up by Sir Kenneth Calman, the Chief Medical Officer, to look at ways in which the arts, including creative writing, might be more extensively used in the National Health Service.

These initiatives still beg the question of the basis for a writing therapy. We do not advocate a future therapy as the only way forward for the field. However, we do reiterate our suggestion, made in the Introduction, that unless the case can be made for such a therapy, the case for other writing and personal development practices is seriously weakened. For if we can argue strongly that creative writing may produce personal development benefits, we must answer the challenge of why those benefits should not be formalised into a writing therapy.

Research is already underway in writing-related therapy activities which will help us work with this question. Of particular significance here is the growth in Britain of narrative counselling or therapy, usefully summarised in McLeod (1996). This derives from developments in social psychology, in particular Jerome Bruner's view that narrative is a way of knowing which is as important as the more familiar 'paradigmatic' approaches to experience: by which he means knowing based on abstract, theoretical models (Bruner 1986, pp.11–43). Much of the practice of narrative therapy takes its inspiration from the pioneering example of Michael White and David Epston, family therapists working at the Dulwich Centre in Adelaide, Australia, and at the Family Therapy Centre in Auckland, New Zealand. They advocate the technique of 're-authoring' – the telling and retelling by clients of their story – which may involve the exchange of letters between patient and therapist (White and Epston 1990).

Closer to creative writing is the technique sometimes suggested by personal construct therapists of 'self-characterisations' to facilitate the formulation of constructs and elements used in the therapy (Fransella and Dalton 1990). A detailed method of therapeutic diary writing is advocated by Ira Progoff. There is no overt intention here of creating a literary end project: the Progoff method relies on a special 'work-book' which is divided into different sections according to the different kinds of writing being done. However, some of the techniques encourage the use of symbols and metaphor for engaging with the self at a deeper level (Progoff 1975). Progoff method workshop leaders usually have therapeutic or counselling qualifications and have undergone special training in the use of Progoff techniques. Oral and written story-telling is advocated as a method of therapy by Alida Gersie, who draws on myths, folk tales and fairy stories to facilitate clients' creative story-making as a means of getting in deeper touch with life experiences (Gersie 1997; Gersie and King 1990).

The most fruitful model for a writing therapy is provided by poetry therapy, which has been well established in the United States for some 20 years. It draws its inspiration from J.J. Leedy and A. Lerner (Leedy 1969; Lerner 1978), and its practice is variously known as 'interactive bibliotherapy', reading therapy, literatherapy and narrative therapy (Mazza 1993, p.56). There is a National Association for Poetry Therapy, which has standards and procedures in place for Certified Poetry Therapists and

Registered Poetry Therapists (p.51). Techniques of poetry therapy include reading poems as sparking-off points for individual, family or group discussions, the writing of poems by individuals, couples, families or groups, and the analysis of metaphors and imagery arising from this writing. Poetry therapy is unique amongst the existing writing therapies in that it has a national organisation, with the ability to accredit practitioners and a programme of research. In particular it is concerned to determine what constitutes improvement and to evaluate methods of work.

We have mentioned the significance of proceeding by analogy in establishing ethical guidelines for this work. Analogy is useful, too, in suggesting how these diverse professional imperatives and initiatives may come together. The early history of the art therapies – art therapy, art psychotherapy and psychoanalytic art psychotherapy – shows a field of diverse practices which preceded those theories and ethical codes, the research and the training, which now underpin them. Waller (1991) surveys this history.

Conclusion

This book has indicated some of the excitement and diversity which informs the field of writing and personal development. Our final chapter has attempted to draw out some of the common themes that underlie this diversity in order to think through how these practices might continue to develop. Although we've highlighted the significance of responsible research, developed ethical codes and training, we cannot predict the many forms these developments will take.

Nevertheless, that writing and personal development will continue to expand, consolidate and develop in some form or other is made clear by present exponential rates of development. In 1988 there were around four committed practitioners in the UK. At the time of going to press, LAPIDUS, the professional organisation for the field, has around 100 members, many of whom are practitioners.

Beyond this, though, future developments – in research as well as practice – are implied as well as endorsed by the close relationship with ethical and reflexive theoretical work which practices in the field seem to be developing. There are many ways forward for writing and personal development and we anticipate them with interest and enthusiasm.

References

Alvarez, A. (1971) *The Savage God.* Harmondsworth: Penguin.

Bastable, M. (1995) 'Doing Lucie's stories and the fictionalysis.' *Auto/Biography 4*, 1, 35–49.

Boethius (1969) *The Consolation of Philosophy.* Trans. V.E. Watts. London: Penguin Books.

Bruner, J. (1986) *Actual Minds, Possible Worlds.* Cambridge, MA and London: Harvard University Press.

Chandler, M.R. (1990) *A Healing Art: Regeneration through Autobiography.* New York and London: Garland Publishing.

Davies, C. (1997) *Occupational Therapy and the Visiting Writer: A Comparative Study of Attitudes to Facilitating Creative Writing Groups in Mental Health Settings.* Unpublished dissertation for the Postgraduate Diploma in Writing and Personal Development, University of Sussex (pp.5, 34).

Dickens, C. (1992) *David Copperfield.* Harlow, Essex: Addison Wesley Longmans.

Eakin, P.J. (1985) *Fictions of the Self: Studies in the Art of Self-Invention.* Princeton, NJ: Princeton University Press.

Freud, S. (1976) *The Interpretation of Dreams.* Trans. J. Strachey. Volume Four in The Pelican Freud Library. London: Penguin Books.

Fransella, A. and Dalton, P. (1990) *Personal Construct Counselling in Action.* London: Sage.

Gersie, A. (1997) *Reflections on Therapeutic Storymaking: The Use of Stories in Group.* London: Jessica Kingsley Publishers.

Gersie, A. and King, N. (1990) *Storymaking in Education and Therapy.* London: Jessica Kingsley Publishers.

Harthill, G. (1994) *Creative Writing: Towards a Framework for Evaluation.* Occasional Papers No. 4. Edinburgh: University of Edinburgh.

Harthill, G. and Sampson, F. (1996) *Report to the Poetry Society Project on Issues of Health, Healing and Personal Development.* Unpublished.

Hoar, M. *et al.* (1994) *Life Histories and Learning: Language, the Self and Education.* Brighton: University of Sussex.

Hunt, C. (1998) *The Use of Fictional Autobiography in Personal Development.* Unpublished thesis in progress for DPhil, University of Sussex.

Jackowska, N. (1997) *Write for Life.* Shaftesbury, Dorset: Element Books.

Killick, J. and Schneider, M. (1998) *Writing for Self-Discovery.* Shaftesbury, Dorset: Element Books.

Leedy, J.J. (ed) (1969) *Poetry Therapy.* Philadelphia: Lippincott.

Lerner, A. (ed) (1978) *Poetry in the Therapeutic Experience.* Elmsford, NY: Pergamon Press.

Mazza, N. (1993) 'Poetry therapy: toward a research agenda for the 1990s.' *The Arts in Psychotherapy 20*, 51–59.

McLeod, J. (1996) 'Working with narratives.' In I. Horton and J. Bimrose (eds) *New Directions in Counselling.* London: Routledge.

Morrison, B. (1994) *And When Did You Last See Your Father?* London: Granta Books.

Morrison, T. (1994) *Beloved.* London: Chatto and Windus.

Philipp, R. (1996) 'The links between poetry and healing.' *The Therapist 3*, 4, 15.

Progoff, I. (1975) *At a Journal Workshop: The Basic Text and Guide for Using the Intensive Journal*. New York: Dialogue House Library.

Rose, J. (1991) *The Haunting of Sylvia Plath*. London: Virago Press.

Sampson, F. (1997a) 'Some questions of identity: what is writing in health care?' In C. Kaye and T. Blee (eds) *The Arts in Health Care*. London: Jessica Kingsley Publishers.

Sampson, F. (1997b) 'Poetry and the position of weakness: some challenges of writing in health-care.' In V. Bertram (ed) *Kicking Daffodils: Twentieth Century Women Poets*. Edinburgh: Edinburgh University Press.

Sampson, F. (1998) *Towards a Theoretical Foundation for Writing in Health Care*. Unpublished thesis in progress for PhD, University of London.

Senior, P. and Croall, J. (1993) *Helping to Heal: The Arts in Health Care*. London: Calouste Gulbenkian Foundation.

Stanley, L. (1991) *The Autobiographical I*. Manchester: Manchester University Press.

Utting, S. (1997) *The Craft of Writing – a Skill for Life: Creative Writing and Personal Development in the Non-Specialist Writing Group*. Unpublished dissertation for the Post-graduate Diploma in Creative Writing and Personal Development.

Waller, D. (1991) *Becoming a Profession: The History of Art Therapy in Britain 1940–82*. London: Routledge.

White, M. and Epston, D. (1990) *Narrative Means to Therapeutic Ends*. New York: W.W.Norton.

Woolf, V. (1927) *To the Lighthouse*. London: Hogarth Press.

work throughout a District Health Authority, for the Isle of Wight Health Authority. Other long-term residencies have included Stone House Psychiatric Hospital, Dartford; Age Concern, Swindon; and Dyfed Probation Service. Awards for her poetry include the Newdigate Prize, a Southern Arts Writer's Award and a Residency at the Millay Colony in New York State. Her first collection, *Picasso's Men* (Phoenix Press), was published in 1994. She writes, and is engaged in doctoral research, on the theoretical foundations of writing in health care.

Mary Stuart is Assistant Director of the University of Sussex Centre for Continuing Education, where she is also Lecturer in Social and Cultural Studies. She is the author of articles on the use of life histories in further education and is particularly concerned with providing access to higher education for those previously excluded, such as adults with learning disability, slow learners and working-class women.

Subject Index

abandonment 125
Age Concern, Thamesdown 72
Althusser, Louis 143
Alzheimer's disease 105, 108, 131
Alvarez, A. 202
anima/animus 38
Anthony, Saint 122
Anthropologist on Mars, An 109
anxiety 79, 82
anxiety, basic 187
Ariel 166
Arnold, Matthew 136
Artemis, Temple of 118
Artscare 204
Atkinson, Kate 154
Augustine, Saint 15, 118, 120–123
Austen, Jane 189
author implied 190, 191
author/character relationship 189–191
Autobiographical, The 205
autobiography
  birth of 120–123
  cultural context 15, 117–128
  fictional 9–12, 21–33
  historical context 15, 117–128
  psychotherapeutic process 181–196
  term coined 127
  theory of 17
autobiography, compared to psychoanalysis
  author values 191, 192
  autobiographical pact 192
  chronology 185, 186
  defensive strategies 188, 189, 193
  fictional narratives of self 181, 184
  fragmentation 184
  free association 186
  identity problems 193
  language emphasised 186
  multiplicity of selves 182
  psyche structure 189
  quest for truth 182, 183
  revisioning 183, 184
  self-analytic reflection 194, 195
  self-sacrifice 194, 186
autopsychography 185
Avon Foundation 132

Baelz, Professor Peter 81
Balzac, Honoré de 157
Barbara, Toni Cade 177
Barthes, Roland 157, 158, 164, 178, 182
Baudelaire, Charles Pierre 174
BBC Radio Four 64, 84
Behind the Scenes at the Museum 154
Being and Time 161
Beloved 16, 176, 177, 200
Belsey, Catherine 136
Billy Cotton's Bandshow 57
Boethius 198
Bollas, Christopher 172–174, 178
Booth, Wayne 191
brainstorming 36, 55
Britton, James 33
Brooks, Peter 166–168, 171, 184
Bruner, Jerome 207
Bunyan, John 122

Calman, Sir Kenneth 81, 206
Canetti, Elias 135
catchphrases 131
Cedars, Ryde, Isle of Wight 139
Chandler, M.R. 205
character creation 36, 39–40
character naming 41–43
character/author relationship 189–191
Cherwell Age Arts Project 130
Childhood 23, 25
Cixous, Hélène 133

collaborative writing 12–13, 47–61
collective consciousness 38
Community Arts 17
confession, sacrament of 124
Confessions (of J-J. Rousseau) 118, 124, 135, 181
Confessions (of Saint Augustine) 118, 120–123, 125–127
consciousness 119
Consolation of Philosophy, The 198
Conway, Martin 22
Corradi Fiumara, Gemma 135
Creative Writers and Day-Dreaming 35
Critical Practice 136
critical faculty hypertrophy 162
critical thought 118
Crompton, Richmal 103
Crossing the Bar 96

Daily Mail 91
Dante 51
David Copperfield 200
de Bergerac, Cyrano 137
de Saussure, Ferdinand 164
death 86
Death and Dying, On 101
Death of the Author 158, 159, 164
deconstructive suspicion 154
deferral 161
deformative experience 127
dementia 13–14, 71–72, 104–114
denial 156
depression 49, 79, 82, 84–86
Derrida, Jacques 148, 149, 161, 182
diachronic theory 187
diary writing 17
Dickens, Charles 200
discourse 147
discursive
  conflict 135–137
  participation 140

reification 137–141
survival 136
Donne, John 43
Down's syndrome 63
Downie, Professor Robin 81
Downing, Christine 185, 192
Dudley, Katie 88
Dulwich Centre, Adelaide 207
Dunn, Laura 159

Eakin, John Paul 22, 182, 183, 205
early memories
    episodic nature 22
    expansion through imagination 23
    formulation 23–28
    reconstructive dialogue 25–28
    sensual quality 23–25, 28
    shaped by present consciousness 28–32
    triggered by visual imagery 22
earnest insincerity 161
ego 38, 172
Elderly Severely Mentally Ill (ESMI) 131
Eliot, George 193
emotional engagement risks 33
enactment 155, 156
Enheduanna 41
Ephesus 118
Epston, David 207
ethical practice 17
exhibitionism 125
existential testimony 122

Family Therapy Centre, Auckland 207
Felman, Shosana 171
feminine unconscious 165
feminist linguistics 133
fiction, emotional access role 32–33
Finding a Voice – Exploring the Self 159

Finnegan's Wake 103
fits 84
Fonction et Champ de la Parole et du Langage en Psychanalyse 160, 161
formative experience 125, 127
Forster, E.M. 102, 190
Foucault, Michel 67, 143, 147, 148
Frame, Janet 199
Frankenstein 43
Freud, Sigmund 35, 38, 127, 162, 165, 168, 171, 172, 176, 181, 183–185, 199
Freudianism 183, 187

Gables Day Hospital, East Dyfed 139
Gadamer, Hans-Georg 166
Gellhorn, Martha 114
Gersie, Alida 207
Giddens, Anthony 143
Glamis Court Group Home, East Cowes, I.o.W.
Glebe House, Kidlington 130
Goffman, Erving 145
Gore Grange, New Milton 138
Green Fuse, The 73
Gunn, Janet Varner 182
Gusdorf, Georges 182

Hannay, Professor David 82
Harré, Rom 155
Harrison, Bernard 176
Haunting of Sylvia Plath, The 205
Healing Arts 76, 132, 139
healthcare, primary see primary healthcare
Heaney, Seamus 68, 137, 174
Hebraic parataxis 120, 121
Heidegger, Martin 132, 133, 137, 140, 161, 166
Hellenic hypotaxis 121
Heraclitus 15, 118

hermenuetic reader theory 166, 167, 178
hermenuetics 169, 178
Hesse, Herman 10, 18
Hillman, James 12, 14, 49, 52, 183
historicity of self 117
Hölderlin, Friedrich 133
Homer 119
Horney, Karen 16, 187–190, 192, 193, 195
Hospital Arts 202
Hughes, Ted 69–70, 166
humanism 164, 166

I Ching 60
id 38
identity and social experience 134–135
idiosyncratic insightfulness 139–140
illness, source of strength, creativity 47–48
imaging 40–41
Imperial War Museum (London) 101
Impressionist Painters 157
individuation and writing 117, 132–135
insincerity, earnestly expressed 161
Interpretation of Dreams 199
introspection 122
Iragaray, Luce 133, 176
Islecare 68
Ivanic, Roz 143, 147, 149–151

Jekyll (Dr.) and Hyde (Mr.), The Strange Case of 12, 37, 39, 43
Joyce, James 103
Jung, Carl Gustav 38, 49, 127
Jungianism 183

Keats, John 52, 137
Kids' Guide to Newport 70
Kitwood, Tom 108, 114
Kivy, Peter 157

Klein, Melanie 134
Kleinian theory 183
kleptomania 125
Kristeva, Julia 134, 137, 165
Kübler-Ross, Elizabeth 101
L'Age d'homme 186
L'Internelle Consolacion 160
LAPIDUS (Association for
    the Literary Arts in
    Personal Development)
    11, 208
La Regle du Jeu 186
Lacan, Jacques 134, 160,
    165, 166, 170–172,
    176–178
Lakeland Poets 135
Lambercier, Madame 125,
    126
language
    abstraction made concrete
        137–141
    authentically representing
        life 133
    determining individual
        experience 133–134
    ideological use 133
    and individual discursive
        space 15
    individually recognisable
        131, 137
    personal usage and creative
        writing role 132
    verbatim transcription
        129–131
Language of Self, The 160
Latin, classical 121
Lazarus 50–51
learning disability 13, 63–76
Leavisite criticism 164
Leedy, J.J. 207
Leiris, Michel 185–187, 194
Lejeune, Philippe 185, 192
Lerner, J. 207
Lethe 96
Levi-Strauss, Claude Gustav
    164
Lewis, Helen 146

linguistics 147, 148, 168,
    169, 171, 178
listening 55
literary archeology 175
literary theory 164–166,
    178
literature, transferral
    relationship with
    psychoanalysis 171
Livy 186
Lockhart, Russell 52
Lukàcs, György 157
Lyotard, Jean Francois 147,
    148, 169
Lyrical Ballads 134
MacCaig, Norman 40
MacNeice, Louis 159
Madness and Civilisation 67
Manhood 186, 187, 194
manic-depression 53
Marxist thought 133, 136
masochism 125
masturbation 125
McDougall, Joyce 44–45
Mead, George Herbert 144
mental health 13, 47–61
metaphor
    and the dying 94, 96
    fuel of poetry 53
    handled with ease 71
    heart as lead 120
    liberating mask 139
    liberating repressed material
        159
    of performing individual
        145
    subject to truth 160
    voice of writer 156
    written text as 183
Milan 120
mimetic characters 189, 190
Monty Python 64
Morrison, Blake 201
Morrison, Toni 16,
    174–179, 200
Morton, Angela 49–52
Moses and Monotheism 184
motor neurone disease 94

mutual attention 53
NAWE see Writers in
    Education, National
    Association of
narrative and self-esteem 148
Narrative Truth and Historical
    Truth 184
narrative, psychoanalysis
    inverted 167–169, 173
National Health Service
    (NHS) 35, 206
Nature, On 118
Naylor, Gloria 177
Neisser, Ulric 182, 184
New Historicist Movement
    205
new meaning 171
Nietzsche, Friedrich 127
Ntozake, Shange 177
Oedipal myth/model
    see also unconscious,
        structure of the
    alternative paradigms 177
    complex narrative entity
        172
    culturally instituted imagery
        168
    hermenuetic starting point
        170
    historical contingency 176
    linguistic restatement 165
    and pre-Oedipal focus 171
    reconfiguration 178
    universal linguistic structure
        164, 166, 169, 183
Old Testament 186
orientation 71–72
Ostia 120
Other Side of Language, The
    135
Our Inner Conflicts 190
Oxford Brookes University
    11
paradox 53
Paris, Bernard 16, 189–193,
    195
Paul, Saint 122

persona 38
personal development
    through writing 17
    see also writing and personal
    development
personal meaning 22
personal reflection 12,
    35–45
personal truth, fictional nature
    17
personality, aspects in conflict
    32
phallic metaphor 165, 167,
    168, 171, 177
Phillips, Adam 154, 181,
    183–185
Plath, Sylvia 166, 177
Plato 118, 119, 134, 140
Playing in the Dark 175
Plummer, Ken 148, 150
Poe, Edgar Allen 174
poetic discourse 136–139
poetic images 174
Poetically Man Dwells
    132–133
poetry, commonality with
    healing 47–49
Poetry Society 11
Poetry Therapy, National
    Association for (U.S.)
    207
post-modernism 164–166
post-structuralism 164–167,
    171, 172, 178, 182
    see also structuralism
postnatal depression 84
Potter, Denis 98
Pound, Ezra Loomis 174
Practical Parenting 88
primary healthcare 13,
    78–91
Princess Alice Hospice, Esher
    93, 95
Progoff, Ira 207
projection 156
Psalms 120–121
psyche 114, 119, 189
psychic genera 172

psychoanalysis 45, 161,
    165–172, 178, 179, 181
psychoanalysis and
    autobiography 16, 17,
    181–196
psychoanalysis and the nature
    of writing
    acting out unresolved
        conflict 155
    discovery and invention
        153
    emotional animation 157
    emotional depth 156–157,
        160–163
    experience reservoirs 158
    expressive qualities 159
    internal properties 159
    modes of attention 159
    mood and vision 157
    reminiscence and
        self-discovery 154, 160
    repressed experience
        158–159
    scriptor strategy 158
    the unconscious and the
        emergence of Truth
        156, 157, 160–163
        elaboration thereof 163
        obstacles thereto 162
psychoanalysis of feeling
    121, 126
psychoanalytic method
    123–128
psychobiography 159
psycholinguistics 108
psychological distress 79
psychology 119, 123
Psychology of Everyday Life, The
    162
psychosis 85
psychotherapy 156,
    181–196

Rabinow, Paul 143
rationalisation 156
reader, participatory
    interaction with text
    175, 176
reading

less creative than writing
    164
transformative and creative
    174–178
transformative experience
    and language 16,
    168–171
transformative linguistics or
    poetic unconscious?
    171–174
transformative meaning
    historically connected
    167, 173
reflection, personal see
    personal reflection
reflexively monitored action
    155
repression 16
Republic 119, 134
resource scarcity 135
rhetoric, classical 154–155
rhetoric/referent tension 178
rhetorical tripartition 155,
    158
Ricoeur, Paul 166, 169–171,
    173, 174, 178
Rigler, Dr. Malcolm 80
Rimbaud, Arthur 174
Rimmon-Kenan, S. 191
rite of passage 147
Roberts, Christine 31, 32
Roe, Sue 25
Rose, Jacqueline 205
Rousseau, Jean-Jacques 15,
    118, 122–127, 135, 181
Royal College of General
    Practitioners (RCGP) 79,
    81

Sacks, Oliver 109
Sappho 119
Sarraute, Nathalie 23, 25,
    27, 28
Savage God, The 202
Scheff, Thomas 146
schizophrenia 53
self, textuality of 17
self development, language
    influence 148

self
    plurality of fictions 166
    real as authentic 166
    socially constructed
        143–144·
    socially defined 142–144
self-analysis 121, 122, 125,
    126
self-consciousness 123
self-deception 156
self-definition 15
self-development
    classification process 147
    narrative and language role
        147–149
    ongoing process 142–151
    social interactional role
        144–146
self-expression 10
self-figuration 118–120
self-improvisation 154, 155
self-invention 154, 155
self-understanding 170
selfhood enacted 16
selfhood reconfigured 16,
    164–179
semiotic 165
sexual activity 125
shame and social interaction
    146
Sheffield Hallam University
    79, 89
Shelley, Mary 43
shyness 125
Sketch of the Past 23, 25
Social Contract 135
social experience and identity
    134–135
social interaction 15, 16,
    146
    see also symbolic
        interactionism
social process 15–16,
    142–151
social psychological
    (dramaturgical) theories
    142, 145
Socrates 118, 119
somatisation 79

Song of Solomon 177
Sontag, Susan 187
speculation 118
Spence, Donald 183, 184
Spender, Dale 133
Spikenard and Jasmine 51–52
spontaneous intermittant
    remission 113
sprezzatura 101
St. Cross House (Isle of
    Wight) 63, 67, 70, 74
Staffordshire 124
Stanley, Liz 205
Stevenson, Robert Louis 12,
    37–39, 43
Stoicism 119–120, 122
stories and momentary
    truthfulness 148
story components 43–44
story resolution 44–45
storymaking, character
    integration 43–45
stress 86
structuralism 15, 143, 164
    see also post-structuralism
Sturrock, John 185, 186,
    194
subjectivity
    construction of 166
    cultural understanding of
        169
    reconfigured 168
Sun (newspaper) 49
super-ego 38, 162
surrealism 174, 186
Survivors Poetry 14
symbolic interactionism 15,
    142, 144–146
    see also social interaction
synaesthesia 71
synchronic theory 187

Tao philosophy 49
Telling of Selves, The 184
terminal illness 13, 93–102
Thackeray, W.M. 190
Thagaste, North Africa 120
theft 125

theology 125
therapeutic claims
    inappropriate 18
Thinker as Poet, The 132
Thomas, Dylan 73
To the Lighthouse 9, 174, 198
Traherne, Thomas 98
transformational experience
    173, 178, 179
transformational space 16
Treasure Island 57
truth in writing 16,
    153–162
truth, personal see personal
    truth

unconscious experience 173,
    174, 178
unconscious, structure of the
    169, 170, 172
    see also Oedipal
        myth/model
University of Glasgow 11,
    81
University of Sheffield 78,
    82
University of Sussex 11, 21,
    176, 204
Unspeakable Things Unspoken
    175
urinary problems 125

Vanity Fair 190
violence 85
voluntarism 146

Waghorn, Tania 28, 29, 30
Wales, West 139, 204
Walker, Alice 177
Weybridge Hospital, Surrey
    93
When Did You Last See Your
    Father?, And 201
White, Michael 207
Wight, Isle of 139
Wight, Isle of, District Health
    Authority 63, 66, 68
Wight, Isle of, Tourist Board
    70
Wilden, Anthony 160, 161

William the Outlaw 103
Williams, Linda 171
Winnicott, Donald 161, 172, 173
Winnicottian transitional environment 14, 33
Wintering Out 68
Withymoor Village Surgery 80
Wittgenstein, Ludwig J.J. 135
Wollheim, Richard 157
Woolf, Virginia 9, 11, 18, 23, 24, 174
Wooton Hall 124
Wordsworth, William 98, 134, 140
workshop collaboration
    facilitation 54–61
    generating ideas 55–57
    group dynamics 61
    introductory technique 54
    symbiosis 58–61
    vulnaribility of participants 55
    writing without inhibition 57–58
writer anxiety 150
writer identity 150–151
Writers in Education, National Association of (NAWE) 10, 11
writing
    artform-led 17, 18
    blocked 162
    collaborative see collaborative writing
    constraints upon 150–151
    diary 17
    equated with schooling 150
    from personal experience 9–12, 21–33
    as self-expression 9–12
    social interactional process 149–151
    as therapy 17, 18
    see also writing and personal development

writing, truth in see truth in writing
writing and dementia sufferers
    carers' reactions 107–108
    confidentiality 110
    demands on writers 113–114
    editorial considerations 110
    empathetic approach 108
    engagement 106
    facilitation 109–111
    identity crises 104–106
    illustrative examples 111–113
    inventiveness 108–109
    language control 106
    role of writers 114
    therapeutic? 107–109
    uninhibited nature 109
writing and personal development
    definitions 199–200
    ethics 203–205
    excluding elements harmful to participants 202–205
    future 208
    polyvalent field 198–199
    process-oriented work 201
    product-oriented work 201
    research 205–208
    therapeutic work 201, 202
writing and the terminally ill
    autobiography 99, 100
    barriers 94–95
    bequeathal 101
    catharsis 101–102
    communication initiation 98–99
    communication problems 94–95
    diversion 97
    frailty 94
    groupwork 95–96
    life-story highlights 99
    living fully 98
    one-to-one work 95

rating benefits 102–103
    reflections on life 100
    self-presentation 100–101
    signing-off 102
    time limits 95
    underestimating abilities 94
writing in healthcare
    access forms 70–74
    aims and objectives 66
    celebrating ownership 74–76
    complementing care 67–69
    confidentiality 76
    dictation 74–76
    disposition of product 76
    literary quality 69–70
writing therapy in primary healthcare
    background 80–81
    case examples 84–85, 86–88
    emotional expression 84
    evaluation 83
    media reports 91
    nursing training 89–90
    problems 85–86
    RCGP research project 81–88
    rationale for 78–80

Zola, Emile 157

Author Index

Abbs, P. 128
Abbs, P. and Richardson, J. 27
Adorno, T. 133
Alexander, L. 97
Althusser, L. 143
Alvarez, A. 202
Anonymous GP 80
Archer, C. 96, 97
Arnold, M. 136
Atkinson, K. 154
Augustine 118, 120

Barthes, R. 157, 158, 159, 164, 182
Bastable, M. 205
Belsey, C. 136
Berne, E. 45
Boethius 198
Bollas, C. 172, 173, 174
Bolton, G. 79, 80, 84
Booth, W. 32, 191
Brooks, P. 167, 168, 171, 180, 184
Bruner, J. 207
Burnet, J. 119

Callanan, M. and Kelley, P. 96, 98
Cameron, D. 141
Campbell, J. 167, 173, 177
Chandler, M.R. 205
Cixons, H. 133
Conway, M.A. 22
Cooley, C.H. 144
Corr, A. and Corr, D. 97
Corradi Fimura, G. 136

Davies, C. 203, 206
Derrida, J. 148, 149, 182
de Saussure, F. 164
Dickens, C. 200
Downie, R.S. 80
Downing, C. 185
Dudley, K. 88

Eakin, P.J. 22, 182, 205

Fairfax, J. and Moat, J. 22
Felman, S. 171

Forster, M. 114
Fortuna, J. and Hodgson, H. 97
Foucault, M. 67, 143
Fransella, A. and Dalton, P. 207
Freud, S. 35, 46, 162, 184, 199

Gellhorn, M. 114
Gersie, A. 207
Gersie, A. and King, N. 207
Giddens, A. 143, 155
Gittins, C. 97
Goffman, E. 142, 145
Goldberg, N. 32, 61, 80
Goldsmith, M. 114
Gunn, J.V. 182
Gusdorf, G. 182

Harré, R. and Madden, E. 155
Harrison, B. 176
Harthill, G. 206
Harthill, G. and Sampson, F. 206
Healing Arts, Isle of Wight 76, 132, 139
Heaney, S. 68, 137
Heidegger, M. 132, 133, 141, 161
Hesse, H. 10,
Hillman, J. 62, 183
Hillman, J. and Ventura, M. 52
Hoar, M. et al. 205
Horney, K. 187, 188, 189, 190, 195
Hughes, T. 70, 166
Hunt, C. 21, 32, 157, 159, 188, 192, 193, 206

Ignatieff, M. 114
Irigaray, L. 133
Ivanic, R. 142, 143, 146, 147, 148, 150, 151
Jackowska, N. 80, 206
Jamison, K. 62
Jung, C.G. 46

Kearney, R. and Rainwater, M. 166
Killick, J. 114

Killick, J. and Schneider, M. 80, 206
Kitwood, T. 108, 114
Kivy, P. 157
Klein, M. 141
Kristeva, J. 134, 141, 165
Kübler-Ross, E. 101

Lacan, J. 134, 141, 165
Laclau, E. and Mouffe, C. 136
Laing, R.D. 46
Le Shan, L. 97
Leedy, J.J. 207
Leiris, M. 186, 187, 194
Lejeune, P. 185, 192
Lerner, A. 62, 207
Levete, G. 77
Levi-Strauss, C. 164
Lewis, H. 142, 146
Lockhart, R. 52
Lukács, G. 157
Lyotard, J.F. 147, 169

MacCaig, N. 40
MacNeice, L. 159
Mazza, N. 207
McCracken, L. 23
McDonnel, B. 80
McDougall, J. 45
McLeod, J. 207
McLoughlin, D. 10
Mead, G.H. 142, 144
Meaney, J. 97
Miles, I. 98
Miles, M. 77, 80
Moi, T. 180
Morgan, P. 10
Morrison, B. 201
Morrison, M. 62
Morrison, T. 175, 176, 200
Mugerauer, R. 141

Neisser, U. 182, 184

Palmer, J. and Nash, F. 77
Paris, B. 187, 189, 190, 191, 193, 195
Partnow, E. 46
Pateman, T. 21, 33
Phillip, R. 206
Phillips, A. 154, 181, 183, 184, 185

Pierce, C. 144
Plato 134
Plummer, K. 142, 148, 150
Poole, H. 99
Progoff, I. 207

Rabinow, P. 143
Rainer, T. 80
Rancour-Laferriere, D. 193
Ricoeur, P. 166, 169, 170
Rigler, M. 80, 81
Rimmon-Kenan, S. 191
Ritchie, C. 80
Roberts, M. 100
Roberts, S. and Bond, A. 80
Roe, S. 23, 25
Rose, J. 205
Rousseau, J-J. 118, 124, 126,
    127, 135, 181

Sacks, O. 109
Sampson, F. 77, 141, 206
Sarraute, N. 23, 27, 28, 31
Scheff, T. 142, 146
Scholes, R. and Kellog, R.
    189
Sellers, S. 80
Senior, P. and Croall, J. 77,
    80, 202
Shelley, M. 43
Smith, B.H. and Taylor, R.J.
    80
Smyth, T. 89
Spence, D. 183, 184
Spender, D. 141
St. Cross House Writing
    Group 63, 70
Stanley, L. 205
Stedeford, A. 94
Stelzig, E.L. 10
Stevenson, R.L. 37
Street, B. 150
Sturrock, J. 185, 186, 194

Taylor, C. 128

Utting, S. 206

Waller, D. 208
Weintraub, K. 128
White, M. and Epston, D.
    207

Wilden, A. 160, 161
Williams, L.R. 171
Wilson, G. 91
Winnicott, D.W. 46
Wittgenstein, L. 141
Wollheim, R. 157
Woolf, V. 9, 23–25, 28, 46,
    174, 198
Wordsworth, W. 134
Wright, A.F. 80
Wyatt-Brown, A.M. 33